GOD STILL SPEAKS

The Miracle at Fall Creek Falls

GOD STILL SPEAKS

THE MIRACLE AT FALL CREEK FALLS

Timothy M. Brown, Jr.

Wholehearted Press
Nashville, TN

Copyright © 2016 by Timothy M. Brown, Jr.

Wholehearted Press
P.O Box 332
Gallatin, TN 37066
www.timothybrownjr.com

ISBN 978-0-9970138-0-1 (Softcover)
ISBN 978-0-9970138-1-8 (Hardcover)
SIBN 978-0-9970138-2-5 (eBook)

Printed in the United States of America
First Printing, 2016

All scriptures quotations, unless otherwise notes, are taken from THE HOLY BIBLE, NEW INTERNATIONAL VERSION®, NIV® Copyright © 1973, 1978, 1984, 2011 by Biblica, Inc.® Used by permission. All rights reserved worldwide.

All rights reserved. No part of this publication may be reproduced, distributed, or transmitted in any form or by any means, including photocopying, recording, or other electronic or mechanical methods, without the prior written permission of the publisher, except in the case of brief quotations embodied in critical reviews and certain other noncommercial uses permitted by copyright law. For permission requests, write to the publisher, addressed "Attention: Permissions Coordinator," at the address above.

Ordering Information:
Quantity sales. Special discounts are available on quantity purchases by corporations, associations, and others. For details, contact the publisher at the address above.

Editing by Siobhan Gallagher, www.yourbesteditor.com
Cover design by Emem Habuti, www.redundantdesigns.com
Book design by Sarah Thomsen, www.sarahmariedesigns.net

To Tiffany, Colby, Caleb, Connor, Chloe, and Camden…
to our family and friends…
to all who prayed…
…for His glory.

CONTENTS

Foreword .... *ix*
Preface .... *xi*
Prologue .... *xiii*

Part I – Faith
1. Let's Go Camping 3
2. Fall Creek Falls 11
3. "Someone Please Help My Baby!" 19
4. Life Flight 25
5. P.I.C.U 33
6. "Don't Talk To Me About God!" 41
7. Fingerprints Everywhere 55
8. Let Me Help You 63
9. Of Dreams and Visions 71
10. Finally, Some Good News 81
11. Todd and His Guitar 89
12. "Caleb's Going to Live!" 97
13. Coma Scale: Four 101
14. Honk Your Nose 111
15. The Prayer for Caleb Project 129
16. Scottish Rite 135

Part II – Hope
17. A New Phase 145
18. I…Love…You! 159
19. Rocky Balboa 169
20. The Necklace 183
21. Extreme Makeover: Caleb Edition 189

Part III – Love

22. Reality Hits Hard 203
23. The Heart of the Matter 209
24. A New Kind of "Normal" 215
25. Miracle on 3rd St. 231
26. Missed Warnings 249
27. "It Wasn't an Accident" 259
28. An Unexpected Surprise 265
29. Happy Birthday! 271

Epilogue *281*
Acknowledgments *285*
About the Browns *293*
A Poem for Caleb *297*
Photos *301*

FOREWORD

When God speaks, as followers of Jesus Christ we are called to obey. Sometimes that call will move us into a very uncomfortable and often uncertain situation. We are not promised that it will be easy, but we have the assurance that God will be with us. As Tim clearly heard the call of what was still ahead, there was no way he could imagine how that would impact his son and family.

To have the faith for the journey often means our faith will be tested. To step out of a dry boat onto a stormy ocean may not make sense. But when God calls you onto the water, do you leave your safe surroundings to follow his command?

As Tim and Tiffany left for what was to be a relaxing family weekend together, in an instant it turned into a life changing event. How does God use something so seemingly tragic and turn it into a miracle? How do you find the strength and peace to fully trust God in a time where there are so many questions and uncertainties? As you read about the Miracle at Fall Creek Falls, I encourage you to ask yourself what God is calling you to do, and if you are ready to follow wherever He leads.

Jason McKay
Chattanooga Christian Media Personality

PREFACE

When I consider the reasons why I chose to write this book, I am reminded of a story I heard back when my wife and I were at T.C. Thompson, not long after Caleb's accident. Caleb's story had already broke in the news and thousands were starting to pray for him all over the world. Numerous people were sending us their own stories of encouragement and hope. I never will forget hearing this one story about a pastor who, when faced with the possibility of losing his own son in a tragic accident, made a promise to God. He said in essence, "God if you let my son live, if you let him pull through this, then no matter what, I will never cease to give you glory. I will praise you nonetheless, but I will praise you all the more if you allow a miracle to save my son's life." That night I made a commitment and prayed that same prayer for Caleb.

Soon after that prayer, it became clear through many circumstances that were unmistakably the work of God, that I was being called to write down the story as it happened and to preserve it as a blessing and encouragement for others, as a means to give glory to God. Over the years as I have written, edited, and re-written this book I've learned that Caleb's story is so much more than just the story of a little boy who was tragically injured by a falling boulder. That's the story the media told. It's also more than the story of how tens of thousands prayed for Caleb all over the world and how God heard those prayers. That's the story people experienced on Facebook and on our blog. For our family, Caleb's story is the true story of how God is present with us even today, from the highest mountain peaks of human experience to the darkest valleys of pain and despair. As we learn to listen to God through all the experiences of life,

God shapes, molds, and teaches us incredible life-lessons along the way. It's these lessons and experiences and the overwhelming encouragement they've brought our family that I have a burning desire to share with others. These are the things you will read about in God Still Speaks: The Miracle at Fall Creek Falls. May God bless you as you read.

Timothy. M. Brown, Jr.

PROLOGUE

You are going to need your whole heart for what is coming.

I stirred and then sank back into my pillow willing it to be early, too early—oh, please don't let it be morning yet, I groaned—as the breeze from the ceiling fan overhead caressed my face. The morning light relentlessly insinuated itself through the dark red curtains of the bedroom I shared with my wife, Tiffany. As I floated between consciousness and sleep, as the day's thoughts began entering my mind, I heard it.

You are going to need your whole heart for what is coming.

My eyes shot open. Startled, I sat up and looked around the room in confusion. The voice was clear as a bell, right in the room. It was a man's voice, deep, firm, but gentle. I was now completely alert. I turned to Tiffany but her side of the bed was empty. I glanced at the clock. Six-thirty. She must already be downstairs starting breakfast for the boys who'd still be asleep. Was someone in the hallway?

"Hello?" I heard the trepidation in my voice. There was no reply. Adrenalin sliced through me like quicksilver, a slight bitterness rising up to brush the back of my tongue before disappearing again, suppressed effortlessly by a sudden wave of certainty. I relaxed ever so slightly. Deep in my spirit, I knew what had just happened. I felt an inner confirmation of something extraordinary—I had just heard the voice of God.

Over the last few days I had been spending a lot of quiet time alone with God, seeking His voice, and reading His Word. I had just started a twelve-week spiritual growth seminar and right at the beginning we had discussed how to recognize God's voice and activity around us. At first I'd been extremely skeptical, as hearing God speak in our day and age had never been a part of my faith tradition. God speaking, as well as spiritual gifts, miracles and the like, were considered to be things relegated to the first century only and not for today. But within the first week of the seminar I had begun seeing what I would have ordinarily dismissed as coincidence, now as the unmistakable fingerprints of God's activity in my life. I became convinced that God does indeed speak today. But nothing could have prepared me for this. I was perplexed.

I am going to need my whole heart for what? What's coming?

The spreading global financial crisis had filled the news of late. Was it a possible economic collapse? I thought about my own life. Was it concerning my own spiritual growth? My marriage? My kids? What?

I jumped out of bed and headed downstairs to find Tiffany. Little did we know that this would only be the beginning. God was about to prepare our hearts for something that would shake the very foundations of our family and core beliefs. It was the first time I had ever heard God speak directly to me.

It wouldn't be the last.

PART ONE

Faith

"Now faith is being sure of what we hope for and certain of what we do not see."
—Hebrews 11:1

CHAPTER ONE

Let's Go Camping

Like many American families, the ripple effects of the country's economic problems had hit us hard, like a shovel. By the end of the preceding year, my church could no longer support me as a full-time minister. I was out of work. Our savings were depleted and we were using our credit cards for basic living expenses, so our debt was growing fast. Our car had just died, as had the HVAC unit in our house, and Tiffany was nearly eight months pregnant with our third son, Connor. We greeted 2010 bleakly, broke and despairing. Several times, we had to decide between paying the mortgage and putting food on the table. We prayed intensely. I was convinced this must be what God was talking about when He had warned me more than a year and a half earlier that I would need my whole heart for what was coming. Although I'd not forgotten those words, the pressures of daily life had overshadowed them, pushing them back behind the scenes.

Finally, in mid-February, after hundreds of applications and countless interviews at employment agencies, I got a job at a local company in Franklin, Tennessee. The work was great and the pay was reasonable, but we had a mountain of debt. I dove into my work, which soon consumed me. I grabbed every opportunity for overtime and also began working on a home business venture in the hope it would generate extra income to make a dent in what we owed. I worked seven days a week until about two or three in the morning, sometimes longer.

The days turned into weeks, and the weeks became months. Tiffany and I began drifting apart, with scarcely time for more than a "Hi" or "Bye" as we passed each other. Things became tense. We began to argue. By May, when our ninth wedding anniversary rolled around, we were still in debt and emotionally running on fumes. The strain on our marriage became unbearable. Something had to change. Both of us had agreed that we needed to make more time to spend with God and each other. It was a delicate balancing act because we were still desperate to get out of debt, but we knew that, in our mad dash to pay it off, we had not only neglected each other and our family, but had shown a lack of faith and trust in God as well.

Although 2010 had been one of the most challenging times we'd experienced, it was also when we learned more about God than ever before. At every hurdle, we sensed God teaching, stretching, and preparing us. We could see evidence of Him working in our lives everywhere. The entire year, it seemed that, in every sermon I heard, every Bible class I attended, every book I read, or conversation I had, or song I listened to on the radio, the subject was always about faith. Then, in July 2010, I was asked to speak at a local church during their VBS. The topic? Faith! It was the perfect opportunity, I thought, to sit down and write out everything God had shown us.

As I sat at my computer and began sketching out the notes for my first class, I was suddenly inspired, as the memories of all the experiences and lessons that Tiffany and I had learned that year came flooding back. My fingers could barely keep up with my thoughts and ideas as I pondered all that had happened to us. God's lessons to us through that time centered on how faith works in the life of a believer, and how God uses events in our lives, most often the most difficult, to grow us and make us stronger. As I began writing, I felt that God was calling us to remember those lessons—to remember faith.

~

"Daddy!" A chorus of little voices greeted me as I arrived home from work.

Colby, our oldest son, four, wrapped himself around my leg as Caleb, our two-year-old, came running down the hallway, with a ball in his hands. Tiffany was making dinner while holding eight-month-old Connor, who was crying.

"What's wrong with my little man?"

"Oh, the usual," she said, chuckling. "He's hungry."

I started to ask Tiffany how her day had been when Caleb interrupted. I looked down. He was standing in front of me, his hands outstretched, wanting me to pick him up.

"Hug. I want hug."

With Colby still clinging to my leg, I hoisted Caleb into my arms. Tiffany grinned.

"I'm just about done with dinner."

We took our seats around the dinner table. I glanced at Tiffany.

"You know, I've got a vacation day coming."

It was now the second week of October, and summer still lingered invitingly. Tiffany, who had been encouraging Caleb to use his spoon and fork, looked up.

"We could take a three-day weekend," I continued. "Maybe go on a small mini-vacation or something. How does that sound?" We hadn't been on a family vacation for two and a half years, not since before Caleb and Connor were born. Tiffany thought for a moment.

"My sister could watch Connor and we could take Colby

and Caleb somewhere," she suggested. I nodded. It would have to be something we could afford, which didn't leave us many options.

"Camping? We could leave this Friday and come back Sunday."

"Let's do it!"

∽

That Thursday, my dad unexpectedly called me at work.

"Are you okay?" Dad asked. His voice sounded odd, nervous, apprehensive.

"Of course. Why do you ask?"

"I don't know. I woke up with this strange feeling that something was wrong, terribly wrong." He admitted he had been calling family members one by one. "I just have this overwhelming sense of dread."

"Well, everything's fine here," I replied. "But, let me know if you hear anything, all right?"

The incident continued to nag me throughout the day. It was so unlike my father to worry like that. I thought about the fact that later in the day Tiffany was going to be driving to Murfreesboro with our three boys to visit a friend for the evening. My concern continued to grow, and I hurried straight home after work.

"Honey, I really think you should stay home tonight. I'm afraid that, if you leave, something might happen."

Tiffany tried to reassure me. It didn't work.

"Tiff, honey, I don't know what it is, but I just feel like something is going to happen to one our kids."

"What? Why would you think that?"

"I don't know. I just feel something. Something's not right."

I honestly didn't have an answer. My father's fear had been infectious. All day long the same sense of dread that my father described had been slowly turning my own stomach into knots. I was afraid. Tiffany shook her head.

"We'll just be a few hours, all right?"

I nodded, numbly. "I am going to pray that God protects you guys all the way there."

Tiffany hugged me.

"I'll call you when I get there."

I watched as our car's taillights disappeared down the street. I couldn't begin to imagine what I would do if something ever happened to Tiffany or one of the kids. I began to pray in earnest, borrowing the words from Psalm 91:11, asking God to command His angels to watch over Tiffany and the boys, to guard and protect them and to see them safely home. When Tiffany finally called to say she'd arrived, I felt relief wash through me.

"God, thank you," I whispered.

That night, after we tucked the boys into bed, Tiffany put her arm around my waist.

"Let's get some rest, sweetheart. I'm really looking forward to our camping trip tomorrow."

∼

We had waited until the last minute to decide which campground we wanted to go to. I wanted to go to Fall Creek Falls, as it had been a place I had visited a few times before and had loved. What we hadn't realized, however, was that we had somehow managed to pick the busiest weekend of the season to go camping. All the state parks were full.

We had originally planned to leave Friday morning and arrive at our campground sometime in the afternoon. Instead we spent the entire day jumping over one hurdle after another. After spending hours trying to find a campground with a vacancy and an available rental car, Tiffany said, "Honey, why don't we just stay home and have a relaxing weekend here at the house?"

"Tiff, it's been a rough year. I've worked so hard over the last seven months just to get one vacation day—just one—and this is the only time that we can actually get away." I felt frustrated. "I really want to make this happen, and I really want to go to Fall Creek Falls."

After having finally found both a car and a campground, we then spent several hours driving around in the dark, hopelessly lost.

"Man, it feels like everything is trying to get in the way of us going on this trip!" I exclaimed. It was two in the morning when, bleary-eyed, I eventually spotted a sign that read "Entering Fall Creek Falls State Park." Our frustration levels were so high that we had nearly turned around and headed back home. We were all exhausted. But, finally, we'd made it.

It was three in the morning before Tiffany and I finally found our campsite and got everything situated. To our relief, Darvin Oakes, the campground owner, had thoughtfully set up a tent for us, knowing how late we'd be arriving. The only thing left was to collect the firewood we'd need. Colby volunteered to come with me.

The night was pitch black as we walked down the gravel road. I shivered slightly. The nighttime mountain air was decidedly chilly. I paused and looked up, and felt all the night's frustrations begin to fade. The Milky Way splayed across the indigo sky in luminous grandeur, like an immense handful of silver glitter tossed carelessly across the inky blackness.

"Wow, look at that. That is so beautiful," I said, softly. I kneeled down and wrapped army arms around Colby. "Look up. What do you see?" Colby leaned his face against mine.

"I see stars, Dada," he said, his voice filled with awe. "Wow, lots and lots of stars!"

The words of Psalm 19:1 filled my mind: *The heavens declare the glory of God; the skies proclaim the work of His hands.* I was reminded that this was why we were here. This was why we were taking this trip as a family, to get away and spend time with each other. As we spent a few moments in silent worship, God seemed to be saying, "Just be. Enjoy this gift of being together."

"How about tomorrow night we come out here with our sleeping bags?" I whispered. "We can all lie down out here together and look at the stars." It would be the perfect opportunity to teach the boys a little about God and His creation, I thought. "We could do it tomorrow after we get back from the falls." Colby nodded, still staring at the sky, entranced.

It was another hour before we were finally settled, ready to get some sorely needed rest.

"I want Dad-dy," chirped Caleb's sweet baby voice from the far side of the tent. I was surprised. Caleb typically slept with his mother when we were away from home. Tiffany shrugged and smiled, as Caleb crept over to lie on my air mattress. He snuggled against me as I pulled the covers up and asked him if he wanted me to do "tuck-tuck."

"Tuck-tuck!" he giggled in delight.

I tucked him in on each side, making sure to tickle him as I went, his favorite part. Caleb giggled again. We said our evening prayer and kissed the boys goodnight.

"Night, night, Caleb," I whispered. "I love you, buddy. We're going to have so much fun tomorrow," I promised, as I turned off the light.

CHAPTER TWO

Fall Creek Falls

Colby and I were the first to wake up Saturday morning. Since we had arrived so late the night before, we had decided to sleep in, go with the flow, and enjoy the day at a snail's pace. We crept out of the tent. The scenery was stunning. All around us was the lush panorama of autumn in all of its grandeur. Trees of every kind reached high into the sky with colors too numerous to count. The ground was covered with a blanket of leaves that crunched beneath our feet as we walked. Colby couldn't resist. He reached down and grabbed handfuls of leaves and threw them up into the air, shouting "Whee-e-e-e!" His laughter was infectious.

"Hey, buddy, are you ready to help me gather some twigs so we can get a fire going and start making breakfast?"

"Yeah!"

I showed Colby how to lay the kindling. Colby was fascinated and insisted on placing each stick himself. The wood, however, was still quite wet from the morning dew and we struggled to get the fire going. I looked up at the sound of crunching leaves to see two men from the adjacent lot approaching.

"I'm trying to teach my son how to light a fire," I explained, "but the wood's a little wet. Hi, I'm Tim, and this is my son Colby."

"Jason," the man said, extending a hand. "Jason McKay, and this is Brian Smith." In Jason's other hand was a blow dryer, connected to a very long extension cord. "Here, I brought this for you." At my puzzled expression, he chuckled. "If you point it up under the fire pit while you light it, it helps get the fire going. We had trouble getting our fire going too." I tried it. Sure enough, it worked. Slightly embarrassed, I chided myself for not being more of an outdoorsman, until it occurred to me as they made their way back to their campsite that maybe Jason and Brian were more like me than I thought. After all, they'd probably only packed the hairdryer to light their fires. I chuckled as I watched them go.

When Tiffany came out of the tent, I gave her a kiss and slid my arm around her waist. She nestled her head against mine as we watched our kids who were both now hard at play, creating a construction zone in the dirt with their toy dump trucks and diggers. I breathed in deeply and drank in life and love.

As we sat down to breakfast together, Colby volunteered to say the prayer first. Caleb's eyes were fixed intently on his brother.

"God is great, God is good. Let us thank—"

"And Him food!" Caleb finished, triumphantly.

Caleb loved to pester his older brother by cutting him off and finishing his prayers for him. Colby glared.

"Caleb! I'm saying it first. Wait your turn." We all laughed.

By the time we had finished breakfast and washed the dishes, the midday sun was directly overhead. I walked over to the car and opened the trunk.

"Hey, guys, I have a surprise for you." I pulled out a brand new baseball and bat as the boys came running over. The boys had never played baseball before. This would be their first lesson.

I explained to Colby the basic concepts of hitting the ball with the bat and running around the bases, which I marked out using a few nearby trees, and designated an old hickory stump as home plate. I positioned Colby in front of the tree stump.

"OK, Colby, I'm gonna let you hit the ball first." I leaned down and wrapped Colby's hands around the bat. "OK, buddy, are you ready? I'm gonna pitch the ball up in the air and, when I do, we're gonna swing the bat and hit it. Got it?"

"Got it!"

I pitched the ball and together Colby and I swung the bat. *Bam!*

The ball flew across the campground.

"Good job, Colby! Awesome! All right, let's run." Colby jumped up and down, clapping his hands with glee before setting off to run around the makeshift bases, with Tiffany cheering him on.

"OK, let's give Caleb a turn."

I led Caleb over to home plate. He tucked his chubby chin to his chest and peered up at me with shy eyes, giggling. I squatted behind him and readied his hands on the bat while Tiffany pitched the ball. Caleb and I swung.

Boom!

The ball sailed as far as Colby's had. Caleb's eyes lit up.

"Wow! Good job, buddy! OK, now, you have to run. Run! Run, run, run!" Caleb ran out into the field and began running in circles, oblivious to the bases and completely delighted with himself. I grinned as my eyes met Tiffany's. It was one of those moments where time seemed to slow down. I drank in every moment—the smiles, the laughter, the way our boys' eyes squinted as they laughed. I was thankful for every little second. This was going to be the best trip ever, I vowed.

A little while later, we loaded the boys into the car and headed over to see the falls. We were all still tired from yesterday's late arrival and I was having a bit of trouble finding the place. The boys began to get restless in the back of the car. I pulled in to the park only to discover that, instead of Fall Creek Falls, the main falls, we had somehow ended up at Cane Creek Cascades and Falls.

"Wait, this isn't right," I said. "We're at the wrong place." I put the car in reverse. Colby looked visibly upset and Caleb began to cry. Tiffany put her hand on my arm.

"Honey, wait. Why don't we just stay here? There's a playground over there next to the nature center. Why don't we just let the kids play for a little while, and then head on back to the campground?"

"Honey, seeing the main falls is one of the reasons we came all the way out here in the first place. The boys will be fine once we get there." Tiffany nodded, not quite convinced, as we pulled out of the parking lot.

When we reached Fall Creek Falls, the kids had started to calm down somewhat. I pulled into a parking space just across from the entrance.

"Honey, would you hand me my Bible?" Tiffany thumbed through it to a psalm that had to do with God's creation and began reading. When she finished, she looked at Colby and Caleb.

"Boys, we wanted to bring you out here today so you could see the falls and have some fun. But another reason is because we want to show you some of the beautiful things that God has made." She paused. "Colby, look at all the trees around us. See how pretty they are? See all the leaves, the colors, and how pretty the sky is? Did you know God made all this? And just like God made all this, God also made you and Caleb." The boys sat looking at her, silently absorbing her words.

"Colby, Caleb, there is one thing we always want you to know. Mommy and Daddy love you so much, but God loves you even more. Did you know that? That's a lot of love isn't it?" Colby smiled and nodded. I smiled too.

Turning to me Tiffany said, "Alright you ready to go honey?" I laid the Bible on the seat. "OK, let's go!"

When we reached the main overlook for the falls, the boys' moods began to lighten, their tiredness forgotten. Tiffany put Caleb down and he walked straight to the metal railing, stepped up onto the bottom rung and looked at the powerful falls below, the water thundering and splashing.

"Water! Water!" Caleb yelled delightedly, waving his hands up and down as if he could splash them in it.

As we began navigating down the rocky path, the view was amazing. From where we stood, there were gaps between the trees where the steep rocky crags of the gorge lay exposed. Lush evergreens formed a thick blanket of foliage all around us, as the mountain maples and oaks, yellow birch, and tulip poplars competed in beauty, trumpeting their red, yellow, purple, and auburn colors. We stopped along the way a few times to take a few pictures, pointing out to the boys the beauty of what we were witnessing, showing them the wild ferns that grew off the sides of the trail, and the mountain laurel that decorated the landscape of the forest floor. We weren't in a hurry to get to the bottom. We just wanted to take our time.

Finally, after spending about forty minutes hiking the winding and rocky trail two hundred and fifty feet below, we made it to the end of our scenic journey.

"Look, Dada, there's the water!" Colby shouted, pointing excitedly toward the falls.

The magnificent beauty of Fall Creek Falls appeared before us in all its glory. Water rumbled over what looked like oversized white stepping stones, down a majestic drop of more than two hundred and fifty feet. At the bottom foamed a large pool of turquoise water. A light mist bathed our faces.

I thought about all the things I was planning to do with my boys in the next few hours, like dangling our feet in the water, skipping rocks, and playing in the stream at the bottom of the gorge. I had waited so long for this chance to take a weekend to spend with Tiffany and the kids, and now, despite the incredible amount of obstacles that had hurled themselves in our way over the past twenty-four hours (not to mention months), we were finally here. We were at Fall Creek Falls, the tallest falls in the eastern United States. This was the boys' first camping trip and we wanted this excursion to be an experience to remember, an adventure into the great outdoors, and a time to focus on the beauty of God's creation.

Caleb began jumping up and down, pulling at his mother's hand to hurry.

"All right, boys, let's go have some fun!"

We began making our way down through the rocks to the pool that lay invitingly just a few feet below. The surface of the water glistened. Caleb decided to walk with me and Colby while Tiffany followed, just a few paces behind. Caleb clung tightly to my one hand as Colby held the other. After a couple of steps, I felt my feet begin to slide. I looked back at Tiffany.

"It's a little bit slippery here. Would you mind grabbing Caleb?"

Tiffany hoisted Caleb into her arms while I walked with Colby. I kept a firm grip on his hand, picking my way carefully and cautioning Colby to do the same.

As we neared the pool below, we heard a huge crash from the top of the gorge, like a truck at top speed slamming into an unmovable concrete wall. Everyone around us looked up and froze. I looked back at Tiffany, about ten feet behind me, dread surging up into my throat with the force of the falls. I knew immediately what it had to be—a falling rock. A large boulder was barreling down the side of the gorge. My eyes raced back and forth frantically across the tree line, but most of the trees still had their leaves and I could hardly see through the canopy. I held my breath as the silent enemy thudded along its deadly path, slamming against the rock facing. It sounded like it was coming right toward us, but the deep pervasive echoes from the gorge made it impossible to tell from which direction the rock was coming from.

We'll just move out of the way, I reassured myself. I glanced down at Colby, who stood like a statue next me, terrified. I instinctively thought to grab him, to shield him and protect him. But, before I could move, I saw it at the corner of my eye. A large jagged rock, roughly the size of a beach ball, was tumbling out of the tree line at a shocking speed, spiraling madly toward Tiffany, who was clutching Caleb in her arms. As I opened my mouth to warn her, the rock crashed violently into the earth just behind her. The impact was like a cannon firing, the dull echo resounding through the hollow gorge. I flinched as the boulder shot past a mere six feet from my chest and continued raging on its deadly path toward the water. It had all happened within mere seconds. I hadn't even had time to shout a warning, let alone grab Colby.

I took a ragged breath, feeling a sense of relief that the rock had missed us. Confused, out of the corner of my eye, I saw my wife lunging forward, trying to regain her grip on Caleb, who looked as if he were being pried from her arms by some invisible enemy. It was only then that I realized what had happened.

The rock had hit our two year old, Caleb, in the head.

CHAPTER THREE

"Someone Please Help My Baby!"

"Help my baby! Someone please help my baby!" Tiffany's panicked screams echoed through the gorge. Even the pounding waterfall seemed to have been shocked into silence. The force of the blow as the rock hit Caleb's head was so strong that it had nearly flung Caleb out of Tiffany's arms.

"No!" I shrieked, over and over, my cries mingling with Tiffany's screams, as I raced toward her. Blood poured from an open wound on the back of Caleb's head, drenching Tiffany and pooling on the ground at her feet. Caleb's eyes had rolled back in his head and his face had turned deathly pale, with an almost bluish hue. His lips were dark purple.

"Tim, he's dead! He's dead!" Tiffany screamed. I pleaded with her to hand him to me. She couldn't hear me.

"Give him to me, please. Now!" As I took his limp body into my arms, my first thought was to call 911. A sickening feeling of helplessness washed through me as it dawned on me there was no cell phone service at the bottom of the gorge.

"Please help!" I shrieked, looking around in desperation. "Someone call 911! Call 911! Get help now!" I was praying that somehow somebody might be able to call for help.

Everyone around us was crying and screaming. I looked down at Caleb. My tears began to drip onto his lifeless face. I clutched him close and prayed, "Oh, please, buddy, don't go. I love you so much, sweetheart. Please don't go." I looked up at Tiffany and gasped, "We have to get him back up to the top now!"

As I turned toward the path, I glanced down at Colby who was looking up at me, sobbing.

"Daddy! Daddy!" he cried in horror, his arms reaching upward for me. Caleb's blood was now dripping on him. I felt full of pain for Colby. I wanted to be able to hold and comfort him, but I had to move. Now.

I began running up to the rocky area where the trail ended, slipping as I went. Within minutes, I was gasping for air, fatigue settling into my muscles with distressing speed.

"Oh, God," I gasped in terror, "I'm never going to make it. Please, God, help me!" A voice behind me called out.

"Is he breathing?" As I turned, another voice shouted, "It's OK, he's a firefighter!"

"I don't know," I choked in reply, as I looked down at Caleb.

"Let me see." The young man checked Caleb's pulse and breath.

"Is he ok, is he alive?"

"He's breathing, but barely," the firefighter said, his eyes dark. "We've got to go. We've got to go now!"

I clutched Caleb and began running as fast as I could, fearing that at any moment he might die in my arms. Blood was running down my arm and my leg, dripping a telltale trail behind us, as Caleb began to turn blue.

"Caleb," I grunted, "You're going to be OK. Daddy's got you. It's just a boo-boo. Stay with me, buddy. You're going to be OK. I love you so much, Caleb. Stay with me!" Faint gurgles were coming from his mouth. I tensed. *Oh, please, God, don't take him from me. Please don't take my son!*

My arms and legs felt chained to weights. I gasped for

air that never seemed to make it past my lips. Caleb was now unconscious, his deadweight felt three times as heavy.

"You have to hold his head to keep him from bleeding!" the young man shouted over my shoulder. I thought I had been. Fear raced through my veins as I cradled Caleb's head firmly in the crux of my arm to slow the bleeding.

I was only dimly aware of others along the trail, stepping aside to let me pass. I could hear the sounds of bystanders crying and praying, some shielding their crying children from the sight of us. Cries rang out further up the trail.

"Call 911! Call 911!"

The people along the trail were relaying my message further up the mountain with each yell. I prayed that someone near the top would find a signal and be able to get through for help.

Near collapsing, I thought to myself, "I'm not going to make it. I'm just not going to make it." I heard the firefighter behind me a second time, telling me that I had to change my grip again. I suddenly knew that I would never be able to get my son all the way back up the trail safely. Desperate, I turned back to the young man, who looked barely out of his teens. He wasn't even out of breath.

"Will you take him? Will you please take my son? I can't … I can't make it!"

The young firefighter tore off his shirt and hurriedly bandaged Caleb's head with it. Hoisting Caleb into his arms, he started running. I bent over, gasping, my hands on my knees as I watched the young man vaulting up ahead, now almost out of sight, leaping over rocks like some mythical superhero.

"God, please be with my son." I whispered. "Protect that man. Guide his feet so they do not slip, and see him safely to the top." I suddenly thought of Tiffany and Colby and glanced behind me. They weren't far behind. Two men were taking turns carrying Colby while several women were helping Tiffany, holding each arm. I hadn't heard anything but the blood pounding in my ears before this, but now her cries pierced the air.

"Is he OK? He's going to die, isn't he?" she wailed.

"Honey, I don't know. I don't know."

"Tim, you knew! You knew! You knew something was going to happen to one of our boys! Why did God let this happen to our son?" she moaned. I flashed back to the day my father called, feeling that something bad was going to happen, and then my own feeling that something was going to happen to one of our kids. It was then I heard those haunting words again echo in my heart.

You are going to need your whole heart for what is coming.

Now I knew what God meant. It was a warning. It was this.

It was Caleb.

∾

When Colby caught sight of me, he shrieked.

"Daddy, Daddy!"

I descended past Tiffany, taking her hand in mine for a fleeting moment, both slippery with blood, before continuing toward Colby. He struggled to throw himself into my arms. I kissed him and tried to carry him but I was just too exhausted. I cupped my hand against his cheek.

"Colby, it's OK. Listen, son. I'm right here. This man's helping me carry you. I'm not leaving you. I'm right here. But Caleb is hurt and we have to get to the top so we can take Caleb to a doctor, OK?" The hurt on his face pierced my heart.

"OK, Daddy," he mumbled, tears streaking his blood-smeared cheeks.

"I love you so much." With that, I turned and began making my way up the trail to the top. Finally, as the path curved, I saw the lookout point where we had begun our descent.

"You're almost there, you're almost there," I whispered to myself as I continued praying. I felt a resurgence of adrenalin and lurched forward. As we crested the top of the trail, I saw hundreds of people gathered by the park entrance. Then I spotted a frail form on the ground, the young superhero kneeling above it, holding its head. It was Caleb. My eyes darted in every direction. I felt my heart sink as I realized help had not yet arrived.

"Why aren't they here yet?" I muttered as I started to run. I reached Caleb and sank to my knees on the ground next to him.

"Move back," I heard several people saying, "That's his father."

I began crying out to God, pleading that He spare my son's life. I felt that at any moment I was about to watch my son take his last breath. I frantically grasped Caleb's hand as tears wetted the pavement beneath me.

"Please, God!" I cried, "please don't take my son!"

I looked at the young man, his face slightly blurred through my tears. His expression was grave.

"Yes," he said, in answer to my unspoken question, "he's still alive, but he's barely breathing. We've got to get help soon."

CHAPTER FOUR

Life Flight

I became aware of others kneeling beside the firefighter, who told me his name was Michael Tagert and reassured me he was just months from becoming a fully certified EMT. Melissa Lyons, one of the women who had helped Tiffany up the trail, identified herself as a pediatric trauma nurse from Vanderbilt Hospital and was busy monitoring Caleb's vital signs. There were, oddly enough, a handful of doctors and other nurses in the crowd, all of whom happened to be walking the trail that day, and all wanting to help but lacking any equipment.

"Tim! Is he okay? Is he alive?" Tiffany's voice reached me as I searched the crowd to find her. Colby ran over to me and jumped into my arms.

"Daddy, what's wrong with Caleb?"

I sat Colby down with Tiffany.

"He's still alive," I said to Tiffany. She looked at me, desperate for any shred of hope. "We need to pray." I kissed Tiffany and then knelt down in front of Colby. "Stay here with Mommy, OK? I need to be with Caleb right now because he's hurt. You're going to be OK. We're not going to leave you. I love you." I returned to Caleb's side. Each passing minute felt like hours.

"Where is the ambulance?" someone demanded. "This is ridiculous! Where are they?" others shouted.

I heard a faint gurgling sound. Fear gripped my heart and

I searched Michael's face.

"Check his pulse," Michael said to Melissa, as he leaned down to check Caleb's breathing. Melissa's fingers gripped Caleb's wrist. She looked frightened.

"I can't feel anything," she said. Michael grabbed Caleb's other wrist. There was a painful pause.

"I feel it!" he cried. "I feel it. But it's very, very faint."

A doctor, who had been standing by in the crowd, spoke up. "We have to get him to a hospital now!" Several onlookers protested, insisting it was too dangerous to move him.

"I am a doctor and I am saying we need to get him in a car and get him out of here as fast as we can!" he bellowed.

I stared down at Caleb as they argued, feeling helpless. I didn't know what to do. Suddenly, Caleb jerked. Michael ducked down and leaned his ear close to Caleb's mouth.

"He's not breathing—his airway's blocked! We need to turn him on his side now!" With Melissa's help, Michael turned Caleb over. Caleb abruptly vomited, coughing and gasping. Several onlookers cheered.

"Good job, buddy," I whispered. Although still faint, Caleb's breathing sounded slightly stronger. Within minutes, color slowly began to return to his face.

Huge clumps of blood matted Caleb's hair and neck. I couldn't see the wound on the back of his head, but then I wasn't sure I wanted to. Caleb twitched slightly, and his body began to shudder. Horrified, I watched as his eyes rolled back into his head.

"What's happening?"

"He's going into shock." Melissa replied.

I called to Tiffany for Caleb's blanket, which she had carried clenched to her chest the entire way back up the trail.

Quietly sobbing, I knelt down on the cold pavement and

laid his blanket over him.

"Here you go, buddy. I've got your blankie." As I continued to whisper reassurances to Caleb, who lay unconscious, the crowd grew more and more restless. Where on earth were the paramedics? I couldn't stand it any longer. I had to do something. I stood up and faced the hundreds of people who were clustered about.

"If any of you are people of faith," I pleaded, my voice breaking, "if you believe in God, will you please pray for my son right now?" Hundreds of hands immediately lifted skyward and the people around me began to pray.

"I'm Stephanie Rainey," a woman said, coming forward. "This is my friend, Beth Duryea. May we lay our hands on your son to pray?" I nodded, tears in my eyes. I knelt back down next to Caleb and began praying alongside them.

Forty minutes had passed since the first call for help had gone out. I could feel myself starting to get angry.

I heard a shout above the crowd.

"The Park Rangers' office says they're sending a Life Flight helicopter, and there's an EMT truck on its way up the mountain right now."

"Please hurry," I moaned. "Please hurry!"

Michael looked at me.

"This little guy's strong, I can tell you that. He's still struggling to breathe." I gave him a grateful smile.

"That's right," I said to Caleb, "You go, little buddy. You stay strong, you hear me? Mommy and Daddy are right here with you. You stay strong!"

An hour and ten minutes after Caleb's injury, help finally arrived. Several emergency vehicles, including an EMT truck, pulled into the parking lot. One EMT swiftly inserted an I.V. as another began administering oxygen.

"Are you the father?"

"Yes."

"What happened?"

I quickly recounted the events and the EMTs confirmed that Life Flight was on the way, saying that emergency service employees were busy clearing an adjacent parking lot to serve as a landing site. They bundled Caleb onto a stretcher and into the back of the ambulance as we all watched. Tiffany kept asking me why, over and over—why was this happening to us, to Caleb? I had no answers. All we could do now was pray, I said.

Stephanie and Beth helped us to our car, strapped Colby into his car seat, and drove us to the landing site as we sat in the back and sobbed. I pulled out my phone, anxious to call someone, our family, our friends. There was no signal. My phone was useless.

After what felt like an eternity, we pulled into a large empty lot and came to a stop. I leaped out of the car and ran over to the back of the ambulance where a number of paramedics had gathered.

"How is he? Is he still alive?"

"Yes, he's still breathing. He still has a pulse."

One of the EMTs stepped forward and gripped my shoulder.

"I just want you to know that all of us are fathers too, and we feel for what you're going through. These folks who're working on your son are going to take very good care of him."

"They're taking him to T.C. Thompson Children's Hospital in Chattanooga," another paramedic said. "It's one of the best children's trauma units around. There's not a better place for him to go."

We didn't know it yet but we would soon find out that its pediatric intensive care unit staff had just completed a special training session dealing with pediatric trauma cases. Caleb would be their first case since the training.

I peered anxiously in through the back window of the ambulance. Two men were working feverishly on Caleb. I bit my lip. I'd never felt so helpless in all my life.

Within minutes, the back door of the ambulance burst open. As they emerged with the stretcher, a young EMT stood next to my son, forcing air into him through a breathing mask. Wearing only his diaper, Caleb looked frighteningly tiny and fragile on the full-sized stretcher. My heart sank when I was told I couldn't accompany him in the helicopter. We would have to make our own way to Chattanooga.

I took one of Caleb's hands. "Daddy's right here," I choked. "I love you so much. We're going to take you to see a doctor now, okay? We're going to get your boo-boos fixed and then we're going to go home. I love you so much!" I looked at the young man who was helping Caleb breathe. "Please be careful," I pleaded. "You have my son's breath in your hands." He looked at me solemnly.

"Yes, sir, I will."

I could hear the thwack-thwack-thwack of the chopper blades. Dirt and dust filled my eyed as I struggled to shield them. I looked back to see Tiffany and Colby, faces pale, watching intently from the car. Caleb was whisked into the helicopter and we watched as it took off. Within seconds, it was gone. Caleb was gone.

"God, please protect everyone on that helicopter, and help it arrive quickly and safely," I whispered, my eyes glued to the now empty sky.

A policeman approached.

"I'm Officer Walling. I'm not supposed to do this, but, as a father, I can't even begin to imagine what you're going through right now. I'll drive you to Chattanooga." Stephanie and Beth promised to take care of our car while Officer Walling called the campground to secure our belongings. Tiffany and I grabbed a few things from the car and the three of us clambered into the back of the squad car.

∼

The two-hour drive took an eternity. After the first few minutes, we'd lapsed into an uneasy, almost oppressive silence. Tiffany and I sat, lost in our own thoughts, trying desperately to come to terms with what had just happened. Quietly, we took turns praying and sobbing. I thought about everything that had led up to the accident, how so many things had nearly prevented us from going on this trip and how determined I was to go, no matter what. I loathed myself for making the decision to go to the falls in the first place. I felt guilty about how Tiffany had tried several times to persuade me to go somewhere else. Everything felt like it was my fault no matter how I looked at it. I thought about the timing of it all, how so many things had nearly gotten in the way of us going on the trip, how we had arrived at the campground so late after having gotten so lost, and how, as a result, we had left so much later in the afternoon to go hiking than we normally would have done. I thought about the fact that, had we left one minute later or even one minute earlier, or done any number of things differently, none of this would have happened.

I thought again about God's words to me a year and a half earlier.

You are going to need your whole heart for what is coming.

For Tiffany, her initial emotions were confusion and deep, heartfelt pain. I was in pain as well, and deeply confused. But, as the long drive to Chattanooga continued, my emotions began to change. I felt something else welling up inside of me.

It was anger, deep anger.

Toward God.

CHAPTER FIVE

P.I.C.U.

We were unprepared for the horrified looks when we burst into the emergency room. I'd forgotten we were drenched in Caleb's blood.

"Your son was admitted and transferred up to the Pediatric ICU on the fourth floor. He's still being prepped. There's a waiting room up there. They'll come get you when they're ready."

We hurried down the hall to the elevators.

The first thing Tiffany and I noticed when we got off the elevators was a large set of double doors bearing a sign that read "Pediatric Intensive Care Unit (PICU)." I headed for the red phone on the wall to call the nurses' station.

"Ma'am, is he still alive?"

"Sir, we're not allowed to say anything."

"Can we come back and see him?"

"No, sir, I'm sorry, but you can't. You need to go to the PICU waiting room. Once they get him admitted, then they'll come down and talk to you."

I hung up the phone. I felt afraid. I looked at Tiffany whose face fell.

"They can't tell us anything. We have to wait."

For the next agonizing hour, we held each other, cried, prayed, and waited. As I sat with my head in my hands, my legs trembled. Every time I opened my eyes, I saw my blood-soaked khakis. If I had just done one thing differently, I kept thinking, just been a minute later, or gotten to the bottom just a minute sooner, none of this would have happened. The silence in the waiting room was suffocating. You could hear a pin drop. Even Colby by this point was silent and still. All we could do was wonder what the doctors would tell us, and whether Caleb was alive or dead.

The door opened and our heads shot up. Tiffany's sisters, Misty and Chassi, rushed in and we leaped to our feet. We hugged, and each of us began to cry.

"Do you know anything yet?"

We shook our heads.

"They're still prepping him."

We sat down. Through our tears, we explained what had happened.

Finally, a nurse came to escort us down the hall and through the double doors into the PICU, and seated us inside a doctor's office.

"The doctor will be in to see you shortly."

I felt the air leave my lungs. Caleb had died. He must be dead. Why else would the nurses have refused to tell us anything? If he were alive, would we not have been rushed to see him instead of being seated here, waiting for some doctor to calmly and solemnly deliver the bad news in the privacy of his office? I braced for the worst. Tiffany and I clung to each other. I tried to pray but the words wouldn't come.

The door opened.

"Is Caleb alive?" I blurted. The doctor peered at me over his glasses.

"I'm Dr. Keegan." The look on his face was intense, grave. For a split second, I thought I might vomit. Dr. Keegan walked around his desk and sat down in his chair.

"Yes, he's alive."

We exhaled sharply as Tiffany gripped my hand harder.

"Is he still breathing on his own?"

"He was when he arrived, but, as a precaution, because his breathing was quite shallow, we inserted a breathing tube."

"So, he's not breathing on his own at all?"

"For now, his body is letting the machine do the work for him."

I sank back weakly into my chair.

"Before we get started," Dr. Keegan began, "I need to lay out a few things first." He looked at us to make sure he had our attention. "Caleb has suffered a traumatic brain injury. And, based on his CT scan, he has suffered what we call a classic *coup-contrecoup* injury."

Tiffany and I exchanged confused looks.

"What typically happens," Dr. Keegan explained, "with a severe brain trauma is, when you have a point of impact like Caleb had on the back of his head, that initial point of impact is called a coup injury. That's where Caleb's brain was first hit by the rock." He shifted slightly before continuing.

"Your brain sits in a bath of fluid, so it essentially floats. When Caleb was struck by the rock in the back of the head, it caused his brain to slosh around and impact the front part of his skull. So, if you look at his CT scan, you will see an egg-sized spot at both the back and the front of his brain. Caleb has suffered two bleeds on his brain, a parenchymal bleed at the front and another at the back, along with a depressed skull fracture. That's a *coup contrecoup* brain injury."

Dr. Keegan pressed us for details of the accident.

"How long was he on the ground before help arrived?"

"It had to have been at least forty minutes, right, Tiffany?"

Dr. Keegan looked thoughtful.

"Before that, you said that it had taken some time to get him back up the trail? How long would you estimate it was altogether before Caleb got medical attention?"

"More than an hour. At least an hour and ten minutes."

Dr. Keegan grimaced. "That is one of the things that we have working against us here. The fact that he was out there so long without medical help is ... well, it's simply not in his favor. It's within the first moments, really the first hour, that it's most critical to receive medical care. Unfortunately, the fact that he was out there without medical help for such a long period of time will factor into his chances of recovery."

Tiffany began to sob softly. My heart was pounding in fear. It seemed inevitable that Caleb would die. The doctor leaned toward us.

"You should know that I'm a terrible liar. So, I want to be upfront and honest, and let you know what we're going to be facing over the next few days. The next seventy-two hours are going to be critical."

"Because of brain swelling?" I asked, numbly. Dr. Keegan nodded.

"Over the next seventy-two hours, Caleb's brain is going to swell. That's inevitable, because of the trauma his brain has suffered. And, because his brain is inside his skull, a rigid, closed space, if it swells too much, the brain will begin to suffocate, and will suffer even further damage. If it continues to swell, brain cells will start to die." Dr. Keegan looked at us intently. "The patient will become brain dead." At our horrified expressions, Dr. Keegan quickly continued.

"Now, because we do anticipate Caleb's brain swelling, there are a number of things we will do. First, we're going to give him some medications to help with the swelling, to hopefully pull fluids from his body in order to give his brain more room to expand. And we're going to manipulate his ventilator to decrease the carbon dioxide in his body, which should also help with the swelling. Tomorrow, we will likely put in what's called an intracranial pressure or ICP monitor. The monitor will help us calculate how much pressure the swelling is causing on Caleb's brain. It will also help us gauge how much medicine to give him and when to use the various therapies I've just explained to you. Are you following me so far?"

We nodded.

"Do you think the medications will be enough to keep the swelling down?"

"We hope so. That's what we're aiming for. If it doesn't, then there are other options at that point that we may have to consider."

"Like what?" I asked. Dread was eating a hole in my stomach, like battery acid.

"If the medications are not effective, then we may drill a hole into Caleb's skull to alleviate the pressure, and possibly remove a large portion of his skull."

Tiffany gasped and clapped her hand over her mouth. I sat there, rigid. Dr. Keegan held up his hand.

"We're going to try the medications first and hope it does the job we need it to do." He paused. "There's more. Another thing I need to mention is that, over the next few days, especially while his brain swells, it is imperative that he has very limited stimulation, as little as absolutely possible. So, to help with that, we are going to put him into a drug-induced coma. We're also going to give him some medications, as he's now at risk for seizures because of his injury. We're also going to give him some potent sedatives and pain medications so he's comfortable and completely still."

I tried hard to absorb what Dr. Keegan was saying. He

told us how Caleb might need a blood transfusion, how we could expect high fevers, and how he also was going to have a number of lines put in his body: a Foley catheter, a naso-gastric tube, and both femoral and brachial lines for intravenous medications and regular lab tests. They would regulate his food intake via a feeding tube through his nose in order to measure the amount of fluid going in and coming out. It was dizzying.

"You mentioned that, when Caleb was on the ground waiting for help to arrive, he vomited?" Dr. Keegan asked. I nodded. "I'm afraid that means there is a chance he may have aspirated."

"What does that mean?"

"When Caleb vomited, because he was unconscious or semi-conscious, there is a very good possibility that some of the fluid in his throat may have entered his lungs. If that's the case, then there's a good chance he could develop pneumonia. But," he hurriedly added, "we've already started Caleb on a broad spectrum antibiotic as a precaution." He looked at each of us.

"There is also one more issue we need to discuss."

My head was spinning. Would the bad news never end?

"When we did an x-ray of Caleb's head, if you remember, I said we'd discovered that, at the point of impact, he has what's called a depressed skull fracture. What that means is that we found a skull fragment pressed against his brain. Now, we can't tell from the x-ray image how much of a problem this skull fragment presents. If it protrudes inward and his brain continues to swell, it might pierce the brain tissue and cause further damage."

"What can we do?" I blurted, before he could finish. "Do we need to do surgery to get it out, or what?"

"Right now we really can't do anything because Caleb is

entering a very critical stage. We don't want to do anything to stimulate him or increase his brain pressure over the next few days. We'll have a specialist look at the x-ray to determine what the next course of action should be."

I sat there, rubbing my eyes. Dr. Keegan gave us a sympathetic look.

"That's all we need to discuss tonight. We'll continue chest x-rays daily to make sure his lines and tubes are all in the right places, and we'll do another CT scan in the morning to see whether anything has changed as far as the bleeds on Caleb's brain are concerned. But, for now, the most important thing is to keep the swelling in his brain down as much as possible, and that's what we'll begin working on tonight."

Dr. Keegan got to his feet.

"We'll meet you in the morning to talk about a few more things, but, for tonight, the best thing for you two—and I know this is hard—but the best thing is for you to get some rest. You are going to have some very important decisions ahead of you this week and Caleb is going to need both of you to be rested and alert in order to make those decisions. OK?" We nodded.

"Can we see Caleb now?"

"Of course." He led us out into the hallway and pointed toward a door. "There. Room number seven." We shook hands.

"Get some rest," he ordered, and strode down the hallway and out of sight.

CHAPTER SIX

"Don't Talk To Me About God!"

Caleb had a private room right in front of the nurse's station. The lights were dim. A perpetual low-pitched hum was pierced by numerous machines beeping and buzzing, machines working hard to keep our son alive. Caleb lay on his side, wearing only a diaper and a neck brace, looking frighteningly fragile. Tubes and wires were everywhere. Patches of his hair were still clotted with blood. Tape was plastered across his cheeks, nose, and mouth, holding the breathing and feeding tubes in place. One arm bore the needle of an IV, the other a blood pressure cuff. A nurse was there.

"Can he hear us?"

"Yes, he can hear you," she said in a low voice. "Speak to him calmly and very quietly. It's important not to upset or agitate him. We need to keep his brain pressure down."

Tiffany and I sat down next to Caleb's bed. Tiffany held my hand and rested her other hand on Caleb. He looked peaceful, as if he was sleeping. His chest moved up and down in a steady rhythm, the breathing machine pumping oxygen into his lungs. His eyes flickered back and forth beneath his eyelids, as if he were dreaming, reassuring us he was indeed alive. Despite the tangle of tubes, he looked like he might wake up at any moment and bounce out of bed. But he couldn't.

"Oh, my baby, my little buddy," I whispered, tears sliding down my face. Tiffany and I placed our hands on his hand, weeping. "Baby, Mommy and Daddy love you so much. Mommy and Daddy are right here. Do you hear me? We're not going anywhere. We're staying right here, with you."

I turned to Tiffany.

"I'm so sorry for being so selfish. We could have just gone back to the campground, like you suggested. If it hadn't been for me, we wouldn't have gone on this trip in the first place."

"Tim, it's not your fault," Tiffany whispered. "You couldn't have known anything would happen."

I looked back at Caleb and grasped his hand.

"I love him so much. I can't lose him, Tiffany. I can't lose my little boy."

"I know. I can't either," Tiffany sobbed.

"Why would God allow this to happen?" I cried.

Tiffany squeezed my forearm.

"Tim, this isn't God's fault. This isn't anyone's fault. We have to have faith. We have to pray and believe that God loves Caleb, loves him even more than we do."

I reached over and gently placed my hand on Caleb's head. I closed my eyes and prayed. I prayed hard.

∽

When we returned to the waiting room where Colby, Chassi, and Misty still sat, most of our family and friends had arrived. Everyone gasped and burst into tears at the sight of our bloodstained clothes. I told them what the doctor had said. My dad knelt and put his hand on my knee.

"We're going to get through this, son. We're going to get through this together."

I began recounting everything that had happened.

"We were hiking," I choked, "going down the trail at Fall Creek Falls." My voice trailed away and I could feel anger welling up inside of me again, anger at God. I burst into tears. "I just don't understand why God would allow this to happen!" Immediately everyone began reassuring me that God had nothing to do with it.

Lost in my thoughts, the voices around me faded.

I thought back to all we'd gone through the past year or more, the lessons on faith that God had taught us. I had thought about them so much over the last year that I had them committed to heart. One by one, I ticked them off in my head. The first lesson was about the substance of faith, what faith is. Faith, I knew, was believing that what God says is true, no matter what, and knowing that God will supply whatever is needed for His will to be accomplished. The second, I recalled, was that God will sometimes allow difficult circumstances in our lives, ones that are designed to grow our faith and bring us into a deeper relationship with Him.

Third, God will sometimes allow humanly impossible circumstances, ones that only He can resolve, not only to teach us valuable lessons and bring us into a deeper relationship with Him, but also to draw other people to faith as well. As I considered the third lesson, I felt a twinge in my spirit. Is this what God was doing, I asked myself? Was God allowing this for some greater purpose? At the moment, it didn't matter. I was angry. This was *our* son we were talking about. I gritted my teeth.

I looked around at everyone.

"Look, I appreciate everyone trying to make me feel better, but the truth is that God is Sovereign. He knows everything. He is everywhere at once and He has all power, right? So, if He is Sovereign, then nothing happens by accident. Nothing! If anything happens in my life as a Christian, it has to first come before the Father before it comes to me. God either causes or allows or denies all things that happen in my life. If this was the work of Satan, then God allowed it. If it was just a rock falling off a cliff, then God allowed it. He could have stopped it, and He chose not to. He knew exactly when and where that rock was going to hit, and He knew it would hit my son. So, I'm sorry, but the blame ultimately lies with God!" I knew I was being irrational, lost in fear and pain.

Tiffany reminded me again that we had to trust and have faith. I interrupted.

"Don't talk to me about God." When another family member encouraged me to keep faith, I shouted.

"Don't talk to me about God!" At their startled looks, I felt guilty and stood. "I have to go. I have to get out of here," I said. "I'm going back to see Caleb."

I walked out. My brother, Travis, followed. As I reached the double doors of the PICU, I broke down and wept bitterly. Travis gripped my shoulder as he caught up with me.

"Tim, remember when we went to Gatlinburg a few months ago? What did you tell me?"

"I don't know," I sniffled. "I don't remember."

"You told me that God had spoken to you, that you were going to need your whole heart for something that was coming. Tim," he said, urgently, "this is it. You have been so strong in your faith for so long. You can't lose it now. If you've ever needed your faith, it's right now. Your son needs your faith."

My brother's words felt like a ton of bricks hitting my soul. "I know," I choked. My knees nearly buckled as I threw my hands in the air. "God, is this what You were talking about? Is this what You meant?" I felt confused. I clung to Travis and wept. "I can't lose my son, Travis. I just can't!"

"I know, Tim. I know."

In a nearby bathroom, I stared at myself in the mirror, my

gaze roaming over my red, tear-streaked swollen face, the filth of my clothes and the blood—so much blood, everywhere. "Is this real?" I whispered, watching my lips move. "Is this really happening?" And what about God? What was He doing? The lessons on faith, my brother's confirmation to me about what God had said, the events leading up to the accident, the fear that something was going to happen—what did it all mean? I knew it was time to get away for a while.

It was time to talk to God.

The Piney Fire Department had left our car in the hospital's parking garage, as promised. I looked inside. Everything was just the way we had left it. Our bags were all still neatly arranged. The boys' toys lay right where they had left them. It was an image of what was supposed to have been the perfect camping trip. But now everything had changed. Our entire lives had changed. I was convinced nothing would ever feel normal again.

I sank down into the back seat, where Caleb had sat just a few hours earlier, and began to sob. To my right was a neatly arranged set of clothes with a tiny pair of shoes on top, a simple, loving gesture from a mother who anticipated her son having fun, getting dirty, splashing in the water and mud. Instead, he was lying in a hospital room, unconscious, close to death.

Why! Why! Why! I sobbed to God. Why would You do this to me? I have served You my entire life! I've tried so hard to follow You and obey Your will. I've tried so hard to live my life for You. You know my heart. You know how much I love my family. I've tried to be a good father and a good husband. I know I've sinned. I know I've done some bad things in my life. I admit I deserve punishment. But why my son? Why not me instead? You had the power to direct that rock to me! Why does my two-year-old son have to be lying in a hospital bed? Why does he have to be the one to die? *Why?*

I picked up Caleb's shirt and breathed in his scent. I tried to imagine him getting through this, of all of us going home as if nothing had happened, but I couldn't. There's no way he can pull through this, I thought. No one gets hit in the head with a huge boulder falling from two hundred and fifty feet and lives to tell about it. This is it. It's the end. I'm going to lose my son.

I felt completely undone. I sat, unaware of time passing, silently crying and pleading with God to answer my prayer and save my son's life. I watched as people emerged from the elevator and walked to their cars, smiling. How quickly life can turn on a dime, I thought. They're thinking that today is going to be like yesterday, and that tomorrow is always going to be like today.

I looked away. You just don't wake up in the morning and wonder if by the end of the day you are going to lose one of your children. You just don't. Bad things like this happen to other people.

Except that, today, we were the *other* people.

∽

The hospital had arranged for a couple rooms for us, until they could secure one for us at the Ronald McDonald House across the street. I sent Tiffany off with Colby and her sisters to get some rest while the rest of the group went out in search of a nearby hotel. I stayed alone with Caleb until exhaustion overwhelmed me.

After peeking in on Colby, who was fast asleep in the next room with his aunts, I tiptoed in to where Tiffany lay. She was awake and had clearly been crying for some time. An open Bible lay on the bed beside her. I sat on the edge of the bed and put a hand on her shoulder.

"Hey, how are you?"

"It just hurts. I just wish we could all go home. I miss having our family together. I miss Caleb, and I miss Connor so much."

"I know. I miss them too," I replied. I glanced down at the Bible beside her, picked it up, and gripped it tightly. I closed my eyes and prayed, "I need to hear from You, please. If there has ever been a time when I have needed to hear Your voice, it's right now." I tossed the Bible back onto the bed, praying that whatever page it fell to would be the page that contained what I needed to hear. It was an unorthodox approach, but I was desperate. I looked down and saw Psalm 90 and I felt myself stiffen as I read words about man's sin and God's anger.

"It figures!" I spat. At Tiffany's startled look, I said, "It's about judgment." I felt every wrong thing I had ever done stand accusingly in front of me.

"I just don't understand, Tiff," I said, despairingly, as I sat down heavily next to her. "I don't get it. I know God is loving, and I know He cares about us, that He loves Caleb. I just don't understand why He would let this happen."

Tiffany had no answer. She held me tightly, until we finally fell into a troubled sleep.

∼

Three hours later, bleary-eyed, we woke up, anxious to see how Caleb was doing. When I emerged from the bathroom, Tiffany looked up at me from her Bible, her expression pensive.

"Honey, I think you were supposed to read Psalm 91."

"What?"

"Last night, when you were upset. I don't think you were

supposed to read Psalm 90. I think you were supposed to read Psalm 91. It's on the same page. Look."

To humor her, I glanced at it briefly as I got dressed, but didn't see anything that resonated with me. Tiffany left me to go see Caleb. Moments later, I placed the Bible back on the bed and after pausing to check on Colby, I headed upstairs to Caleb's room.

Caleb lay exactly as we had left him hours earlier. More family and friends arrived and we joined them in the hallway. Tiffany seemed calmer now, still fearful, but hopeful. I, on the other hand felt agitated, pessimistic and angry, very angry. I knew that underneath my anger was a deeper struggle with shame and guilt. I wondered if somehow everything had to do with my own failures in life, my own sins. Maybe I was the one being punished, and this had been all my fault.

Tiffany hugged her friends, Tammy and Donna, while I greeted Tammy's husband James and Ken, both good friends of mine. Just then another figure made her way through the crowd toward me. It was June Price, who led the Wednesday evening women's Bible study that my wife attended. As I looked into her wet aged eyes I could tell she wanted to tell me something. She reached out and took my hand.

"Tim, you must accept that this is not your fault. I know you have feelings of guilt, but you have to remember that Jesus took all of our punishment on the cross—all of it. God is not punishing you. That's not what this is about."

I was stunned. How in the world did she just speak to the very things I was feeling? I knew she was right. I knew in my head that what she said was exactly what scripture taught. I just wasn't feeling it in my heart.

Steve Austin and Allen Morrell from 180 Degrees Ministries were seated in the waiting room. Allen asked whether

Tiffany and I would be willing to talk with them privately for a few moments and pray.

We found an empty room just down the hall. They asked how Tiffany and I were doing together as a couple and how we were doing with our faith, in light of all we were going through. We admitted that we had not been very close to each other recently, and that we had been dealing with our feelings individually, separately, in our own way.

"One of the reasons why we wanted to talk to you," Steve said, "is because we want to encourage you to stand together throughout this ordeal and lean on each other for comfort and strength." They urged us to make sure that, despite all the well-wishers, family, and friends surrounding us, we took time to be alone with each other, to talk and process things together. It was good advice. Tiffany and I hadn't even discussed our feelings about the accident with each other yet.

When the subject of faith inevitably arose, I could feel my anger well up again. It had been at one of Steve and Allen's seminars where I had first learned how to listen for God's voice, and, days later, had first heard God speak. Steve had reiterated many times back then how God allowed difficulties in our lives and that "all things work together for those who love the Lord." This "process," as they put it, was specifically designed by God to teach things that we would otherwise never learn, things meant to help us discover more of who God is and who we are in Him.

"How does this fit into God's plan?" I demanded. "I don't get it! God knew that rock was going to hit Caleb. He knew it! He knew we would be there, and He knew that it would happen, and He didn't stop it." I was railing. I couldn't help myself. "He could have let it hit me. It didn't hit anyone else. Instead, He allowed it to hit Caleb. The Bible says, 'Which of you, if his son asks for bread, will give him a stone? Or, if he asks for a fish, will give him a snake?' I know how to give good things to my precious little boy, but God decided to throw a rock at him?"

As I spoke those last words, I knew I was being unjust. But I couldn't reconcile a loving God with my two-year-old son being near death, especially when I knew that God had all the power of the universe at His fingertips and could have stopped it.

"You're right," Steve acknowledged. "God knew you would be right there at that moment. He knew it and He allowed Caleb to be hit with the rock." He looked thoughtful. "But what if you are looking at this through the wrong lens? What if, instead of seeing this as God throwing a rock at your son because He's angry at you, God actually saved your son's life?" I looked at him in disbelief as he continued. "Tiffany told us earlier that she heard God say, 'Turn.'"

I went numb. In the midst of all the emotions and anger, I had barely heard what Tiffany had told me, what she had told everyone last night in the waiting room, that right when we heard the thundering crash of the rock coming down the gorge, a voice in her heart, God's voice, had said, "Turn." She had turned slightly, which had taken her out of the rock's path, which would have surely crushed them both. I stared at Steve, as his words began to sink in.

"What if God interfered to *prevent* the rock from killing Caleb?" he continued. "And what about Tiffany? God told Tiffany to move and she moved. And what about the young firefighter who just happened to be right there, practically beside you, when it happened? The one who took over for you when you couldn't get Caleb back up the mountain? The one who just happened to be training to become an EMT? The only one by your side who had the strength to carry your son back to the top? The one who saved his life that day at the park?" I stood, frozen, as Steve's words rang in my ears.

"And what about all those medical people, the doctors and nurses who just happened to be hiking the trail that day? And what were the odds that all this happened in reach of one of the best brain trauma facilities for children in the entire Southeast?" Steve put his hands on my shoulders.

"What if God has planned something extraordinary, something involving your son that will not only affect you in your own growth, in your own faith, but also in the lives and faith of many countless other people?"

My mind raced. How quick I had been to lay blame. The fingerprints of God's activity were literally everywhere. God had orchestrated the entire event from beginning to end. I was convinced of it now. I was again reminded of my lessons on faith, particularly the third lesson about how God sometimes allows seemingly impossible circumstances, not only to grow us in our own faith, but also to draw others to Him as well, for His glory. I wondered for the first time whether we were witnessing the beginning of God demonstrating the truth of those lessons.

I held Tiffany close, crying, as we began to pray. It was then I felt Steve's hand move slowly from my shoulder to my left cheek. I immediately began to sob.

"Why did you do that?"

"Because God told me to."

I felt my knees grow weak. No one but Tiffany could have known the significance of such a gesture. I raised tear-filled eyes to him.

"Do you have any idea what that means to me? When I was a little boy, my great-grandmother used to put her hand on my cheek like that. She raised me. Growing up, I always felt alone, but when she did that, it always made me feel loved, accepted. I've always told Tiffany that there is nothing she does that makes me feel more loved than when she strokes my cheek with her hand." At this point I was crying so hard, I could barely get the words out.

Steve put his arm around my shoulder.

"See? God is letting you know that this is not about you or your past wrongs. This is about God, and what *He* is doing. God is using your son for His purposes."

My anger drained away. God had just confirmed to me through Steve that He was here, powerfully, among us, loving and comforting us. Clearly, one of the reasons I'd been given those lessons on faith was because He knew we would need them as a map to navigate through these turbulent waters. God, I was now convinced, was going to use our son to somehow bring glory to Himself.

When we made our way back to the waiting room, I felt a renewed sense of strength within me, a fire in my bones. Everyone fell silent as we entered. I looked around.

"I know I've been struggling with my feelings recently. I know I've been angry with God, and have wavered in my own faith. But I want you all to know that I'm not going to do it any longer. I will believe. I will not lose faith. We're going to fight!" Everyone cheered. I grinned.

"OK, let's get to work. Let's start getting the word out about prayer. Let's start praying for all the things that are going on with Caleb." I looked around at the eager faces, everyone anxious to participate, to do something. "Call everyone you know, and tell them to tell everyone they know. Get on Facebook and put your prayer requests there. Ask everyone to repost them. Call every church you know and get Caleb's name added to their prayer list. We're going to fight for Caleb!" As everyone reached for laptops and cell phones, I felt a surge of hope.

"Guys, I think we're seeing a miracle in progress here."

CHAPTER SEVEN

Fingerprints Everywhere

"Caleb's brain has begun to swell."

Dr. Keegan removed his glasses, wiping the lenses as he chose his words. "We expect his condition to worsen over the next forty-eight to seventy-two hours, as I warned you before, so there are a number of very important things that we need to do."

Dr. Keegan explained they would insert a brain monitor in Caleb's head to measure his brain pressure, as well as an I.V. trunk line into his abdomen to dispense medicines rapidly, in the event Caleb's brain pressure began to climb. The bone fragment that had broken off in Caleb's skull was worse than originally thought. CT scans had shown that the fragment was uncomfortably close to an artery. Were enough pressure to build up in Caleb's brain, the bone fragment could puncture the artery, causing even more damage.

"I would prefer to avoid surgery at this point because, at such a critical stage, the surgery itself could complicate matters. If they accidentally pierced the artery during surgery, it would damage Caleb's brain."

I glanced at Tiffany, who had gone pale.

"What are we going to do?"

"Right now, the best thing for us to do is to continue focusing on the swelling and make sure we do everything we can to keep it down. Once we get past this critical stage in a few days, and the swelling starts to lessen, then we'll consider our options concerning the bone fragment."

Dr. Keegan took a deep breath and then relayed even worse news. Because of Caleb's head trauma, his brain was no longer regulating his heart and kidneys properly by producing adequate amounts of dopamine and anti-diuretic hormone. Also, Caleb's lungs were starting to show signs of bacterial growth, which meant pneumonia.

Tiffany was sobbing. I was doing my best to remain calm.

"Doctor, is there any chance that Caleb will make it through this?"

"I have to be honest with you. Caleb has suffered severe brain damage. I cannot tell you yet whether he will live or not. I can say with certainty though that, because of the type of injury and the amount of time that Caleb's brain was deprived of sufficient oxygen, if Caleb survives, he will not be the same little boy you had before the accident."

At those words, Tiffany gasped. Leaping to her feet, she bolted toward the door, and was gone before I had even gotten to my feet. I hesitated, standing at the door for a moment staring after her, and then turned and sat back down.

"I am so sorry that you have to go through this," Dr. Keegan said, "but I need you both to be able to make some very hard decisions. This is a very critical time for Caleb."

"What do you need me to do?" I asked. He handed me the release papers granting permission to proceed. As I picked up the pen, I couldn't help but wonder whether I was making a decision that would cause my son to die. I looked at him, pen poised.

"Do you know what kind of damage there will be? To what extent?"

Dr. Keegan shook his head.

"Every brain is different. Although we can see what areas were injured, we cannot, with any real certainty, predict what and how much will be affected. Dr. Keegan pushed back his chair and stood. "My job right now is to create the best possible situation for Caleb in which to recover and, right now, that means getting his brain monitor and trunk line put in."

I signed the release.

∼

Out in the hallway, I bumped into a man who reached out his hand to me.

"Not sure if you remember me, but I'm Jason McKay. My friend and I were camping next to you at Fall Creek Falls." I immediately recognized him as the man with the hair dryer. "I brought some food and some toys," he said, glancing at Colby who was playing nearby. The news had spread around the campground, Jason said, and he asked whether there was anything else he could do. I impulsively hugged him.

"We could really use your prayers. We could use everyone's prayers!"

I got my wish. Jason, as it turned out, was in media and marketing. The "coincidences" were starting to pile up, I thought to myself.

Jason broadcast our plea for prayers on Facebook. After that, calls began pouring in, including ones from local TV stations looking for interviews. I recoiled at the idea of my son's tragedy being just another media spectacle, but Officer Jamie Walling from the Van Buren County Sheriff's Office, the lead investigator on the case, who had driven us to the hospital after the accident, suggested we consider speaking with the media.

"If your story gets picked up, it might produce an eyewitness or two and help us determine what happened." That's when it dawned on me that it might also be a good way to encourage even more people to pray for Caleb.

∼

I looked down at the frail, small body lying curled on its side. It was hard looking at all the tubes that were running into him now, including the new monitor line that exited just above his right temple. Six millimeters mercury (mmHg), the ICP monitor display read. The doctor had told us that five was the average intracranial pressure for a person, and that Caleb's had been varying between five and ten. Under normal conditions, he'd said, brain pressure could fluctuate safely up to as high as twenty-five or thirty, because the brain can regulate itself and bring the pressure back down. However, he'd admitted, Caleb's brain, because of the swelling, wasn't capable of regulating those pressures. That's why having the monitor inserted had been so critical.

"We need to keep him down to between ten and fifteen in terms of pressure. If it goes up to twenty-five or more for a prolonged period of time, he may suffer additional brain damage." He had cautioned us to try not to obsess about the monitor readings, as there were other factors to consider when looking at his overall health.

One of the nurses suggested we provide things that Caleb might find comforting and familiar, such as a favorite stuffed animal or music.

"Would it be okay if we read to him? He loves that. We always read to him at bedtime." My thought was we'd give him something familiar, like doing his nighttime routine, to help calm him.

"As long you don't over-stimulate him, you should be fine. That's the most important thing at this point. We have to make sure his ICP stays down."

Tiffany and I sat down next to Caleb's hospital bed and took turns reading some of his favorite books to him. In the dimmed lights of the room, Caleb looked as though he was asleep. Now in a deep coma, it had been days since we had seen him open his eyes. Every now and then we could see his eyes move beneath his eyelids, or an eyebrow twitch, and sometimes a slight movement in one of his fingers. As we took turns reading to him, Caleb's ICP pressure occasionally increased, making us think that perhaps Caleb was reacting to the stories we were reading him, that he could hear us despite the coma. We studied each movement carefully, hoping these occasional twitches were signs of life—signs that Caleb was still with us.

"Okay, buddy, you want to go tuck-tuck?" I carefully laid his soft blue blanket over him and tucked him in. Tiffany and I both kissed him softly.

As we prepared to leave, a nurse entered the room. Looking at the ICP monitor, which was now hovering between five and six, she gave an approving nod.

"I think it worked well."

"He's still with us," Tiffany said, tears of joy welling in her eyes. "He knew we were here with him."

The hospital had arranged a room for us across the street at the Ronald McDonald House. As I stood washing my hands in the ground floor men's room, I spotted a little plaque above the sink bearing a single line of scripture, Psalm 91:11, the very same verse I had repeated incessantly the night before our trip, when my dad's phone call had had me fearing something bad might happen to one of the kids. It had also been the verse that

Tiffany's mother said she had prayed as she drove from Nashville to Chattanooga the day of the accident. When I mentioned it to Tiffany, she gave me a searching look.

"You do know that that's the scripture I asked you to read this morning, right?" I looked at her, baffled.

"This morning, when I told you that I felt God wanted you to read Psalm 91, not Psalm 90?"

I stood stock-still.

"I never saw it. I was so angry, so caught up in my emotions, that I never made the connection. You're right. And I never saw it." I pulled out my Bible and began to read.

¹ "Whoever dwells in the shelter of the Most High will rest in the shadow of the Almighty. ² I will say of the Lord, "He is my refuge and my fortress, my God, in whom I trust. ³ Surely he will save you from the fowler's snare and from the deadly pestilence. ⁴ He will cover you with his feathers, and under his wings you will find refuge; his faithfulness will be your shield and rampart. ⁵ You will not fear the terror of night, nor the arrow that flies by day, ⁶ nor the pestilence that stalks in the darkness, nor the plague that destroys at midday. ⁷ A thousand may fall at your side, ten thousand at your right hand, but it will not come near you. ⁸ You will only observe with your eyes and see the punishment of the wicked. ⁹ If you say, "The Lord is my refuge," and you make the Most High your dwelling, ¹⁰ no harm will overtake you, no disaster will come near your tent. ¹¹ For he will command his angels concerning you to guard you in all your ways; ¹² they will lift you up in their hands, so that you will not strike your foot against a stone. ¹³ You will tread on the lion and the cobra; you will trample the great lion and the serpent. ¹⁴ "Because he loves me," says the Lord, "I will rescue him; I will protect him, for he acknowledges my name. ¹⁵ He will call on me, and I will answer him; I will be with him in trouble, I will deliver him and honor him. ¹⁶ With long life I will satisfy him and show him my salvation."

Phrases began to leap out at me. *No harm will overtake you, no disaster will come near your tent.* Tent? I was struck by the very things I had prayed for as Caleb was being rescued. *For he will command his angels concerning you to guard you in all your ways.*

I thought of Michael Tagert, the young firefighter who had indeed been like an angel to us, bearing Caleb up the mountain in his arms, up to where help could reach him. *They will lift you up in their hands, so that you will not strike your foot against a stone.* I looked numbly at the word "stone." I remembered praying after Michael took Caleb into his arms and began to run, that he not stumble or fall. *"Because he loves me," says the Lord, "I will rescue him; I will protect him, for he acknowledges my name. He will call on me, and I will answer him; I will be with him in trouble, I will deliver him and honor him.* I drew a shuddering breath. *With long life I will satisfy him and show him my salvation.* I asked myself whether it could be that God was saying through this scripture that Caleb was not going to die, that he would live a long life and eventually see Christ's salvation. I prayed it was so.

That night, once Colby was tucked to sleep and Tiffany and I were getting ready for bed, my mind raced with everything that God had shown us. I wondered about what things might still lie ahead. With the sounds of Tiffany's soft, rhythmic breathing as she slept in the background, I replayed the epiphany I'd had earlier and prayed for God to give us the wisdom and strength we needed to weather the days ahead, to keep our faith strong. I felt exhaustion wash over me, pulling me into sleep.

As soon as I began to close my eyes, it happened.

I opened my eyes and found myself sitting atop a tall swivel chair. Caleb was lying comatose in his hospital bed next to me, eyes closed. I could hear the beeping sounds, so familiar to me now, emitting from the machines surrounding his bed. As I gazed down at him, Caleb's eyes flickered and then opened. He looked right at me. I gasped, as my heart began to pound within me.

I blinked rapidly and looked around the room in confusion. The clock showed I had only been asleep for a few minutes.

"What was that?" I asked myself, as I lay panting, trying to catch my breath.

CHAPTER EIGHT

Let Me Help You

The next morning, I awoke early. I was convinced that the only thing that would save my son at this point would be God Himself, and ever since I had asked my family to start getting the word out about prayer, I had devised a plan of my own.

What if God was doing something behind the scenes, to use our son for His glory somehow? If thousands of people prayed, I reasoned, would God not be more glorified? Perhaps enough to work a miracle for Caleb and heal him? I felt desperate.

My mind wandered back to the days prior to Caleb's accident, when I had been working on my marketing business. One of the services I offered was voice broadcasting for churches. It dawned on me that I had a system containing the phone numbers of all twelve thousand churches in Tennessee. All I had to do was log into my system, set up the voice mail with the prayer request, and click send.

Feeling almost jubilant, I strode into the family room of the Ronald McDonald House and sat down in front of one of the desktops they made available, fingers twitching in anticipation. That's when the problems began. I clicked onto Internet Explorer.

Nothing. I couldn't get online.

I quickly switched to another computer. The same thing happened. I couldn't believe it! I tried all the computers and none of them would access. I checked the network connections, made a few adjustments, muttered a prayer or two, and then finally I accessed the Web. Exhaling, I typed in the URL for my online marketing account. The login page popped up. I typed in my login information and clicked enter. An error message popped up, asking me to re-enter my user name and password. I chided myself for my haste and typed it in again. The same error message popped up.

What on earth was going on?

Over and over, I tried. Finally, after numerous issues and frustrating attempts, I felt ready to scream. Here I was, having been divinely inspired, being prevented from doing the very thing I knew I should be doing. Angrily, I hit enter again.

I was in.

Heaving an audible sigh of relief, I glanced at my watch. Three hours had passed. For a fleeting moment, I was reminded of the previous time I'd been so dogged, so determined, overcoming the onslaught of obstacles that had lain between us and taking this trip. I brushed that troublesome thought away and clicked through the site pages to access my database, those precious twelve thousand church telephone numbers that I felt God had had a hand in providing me, the numbers I needed to secure those heartfelt prayers to God to help Caleb.

They were gone. I couldn't explain it, but somehow they were gone.

∼

I trudged back to the hospital, my mood alternating between rage and despair. I had wasted more than three hours, hours I could have spent with Caleb--and achieved nothing. Every possible thing that could have gotten in the way of my sending out that massive prayer request had been placed in my path. What on earth was the point? I had been convinced that, if I could solicit hundreds of thousands of people to pray for Caleb, he might survive, even be healed. I felt hopeless.

That afternoon, I was thrown a life preserver.

Jennifer Homa, the hospital's public relations coordinator, came looking for us. Channel 3, WRCB, in Chattanooga, was pressing for an interview. I thought about my thwarted attempt to rally widespread prayer and made up my mind.

"Okay, we'll do it."

"Great! I'll set it up right now, here at the hospital."

An hour or so later, Tiffany and I were squinting under bright lights opposite a reporter and cameraman. As we fielded questions, it felt surreal, as if we were in a movie rather than real life. I could see myself in front of the television on a typical evening watching a report like this and thinking, "Wow, that is so sad," before turning off the television and returning to the daily distractions of my own life, of my family's life. But, this time it wasn't just a story on TV—this was *our* life.

As the interview wrapped up, we noticed two police officers watching us from the sidelines. Assistant Chief Mike Williams and his wife Heather, both of the Chattanooga Police Department, told us that they, too, had been at the park that day, and had come by to see how Caleb was doing. After giving them an update, Mike Williams asked if he might speak to me privately.

"I have an e-mail newsletter that I send out to police officers and their families. With your permission, I'd like to include a prayer request in it for Caleb." I gave him a grateful smile. "The newsletter goes out to twelve thousand officers and their families," he added.

I froze.

"*How many?*"

"Twelve thousand."

I had just spent the entire morning unsuccessfully trying to send out a message to twelve thousand churches. Now, standing in front of me was a man who was offering to send out a prayer request to the same number of families, many, I was sure, who were members of those same churches. Tiffany looked at me.

"I think God is telling us that He is in control."

She was right, I realized. God, I felt, was saying, *Let Me help you. Step back, focus on your son, and let Me do the rest.*

When we got back to the PICU waiting room, I was surprised to see Darvin Oakes, the owner of Sunrise Campground where we had camped, and his daughter, Jana. As we chatted, Darvin handed me a neatly folded list of more than twenty churches.

"When we first heard the news, it spread through the campground like wildfire and the surrounding campgrounds as well. People are constantly coming in asking about Caleb. Everyone, and I mean everyone, is praying for Caleb and adding him to their church prayer lists. So far, here's twenty, and there are more coming in every hour."

I scanned the list that Jana had compiled. It contained all different denominations, believers from every background imaginable.

"This is incredible."

"I know," Darvin replied. "I've never seen anything like it."

Cards, calls, and even visitors began pouring in from all over the country. One woman had driven all the way from Dalton, Georgia, to pray with us and offer encouragement. Ministers from churches all over the Southeast were arriving to pray over Caleb. The love and support of strangers everywhere was both astonishing and humbling.

By this stage we'd had to designate family members to answer phones and take messages. News media agencies from Nashville and Chattanooga were among the calls. Jennifer Homa, the hospital's PR coordinator, was getting more and more media requests, and asked whether we would consider doing a press conference the next day.

Tiffany and I were humbled by what we were witnessing. What I had hoped I would accomplish by my own efforts, God had apparently intended to accomplish Himself all along. God was indeed doing something behind the scenes. He was now getting the attention of tens of thousands of people from all over the country. The third lesson on faith, I thought, was about to be fulfilled.

By the end of the day, Tiffany and I were exhausted and sought some quiet time together. As we sat in a dimly lit room in a quiet section of the PICU, Tiffany and I began talking about the day's events, particularly where we had seen God's fingerprints.

"I've noticed a change in you," I confided to Tiffany.

"You have?"

"You seem calmer, more at peace."

"I do," she sighed and took my hand. "Remember in the car at the falls, when we told Colby and Caleb that we loved them, but that God loved them more? I've been thinking about that over the past few days. God really does love Caleb, more than we will ever know."

She began to cry.

"One thing I've always struggled with is the idea of loving God more than anything else, even more than my family, my kids. I feel like God is calling me to love Him more than anything else right now, to trust Him with our son. If God chooses to let Caleb live and come home with us, of course I will love God. But, if He doesn't, if He takes Caleb home with Him, I will still love Him."

I was startled by the depth of my wife's faith even in the midst of her fear. I admired her, but knew I didn't feel the same way. I was unwilling to consider the possibility of Caleb dying.

"This peace I feel, this acceptance," she said, her concerned eyes on mine, "I know it's not me. I know that God has placed it in me."

Tiffany related how her friend Tammy had played her a song earlier—*Cry On My Shoulder*, by Overflow. She said the song spoke about God's love and our ability to cast our burdens on Him, to cry on His shoulder, and the promise that the pain we go through in life would not last forever. She said the song had really moved her and she felt it was God speaking to her. She also said that, in their prayer time together, Tammy had heard a voice within.

Listen! Listen past the voices of everyone else, even the doctors. Listen to Me. I am the Great Physician.

"So what do you think it all means?" I asked as Tiffany leaned her head against my shoulder.

"I don't know, but I do feel that God is calling us to trust Him."

We sat and hugged each other in silence. The warmth of her body against mine was comforting.

That evening, I sat quietly at Caleb's bedside. After we finished our bedtime ritual with Caleb, Tiffany took Colby back to the Ronald McDonald House to put him to bed. I felt wiped out. Over the course of the day, amid all the activity, Caleb's ICP numbers had begun to climb. The love, support, and prayers of everyone we encountered, while enormously encouraging, weren't enough to extinguish the dread I felt toward what the coming days would bring.

I sat, with eyes glued to Caleb's face, recalling the dream I'd had the previous night. The machine was pumping slow, measured breaths into Caleb's lungs. I watched as his eyes moved ever so slowly beneath his eyelids and thought of how he'd opened his eyes and looked directly at me in the dream. Would I ever see him open his eyes again?

I rubbed my tired eyes and stood to give Caleb a kiss goodnight. As I leaned over him, Caleb's eyes flickered open. I gasped and tears filled my eyes.

"Caleb! Hey, Caleb, my sweet boy, can you see me?"

Caleb's eyes stared fixedly forward. I moved to where he could see me.

"I don't know if you can see me or not, baby, but I want you to know I love you so much!" There was no response, just an empty stare. Then he blinked, closed his eyes, and drifted back to oblivion. I ran back to the Ronald McDonald House to share the news with Tiffany.

Tiffany was skeptical.

"Honey, the doctors told us that, with him being in a coma like this, he can't see. He probably didn't even know he was opening his eyes. You said it yourself. He wasn't looking at you. And he closed them without any indication he'd seen anything."

"But it was just like my dream," I insisted. "I dreamed he'd open his eyes and he did."

Tiffany refused to be convinced and I really couldn't blame her. Maybe I was getting my hopes up a little precipitously. She was cautiously protecting her heart. I didn't want to hurt her further.

After tucking Colby in and reading him some bedtime stories, I sank down onto the bed next to her.

"Maybe you're right. But I still don't think the dream was an accident."

She said nothing. As we lay there, shoulder to shoulder, I felt my eyes grow heavy. Sleep had been doing nothing to erase the incredible weariness I felt, the weariness I was sure we both felt. Within seconds I nodded off. And then it happened. Again.

I saw Caleb lying in his hospital bed with his eyes open. He was staring at Tiffany, who was leaning in close, sitting in the high swivel chair next to him. I stood behind her, smiling down at him over her shoulder. I touched Tiffany's shoulder and leaned in more closely as Caleb's eyes moved from Tiffany to me. My heart was bursting with love for him. Expressionless, he gazed into my eyes.

I awoke abruptly with my heart racing in my chest. What could this mean? Would Caleb look at us tomorrow? I didn't know what to think. Was I just being hopeful, or was God actually showing me something? I didn't know what to do except pray. I prayed until I fell asleep.

CHAPTER NINE

Of Dreams and Visions

The next morning, we headed straight for the PICU and our third morning meeting with the staff. There was both good news and bad news. Caleb, they predicted, might be nearing the peak of his brain swelling and we would likely know as early as that evening whether it was true. Although the brain was still continuing to swell slightly, Caleb had exhibited moderately low ICP levels throughout the night.

The bad news was that Caleb's brain had not yet started producing dopamine, which would have a negative effect on his heart. If Caleb's brain didn't start producing its own dopamine by the following day, they said, they would begin weaning him off the dopamine drip to encourage him to produce it on his own. The concern, they said, was that his body might well become dependent on receiving it artificially, thereby impairing his progress. As I sat trying to absorb all the information, another doctor spoke.

"One thing we want to see as we come over this peak, as Caleb's brain swelling starts to come down, is purposeful movement. We want to see him move his hands, feet, and body in a meaningful, deliberate way. We know that some neurological damage has occurred, but we don't know how much. Right now, he's in a coma because we've given him drugs to keep him that way, to reduce stimuli. But, as the swelling goes down, we're going to start backing off the meds and allow him to wake up a little at a time…"

The doctor looked at us both and I couldn't help but feel my heart sink at his next words: "…then we'll see how much of Caleb is still there."

"Now, about the bone fragment," another doctor began. I braced myself. "It appears that, when the bone fragment broke off, it did not cause an intrusion into Caleb's brain as we'd feared—it broke off flat, more like a plate. What we're hoping will happen over time is that the plate will eventually fuse back together with the rest of Caleb's skull." Tiffany and I glanced at each other, exhaling sharply. I hadn't realized I'd been holding my breath. I took her hand.

"Isn't the bone fragment still lodged up against the artery?"

"The specialist doesn't think we need to be overly concerned about it." At my expression, he added, "Of course, we'll keep monitoring it."

I thought back to what they had said about purposeful movement and told them about Caleb opening his eyes the night before. They shook their heads. An involuntary, reflex-type movement they called it.

After the meeting ended, Tiffany and I spoke to the nurses about Colby. He'd been struggling understandably with all that had been going on and was fearful that his brother would never be the same, that none of us would ever be the same. We weren't sure how to reassure him so we asked about possibly meeting with one of the Child Life Specialists they had recommended when we'd first arrived. As it turned out, there was one onsite in the PICU.

The Child Life Specialist listened to how we had been handling Colby, letting him express his feelings. Not knowing what else to do, we'd simply let him express to us exactly how he felt, and repeated that we loved him, that we were there for him, and that he was safe.

"Keep it up," she advised. "That's exactly what he needs. Do you think Colby would like to go back and see his brother?"

"Absolutely!"

We headed to the library where Colby was playing.

"Colby, why don't you come over here and play with me for a minute," the specialist suggested. As we sat at a nearby table she had Colby choose from several stuffed animals, one for him and one for Caleb.

"Colby, do you know why Caleb is here in the hospital?"

Colby nodded, shyly.

"Okay, so tell me why."

"'Cause Caleb got hit in the head with a rock."

"He did, didn't he?"

"Yeah, but the doctors are going to make him all better."

"You're absolutely right," she said. "We want Caleb to get all better. That's why he's here and why the doctors are doing things to make him feel better."

She described some of the things he'd see in Caleb's room: the breathing machine, the tubes that ran from Caleb's nose, and the numerous wires attached to his body.

"Do you want to see your brother?"

Colby nodded.

Caleb was covered to the waist by his blue baby blanket. The nurses had surrounded him with stuffed animals to help prop up his arms and legs and keep the numerous tubes and lines from getting tangled.

"I think he's sleeping, Dada." Colby whispered.

I glanced at the ICP monitor. The pressure was low, which meant Colby was right, he was most likely sleeping. I put my arm around Colby's shoulder and hugged him.

"Yeah, I think he is too, buddy. But why don't you say hi to him anyway? He can still hear you."

"Hi, Caleb." Colby's voice was barely a whisper.

"You can tell him you love him, too, if you want."

"I love you, Caleb." Colby glanced at me before adding, "The doctors are going to make you all better."

I tried not to cry. Colby took the toy bear he'd picked out as a gift for Caleb, whispered something into the bear's ear, and then placed it snugly near Caleb's head.

"I'm ready to go now, Dada," he said, looking up at me.

Tiffany's sisters were leaving that afternoon, and Tiffany and I had decided earlier that Colby should go with them to reunite with his baby brother, Connor. We spent several hours trying to give him our undivided attention, but it was a struggle. Caleb's ICP pressure had begun spiking to its highest levels yet, and the nurses were now restricting visitors, afraid that any stimulation might raise the pressure in his brain and cause further damage. We hoped he was nearing the peak the doctors had told us about, but it was hard not to feel uneasy.

"It's time to go now," Tiffany said, hugging a tearful Colby one more time.

"We'll see you on the weekend when you come back up," I said, the tone of my voice far more upbeat than I felt. "And listen, I'm going to call you every night and read you some nighttime books and we can say our prayers together, all right? And you can call me anytime you want." As I cupped my hands on his cheeks, I could see the weight of our words were breaking his heart. He bawled, not wanting to leave us. With one more heartbreaking hug and kiss we said goodbye.

We had been convinced that because of the uncertainty of what the next twenty-four hours would bring, sending Colby home with Tiffany's sisters was the right thing to do. Colby would get the attention he needed while we could focus solely on Caleb without Colby feeling neglected. After he left, however, we felt worse instead of better, unsure whether sending him off had been the right thing to do, and worrying whether he'd feel even more abandoned. We looked up when we heard a tap on the door. It was Jason McKay and his friend Brian, who stopped by to see how we were doing.

"Tim, you remember I told you I was in media relations? Well, I'd like to start a website on Caleb's behalf, as a place for people and news agencies to go to for the latest information."

I loved the idea and explained we'd already created a Facebook page for updates.

"Perfect!" Jason said. "We can put a blurb on the site and provide a link to Caleb's Facebook page for updates. I thought we might call it HelpCaleb.com."

"We really only care about two things beyond letting everyone know how Caleb's doing," I admitted. "One is getting the word out about the police investigation, and the second is getting the word out about prayer."

"That sounds good. Let's do it!"

Tiffany and I sat silently praying near Caleb's bedside, the lights dimmed, watching the ICP monitor anxiously. Nurses tiptoed in and out as Tiffany and I sat holding hands. The air was thick with concern at this critical stage.

And then it happened.

Caleb opened his eyes and looked right at Tiffany. Tiffany's sharp intake of breath pierced the quietness of the room.

"Hey, baby, can you see Mommy?" she whispered, leaning down over him. "I love you so much."

I stood behind Tiffany looking at them both for a moment, my heart bursting with affection. I then placed my hand on Tiffany's shoulder to lean in over her and get closer. Caleb shifted his gaze from Tiffany up to me.

Déjà vu. My jaw dropped.

"Tiffany! Oh my goodness!" I whispered, as I stepped back, "This was my dream last night!" I tried to be quiet, but it was hard to contain my excitement.

I switched places with Tiffany and held Caleb's hand. He blinked several times before his eyes slowly drifted closed. I was ecstatic.

"Honey, I'm telling you, this was exactly what I saw in my dream." At her skeptical look, I added, "I think we are seeing a miracle in progress. I really do."

At 5:30 PM, right about the time the doctors had predicted he might peak, Caleb's ICP spiked to twenty-seven, staying there for nearly three heart-stopping minutes. Over the past several days, his cranial pressure had been hovering in the five to ten range, but now it refused to drop any lower than fifteen, occasionally rising to nearly thirty. The drops became less and less frequent. This, the doctors had warned us, was the most critical phase of Caleb's survival. When the pressure spiked, it was imperative that it not last more than five or six minutes. I bit my lip. It was going to be a long night.

Not wanting to disturb Caleb, we waited outside, tiptoeing in throughout the evening to peek at the ICP monitor. I felt sick when I saw it pass the thirty mark. My brother Thomas and Todd, my best friend, were posting prayer requests on Facebook each time Caleb's pressure spiked. There were a lot of requests to post.

Caleb responded well to the medication the doctors gave him after each spike, none of which came anywhere close to the fearsome six-minute duration point. As the prayers poured in, the nurses would invariably say, "It looks like he's coming down off a peak for now." We prayed harder.

By nine o'clock that night, Caleb's pressure was climbing inexorably. His ICP had shot up to twenty-four and remained there for a nerve-shattering four minutes. The medication eventually brought it down to a tolerable seventeen. Every indication, they told us, was that we were now nearing the very top of Caleb's swelling. I rubbed the heels of my hands into my tired eyes.

"Hopefully," I said to myself, "it will all be over soon."

Eventually, the nurses shooed us away, not wanting even the sound of our voices outside to disturb Caleb. For the first time, we couldn't do our nighttime routine or even whisper goodnight to him. Silently blowing him a kiss and a prayer, we headed across the street to try to get some sleep.

When Tiffany and I got back to the Ronald McDonald House, we lay down and held each other close, our first time truly alone since Caleb's accident. It felt strange not having Colby to tuck to sleep. We talked about how much we missed our baby Connor and Colby, and how afraid we were for Caleb. For the first time Tiffany was able to finally connect with a lot of the emotions she was experiencing.

"That day at the falls was such a beautiful day. I keep thinking about Caleb pulling and tugging at me because he was so excited to get down to where the falls were. He wanted to hold your hand instead, because he thought I was moving too slowly." Tiffany smiled at the thought, but then her smile faded.

"Tim, every time I close my eyes, all I see is Caleb's face and his blood everywhere. I don't want that image in my mind, and I know it will never go away!" She began to cry. "If I had just turned a little faster, none of this would have happened." I hugged her close.

"Honey, none of this is your fault," I whispered against her damp cheek.

"I just…. That image keeps playing over and over again in my mind. I can still feel him in my arms. I was holding him so close, and, when that rock hit…"

"Honey, it's okay."

At those last words, the dam holding her emotions in check broke. Tiffany threw her arms around my neck, and sobbed uncontrollably.

"It was like someone was pulling and prying Caleb from my arms and I couldn't hold on. When I screamed, it was as if someone else was screaming. I didn't know it was me. And then time just stood still. That's it. I barely remember anything else that happened afterward. It's like everything that happened since is a blank. It's like I'm here but I'm not here, you know? I'm so scared."

"But God was with us. And you know He is still with us now. Remember how God told you to turn away?"

"Yes, but, Tim, I didn't turn fast enough. If I had turned faster, Caleb would have been safe. He wouldn't have been hit."

"Honey, I was standing right there when that rock crashed behind you. If you hadn't turned, it would have killed you both." We stared at each other. I hadn't truly realized the seriousness of that fact myself until now. Tiffany's face went grey.

"God saved two lives that day. God knew that you had the kind of heart to obey Him and, when He called, you obeyed. You saved our son—and yourself—by listening to His voice. Thank you for being obedient to our Father."

Tiffany gave me a grateful smile.

"Thank you, Tim."

We talked until exhaustion overtook us, as we both drifted

off to sleep. And then it happened, again.

As I opened my eyes I realized that I was face to face with Caleb, every one of his beautiful features before me. There was no breathing tube, and no neck brace; his deep blue eyes as they looked into mine were wide open and sparkling. He smiled a smile so deep that it turned his eyes into crescent moons. I smiled back.

And woke up.

CHAPTER TEN

Finally, Some Good News

We headed toward the PICU, anxiously hoping for news that the swelling had passed its peak and that they could now start lowering the dosage of Caleb's medications. The doctors shook their heads. Caleb had indeed spiked throughout the night, but hadn't definitively reached his peak. We were nowhere near lowering Caleb's medications. It could take as many as five or six days, they admitted, before he might peak. *Five or six days?* I wasn't sure how much more of this we could take.

"Once Caleb's over the peak and his swelling starts to subside, will we be out of the woods then? Will we be able to say that he's going to live?" The doctor looked at me and I felt my heart sink.

"No, we can't say that as of yet. We still have the issue of his heart, kidneys, and lungs."

Caleb's kidneys were still not working correctly. He was still retaining too much body fluid, which was having a counter effect on the medications they were giving him for swelling. For now, they said, Caleb's blood pressure was good and his dopamine levels seemed to be staying at normal levels, another good sign. Then came more bad news. The latest bacteria culture showed at least three different strains of pneumonia in his lungs and they were growing rapidly. He'd been on antibiotics but the ventilator settings that were optimum to help control his brain swelling were not ideal to control pneumonia.

"Right now," they said, "the brain swelling is our top priority." At this point I wasn't sure whether to be encouraged or discouraged. Confused by all the medical jargon going back and forth, I had a simple, pointed question.

"Bottom line, is Caleb better today at all?" The doctors exchanged brief looks.

"No. He's not better, but neither is he worse. He's the same. Today is another critical day."

~

My friend Todd was in the waiting room.

"While you and Tiffany were with Caleb this morning, you had a visit from someone by the name of Camille Ward. She brought this letter for you and left me her contact information. Tim, you've got to read this letter."

I glanced at the letter and then took a closer look. Camille's father and brother had been on a nighttime fishing trip when they collided with another boat, leaving them in critical condition for weeks. She and her family had experienced the same emotional rollercoaster we now found ourselves on. At times, she wrote, all hope seemed lost. As the days turned into weeks, it looked like her father and brother would never emerge from their comas. Only the family's deep faith in God had kept them hopeful. They had prayed earnestly as the weeks passed. Then both emerged from their comas and were now well on their way toward positive recovery.

I looked up at Todd. Neither of us said anything. I looked back at the letter. Camille closed the letter saying that, regardless of what the doctors had told us, we should not lose hope, that we must believe that God can heal, and that she was convinced that Caleb would pull through with God's strength.

I shook my head in wonderment as to how a complete

stranger could feel so compelled to write to us about her experience, and how she could be so convinced that Caleb would pull through. God, I felt, was again speaking to us.

"Thank you," I said to Todd. "This is the most hopeful thing I've heard since we've been here."

That afternoon, when we were permitted to see Caleb again, we were alarmed to hear a muted lullaby playing in the background. Caleb wasn't supposed to have any stimulation whatsoever. What had happened to the noise restriction?

"It's been lifted," the nurse said with a smile. "The doctors said that we could play some music as long as he responded well to it." It would be all right to talk to him again, she said, and read books, as long as we stayed quiet and didn't over-stimulate him. Tiffany and I exchanged a smile. I knew she was sending up the same silent prayer of thanks at that moment that I was.

That day brought a number of small victories. Caleb's ICP pressure had fallen back to a normal range for roughly fifteen minutes, something they admitted was significant. We might be seeing the beginning of the end of Caleb's brain swelling, they said.

"I saw him move."

Our heads shot up and we looked at the nurse, stunned. She held up her hands.

"I can't say for sure that it was purposeful movement, but, when I was turning him over and shifting him a bit, it was as if he was trying to pull his arm away from me. And then he did this—" The nurse tucked her chin down toward her shoulder, while furling her eyebrows.

"Oh, my goodness," Tiffany exclaimed, "that's Caleb! That's what he does when he doesn't like something!" We raced back to the waiting room to share the news.

When we returned, we heard Caleb making an odd noise. Just hearing him make any sound at this point was startling.

"I think he's crying," said one of the nurses. "We removed his neck brace to give him a bath and he started making that sound. He's probably pretty sore."

Caleb's eyes were tightly closed. A small tear rolled down his face. His mouth was open, but only the faintest of sounds were coming out. He was clearly in pain.

"Hey, buddy, it's okay," I whispered, stroking him softly. "Mommy and Daddy are here. It's okay, baby. Don't cry."

Despite his pain, Tiffany and I were overjoyed. He was responding, and making sounds, the first we'd heard since the accident.

"Wouldn't crying count as purposeful movement?" I asked the nurse. "Isn't it an appropriate response to pain?" After all, the doctors had told us proper response to pain would be a positive indicator, and crying when his neck brace was removed seemed pretty darned proper to me.

"I don't want to give you any false hope," she said, "but, yes, to me it looked like a normal response to pain."

That evening, when we returned to the PICU after dinner, one of the nurses approached us.

"We have good news. It looks as though Caleb's kidneys are functioning properly now. We've been monitoring his body fluids all day and they're stable." Smiling at our delight, the nurse added, "Not only is Caleb's brain regulating his ADH for his kidneys, but it's also begun regulating dopamine for his heart." Tiffany and I clutched each other and she leaned her head against mine.

"Thank God!"

That evening, Caleb's story was on every local news program. It felt surreal seeing ourselves on TV, but our desire to get the word out about prayer had clearly worked. Caleb's Facebook page had more than a thousand followers and he was getting two to three hundred friend requests every hour or so. Comments were coming in from all over the world.

"His story is everywhere," I said to Tiffany in wonderment. "People all over the world are praying for him." I shook my head in disbelief. "And from how things went today, I'd say those prayers are being answered."

Despite all the uplifting events of the day, there was an underlying sadness inside me. I had been so sure that, after what happened in my dream the previous night, Caleb would smile at us that day.

"I thought God was showing us things," I said to Tiffany, feeling dejected. "I guess I was reading too much into it."

Tiffany hugged me.

"The only thing we can do is wait and see."

That night, as we curled up together, there was no longer any anticipation of a vision in my dreams. I burrowed my face into the back of Tiffany's neck and reluctantly drifted off to sleep.

And then, for the fourth night in a row, I dreamed.

I was outside. The grass was lush beneath my feet as I walked, like a thick green carpet. I breathed deeply the scent of a freshly mown lawn. The trees and bushes sported emerald canopies and flowers bloomed. Caleb walked slowly, with his hands clasped together against his chest. I could see the outline of the side of his face. He was looking straight ahead, giggling, his face shining with joyous delight. As he moved forward, he looked down at his feet. I loved and longed for the sight that was before me. As my heart came alive within me, it ended.

I woke up. I didn't want to. It was the kind of dream I didn't want to end. I might not ever see Caleb that way again—walking, playing, happy. Tiffany woke up to the sound of my crying.

"What's wrong?"

"Now I know it's all in my head."

"What do you mean? Why?"

I explained my dream. "Now I know it can't be real. Caleb didn't smile today, and I know for sure he won't be walking tomorrow." I prayed that we would again one day get to see our son run, play, and be happy, just like in my dream, but with where Caleb currently was, it was hard to believe it was possible.

∽

Caleb's ICP pressure had spiked a couple of times during the night, once for ten full minutes, the doctors told us the following morning. Although momentarily alarming, they said that Caleb had continued to trend downward throughout the night, so they weren't too concerned. I looked at Dr. Keegan.

"So, are we over the peak now?"

"Yes, we believe so." Tiffany and I both breathed a huge sigh of relief. "Overall," the doctor said, "Caleb is doing better, but we still have a long way to go. We'll remove the brain monitor tomorrow. Now it's time to aggressively attack the pneumonia."

"How are his lungs?"

"They look better today. The antibiotics seem to be working."

It was also time to start weaning Caleb off the narcotics, because the longer he remained on them, the greater the chance would be that he would experience adverse side effects and the pain of withdrawal. The doctor ordered one of his assistants to immediately lower Caleb's medications by half, starting the process of slowly waking him up.

"Hopefully by tomorrow afternoon," a doctor said, "we'll start to see a little bit more of Caleb."

Oh wow!" I replied. Are we really ready for that yet?" The doctor answered.

"We believe Caleb is showing signs of waking up from his coma. When he's so heavily sedated, it's impossible to gauge how much brain damage has occurred or how well Caleb will respond. Caleb's brain is no longer swelling, so, yes, we think it's time. And, now that Caleb's swelling is over, we can focus on the pneumonia and do some more x-rays to get a better idea of what the next course of action should be with the bone fragment."

At this point, we had overcome the first hurdle. Now we were about to confront the second, whether Caleb had suffered extensive brain damage and, more importantly, whether he would live or die.

It was an abrupt switching of gears, going from obsessively watching Caleb's ICP monitor to now carefully observing Caleb himself for positive neurological signs, those purposeful movements and proper responses to pain the doctors had told us about. We noted every movement, the faintest toe wiggle, the twitch of a finger, the slightest change of expression—anything—and wondered whether it was one of the telltale signs. Some of the nurses called what we were witnessing neuro storming, the elevated neurological misfires that normally occur after a traumatic brain injury, and not purposeful movement. Still others were cautiously optimistic, thinking that some of what we were seeing might in fact be purposeful movement. The truth was, it was still too early to know for sure.

That evening, we received another visit from Camille Ward, the young woman who had sent us that encouraging letter the day before. She handed us a rolled up piece of poster board.

"I made this for you." she said. As I unrolled it I saw that every single space bore a handwritten passage of scripture. "I did this last night," she said. "It's all the scriptures that have given me comfort over the last few months." She had obviously put a lot of time and effort into it. It had to have taken her hours.

As I read over the passages, there was one that leapt out at me. Centered on the board, longer, larger, and more prominent than all the rest, was the entire text of Psalm 91. I grinned as I turned to Tiffany.

"Which scripture stands out to you?"

"Oh, my! It's Psalm 91!"

CHAPTER ELEVEN

Todd and His Guitar

Friday we woke up exhausted from a week with little sleep. The following day would mark exactly one week since Caleb's accident. We hurriedly made our way to the hospital to attend the morning rounds. Today was going to be an important day.

"Once we begin weaning him off his meds we can do a neurological exam." This, Dr. Marvin Hall said, would include watching for reactions like hand and foot retractions from pain stimuli. "We would like him to open his eyes more and track people and objects, to follow them around the room." These, he said, would be positive neurological signs.

"What we will also be watching for are signs that he suffered cerebral hypoxia," the doctor continued. At our puzzled expressions, he reminded us of what we had first said about Caleb having stopped breathing after the accident, before help arrived. If a person goes without oxygen for a period of time, around six minutes, he explained, the brain's cells begin to die off rapidly, resulting in permanent damage. Caleb had only stopped breathing for mere seconds, at least that we were aware of. However, the entire time we'd waited for help to arrive, more than an hour, Caleb had had visible difficulty breathing, meaning he still might not have gotten enough oxygen to his brain.

Fear washed over us threatening to knock us off balance yet again. Not only were we dealing with the aftereffects of the two localized, egg-sized bleeds on his brain, but also possibly a broad spectrum of brain damage. I thought of how Caleb's face had turned blue for so long before help arrived. I wanted to weep. I wanted to scream. I desperately wanted to turn the clock back a week.

An MRI was scheduled for later that day to help determine if cerebral hypoxia was a concern.

"But," the doctor cautioned us, "we're really not going to know how he's going to be until he starts to wake up."

Would the MRI at least reveal what parts of the brain were damaged and what effects there might be, I asked? The doctor shrugged.

"When we look at a CT scan," he explained, "all we can see is whether there has been any damage or not, and how large of an area or areas have been affected. What we can't see is the brain cell level of things. We can look down from a bird's eye view and tell that a bomb has fallen on a city, so to speak, but we can't tell if there are any people alive in the buildings."

That was when the reality hit us. The question was not whether Caleb had suffered brain damage, but instead how much, to what extent, and exactly what would be the aftereffects. Caleb was still on a ventilator, after all. If it turned out that Caleb was unable to maintain his most fundamental bodily functions, like breathing, we would be faced with the impossible question of whether or not to leave our son on life support.

Exhausted, our heads were spinning. The media still sought interviews, and well-wishers continued to telephone and drop by the hospital to visit us. We were intensely grateful for the outpouring of support, but at times it felt overwhelming. Wrestling with the news that, by tonight, we might know whether our son would live or die, we didn't feel much like talking to anyone. We simply wanted to share as many precious moments with Caleb as possible. Still, there was one phone call that I had been meaning to make all week.

Michael Tagert, our hero firefighter, was eager to hear all about how Caleb was doing. I filled him in quickly, explaining our latest concern about him possibly having cerebral hypoxia, and that I wasn't quite sure how long Caleb had been unable to breathe.

"Well, I got him almost all the way up to the top of the trail before my legs gave out," Michael said. "I was running so fast I wouldn't have noticed. My Uncle Robert was up there and when he took him from me for a moment to give me a break, it was only then I realized that Caleb wasn't breathing. I didn't even think—I just grabbed Caleb and ran the rest of the way up. I knew we needed to get help fast."

I was silent, thinking back to how Michael had just swooped in and carried off Caleb when I knew I couldn't take another step.

"Tim, I'm pretty sure it couldn't have been more than a minute or two that he wasn't breathing. It wasn't very long."

"If our son lives," I said, my voice choking slightly, "it will be because of you, Michael, because of you and God. I believe in my heart that the reason you were there in that park at that very moment was because God wanted you there."

That afternoon, Caleb's brain monitor probe was removed and they cut his medications back by half. It would be several hours before we would really see the full effects of the reduced meds, but the doctors predicted he would show signs of emerging from his coma before that. Desperate for some shred of hope, I pressed a nurse for her experiences with other kids who had suffered traumatic brain injury. She said some children, after considerable therapy, had actually returned to walk back into the PICU for a visit. But not all were as fortunate, she admitted. Some wound up in wheelchairs, some never emerged from their comatose states, and others, she admitted, had died.

The uncertainty was excruciating. We tried to remain strong, for ourselves, for each other, and for Caleb, but underneath we were dissolving in a pool of inner doubt and fear. We continued to pray harder than we had ever had in our lives, but we also knew that God did allow pain in life, and death, and that both were very real possibilities for Caleb.

One cause for cautious optimism was the latest x-rays of Caleb's spine and neck. They had confirmed that his bone structure was undamaged, so he no longer needed a neck brace. Even better was the news that Caleb wouldn't require surgery to remove or adjust the bone fragment.

"As we thought, the sliver is a thin plate that we believe in time will fuse back to the skull. There's no danger if we leave it as is." When Tiffany and I heard that, we breathed a huge sigh of relief.

It was not long before we spotted slight movement. Caleb's eyelids twitched slightly and his eyes began moving back and forth beneath the lids. He drew one of his legs up and then stretched it flat again. Tiffany's fingers tightened in mine as we watched for more signs of purposeful movement that the doctors wanted to see.

Our excitement over seeing Caleb beginning to wake up was short lived however, when the nurses came in and readied Caleb for an MRI. The necessary sedation meant that Caleb wouldn't be able to undergo a proper neurological exam yet. Even though we were finally seeing Caleb start to awaken, we would have to wait and worry yet another gut wrenching day, as Caleb would likely sleep through the evening.

After the MRI, we sat with Caleb, who didn't move a muscle. I was absentmindedly stroking Caleb's arm while Dr. Hamm was chatting with Tiffany. Suddenly, Caleb's hand gripped mine with surprising strength and he drew it up toward his face. At my gasp, Dr. Hamm dropped her notes and leaned down to check Caleb's pupils and other vital signs. Caleb relaxed his grip on my hand, nodded slightly, and went back to sleep.

"That was purposeful movement, right?" I asked, unable to conceal my elation. My grin faltered slightly at her solemn expression. She seemed to be choosing her words carefully.

"Caleb just had a seizure."

"What?"

"It's common with traumatic brain injuries for patients to suffer seizures as the brain swelling begins to subside."

"I don't understand. You mean right now? Or…" I hesitated, almost too terrified to ask. "Or are we talking long term here?"

"We still don't know. It all depends on the amount of damage that has been done to the brain. Some people can have seizures right afterward, and then be fine, and others need seizure medication on an ongoing basis." She paused. "We think Caleb might also have had a seizure earlier when we took him to get his MRI."

Although the doctors had warned us that seizures could result, I had convinced myself that, because we hadn't seen any previously, somehow he'd managed to escape that.

"So, what's made Caleb start having them?"

"The seizing is from the brain injury itself. He may have been seizing all along, but we couldn't see it until we started lowering the medications. One's an anti-seizure medicine, so we may have to adjust the dose now that he's having seizures."

If we could just get past worrying about Caleb living or dying, I told myself, and not have to worry about the pneumonia and lack of oxygen thing anymore, we could handle seizures. We would happily manage that, I thought.

∼

Later when it was time to bathe Caleb, I decided to give Tiffany some alone time with him while I visited with family in the waiting room. A nurse poked her head through the doorway.

"Your wife wants to know if you'd like to come back. Caleb's got his eyes open." I shot out of my chair and raced back to the PICU. Caleb was lying there, eyes wide open, surrounded by smiling nurses.

"After his bath," whispered Tiffany, "he's pretty much had his eyes open the whole time. And there's more. You know how Caleb's never liked getting a bath? Well, he kept moving his arms and legs slightly as if he was trying to pull away. One of the nurses swears he pushed her arm away with his leg!"

That sure sounded like purposeful movement to me. I looked at Caleb's bright blue eyes and felt like I was seeing them for the very first time, with all the joy of a new father. The joy withered, however, when his eyes rolled back into his head.

"What's wrong?" I cried. A nurse put her hand on my shoulder and said I shouldn't be alarmed, that Caleb's responses were normal for someone who has experienced brain trauma, and were not necessarily permanent.

"So, another milestone, right?"

A chorus of smiles gave me my answer.

∼

That evening, Tiffany's sisters surprised us, walking in with baby Connor. We had not seen him since the night before the accident, a week ago.

"My baby!" Tiffany cuddled him close, his cheek pressed against hers. He wrapped his arms tightly around her neck.

What a blessing, I thought, as I stroked his other cheek. We really needed this. Despite all the ups and downs, overall this had turned out to be the best day we'd had all week. Caleb had no fractures, so his neck brace had been removed, as had the pressure monitor probe, because his brain pressure was continuing its slow descent toward normal. His brain had begun regulating dopamine and ADH correctly, so there were no further worries about his heart and kidneys. His pneumonia was improving. He wasn't going to need surgery to remove the bone fragment. And, arguably, best of all, he was starting to show signs of purposeful movement.

Todd pulled out his guitar.

"When the time was right," he said "I wanted to be able to offer you and you're your family some songs of worship and encouragement. I think, with Connor here, and with all the good news we've had today, I think it's a good time."

For the next couple of hours, with tears of joy, we listened, sang, and gave thanks to God. We ended the night with prayer, committing to God the days and weeks ahead. It was the perfect end to a very challenging week. We felt re-energized, refilled, and ready for the week ahead.

"Thank you," I said to Todd, as I hugged him tightly. "You are and will always be my best friend. I love you, brother."

Little did I realize that, through Todd, God was again preparing our hearts to be strong for what was to come next.

CHAPTER TWELVE

"Caleb's Going to Live!"

"We have the MRI results."

Tiffany and I gripped hands. That morning, we had awoken with a renewed sense of strength. It had now been seven days since the accident.

"There don't appear to be any signs of cerebral hypoxia."

I felt Tiffany's hand relax. Caleb had also breathed over his ventilator for the first time, we were told, a good sign as it meant that the brain was recognizing its responsibility to breathe." The plan at this point, a doctor added, was that, if nothing else changed and Caleb's pneumonia continued to abate, they would begin weaning Caleb off the ventilator to allow him to breathe on his own. The consensus was that, overall, Caleb was better today than he had been yesterday. That was music to our ears.

As the doctors continued to scale back Caleb's coma-inducing medications, Caleb began to move more and emit sounds. One of the nurses came in to turn Caleb over on his side, and Caleb raised his arm up as if to yank his breathing tube out.

"Oh, no you don't," the nurse said, deftly deflecting his hand.

"Purposeful movement, right?" I asked. "Wasn't that purposeful?"

"Well, I can't say for sure, but it looked like it to me," the nurse said, with a wry smile.

Caleb was opening his eyes, but there was no indication

that he could see. The doctors agreed that most likely he couldn't yet, but that this was no cause for alarm. When I would wave my hand gently back and forth in front of him, he stared as if seeing right through me. His pupils weren't light reactive, the nurses said. We would just have to be patient and wait and see.

By mid-afternoon, Tiffany's sister Misty had arrived with Colby. After enthusiastic greetings, we turned to Misty.

"How is he doing?" we asked, in low voices.

"Remarkably well, considering what he's gone through." Misty glanced at Colby, who was playing with some toys on the floor. "He talks about the accident every now and then, but, for the most part, he just plays and is happy and acts normal." What a relief it was to hear that.

Misty took Connor home with her that evening. We'd worked it out with everyone's schedules so that Colby could stay with us a few more days. My and Tiffany's parents would take turns spending time with Caleb so that Tiffany and I could spend as much time with Colby as possible, before he returned home.

∽

"Caleb's going to live!"

Tiffany and I burst into the waiting room the following day, where family and friends were gathered. A cheer erupted.

We had had our daily session with the team of doctors, I explained. Near the end, it had dawned on me that the doctors were now using different language, talking about his recovery, the milestones and things they wanted to see Caleb do.

"So, it's safe to say at this point that you think Caleb will live?" We did seem to be past the worst of everything.

"As long as there are no further complications, yes, we're confident now that Caleb will live."

My mother cried when she heard the news. My father put

his hand on my shoulder and squeezed.

"We are finally leaving phase one, and moving on to phase two—rehabilitation!" We still didn't know how things would be when Caleb finally emerged from his coma, I admitted, but his medications continued to be reduced and we would know more soon. "It's going to be a long, ongoing process now of re-examining and re-evaluating Caleb's abilities and brain functions."

There was something else that required moving forward from phase one to phase two, something that kept getting pushed onto the back burner. Up until this point, Tiffany and I had been running on autopilot. Everything over the last week—Caleb, caring for and worrying about our other two children, the doctors, the interviews, the visits and calls from people everywhere—all of it had been so demanding that Tiffany and I had barely shared our feelings, let alone had had any time to focus on each other. After this past week, we were both spent. We knew we needed to connect more but, as every day brought more fears about Caleb, and as our nerves became more frayed, the friction between us grew evident.

Todd returned that evening with his wife, Emily. Having been married several more years longer than us, we often relied on their Christ-centered marital advice, experience, and encouragement. Todd and Emily wanted to be sure we were navigating these treacherous waters together. The four of us spent some quiet time together, talking and praying, which ended with Tiffany and I reaffirming our love and commitment to each other out loud, and promising each other that we would look for ways to spend time together alone, to share feelings, and support and comfort each other.

"You need each other, now more than ever," Todd reminded us, "for the weeks ahead, and, really, for the life ahead." We agreed, as we ended our time together in prayer.

We entered phase two feeling a renewed sense of direction and unity. After all, the worse was behind us now.

Or, at least, that's what we'd thought.

CHAPTER THIRTEEN

Coma Scale: Four

"He's not responding with purposeful movement."

"What?" I looked at Tiffany, perplexed. She looked near tears.

I had let her go on ahead to sit with Caleb that morning while I spent some time playing with Colby. Today was the first day of phase two. We'd gotten confirmation that Caleb would pull through, that he was going to live. We'd watched as he slowly began to emerge from the effects of the coma-inducing medications and noted every shift and twitch as a potentially deliberate motion versus an involuntary one. I'd woken up hopeful that, by the end of the day, we might even see our son smile, say hello, perhaps even sit up and eat. So, when Tiffany stuck her head in through the library doorway after just half an hour, I was expecting something encouraging. Instead, she looked grim.

"I need to talk to you."

We sat down out of Colby's earshot.

"The doctors told me that the medications are now low enough to see how he is, and he's not responding with purposeful movement."

"That's impossible! What about the fact that he's been opening his eyes and moving his hands and body? Just yesterday you saw him push the nurse's hand away when you were bathing him." I looked at Tiffany who was visibly upset.

"We were wrong."

"What if they're wrong?" I demanded. "What if he just needs a little more time?" Tiffany's eyes welled up as she looked at me and shook her head.

"No. The doctors said that the Caleb we're seeing now is the Caleb we'll be taking home with us."

My world, my hopes, my dreams for the future, were all sucked away in a tornado of confusion, a cataclysmic vortex, leaving nothing behind but shards and debris in my soul. I had a sudden horrible vision of Caleb as a thirty-year-old man lying in a hospital bed in our house in a vegetative state.

"No," I said, my voice barely a whisper. I looked around, trying not to let the panic overwhelm me. I had to escape, steal a few moments to come to grips with this impossible news. I pushed back my chair and got unsteadily to my feet. "I have to leave. I have to go for just a minute."

As I stumbled from the room, I began sobbing. I just didn't understand. Why was it that, after all the fingerprints and signs we had seen, after all we had felt that God was doing, that our hopes had now been dashed again? What did this all mean? And what about those dreams I'd been having? Surely they meant something. I felt like I was in a dream now myself, emotionally numb, as if looking at everything from outside my body. I didn't know what was and wasn't real anymore.

A dull ache began to pulse in my temples. I leaned back hard against the wall opposite the waiting room, hoping the pressure on my back would distract me from the throbbing behind my eyes, which was determined to assert itself. Tiffany approached me gently, her face wet with tears, and wrapped her arms around me.

"Why? Why, Tiffany?" I choked. "Why would God, after all this, after all we've been through, after all Caleb's been through—why would He do this?" I lifted my eyes to hers. "I was so sure we were witnessing a miracle, that God, for His glory, because of all the tens of thousands of people praying for him, would allow Caleb to wake up and be well, to just be our Caleb." I smudged my hands across my cheeks in despair. "What glory is there in this? Tell me, to allow Caleb to live and suffer like this? Why didn't God just take him? I mean, when the rock came down, why not just go ahead and take his life instead of making him suffer like this the rest of his life?" Tiffany grabbed my arms and gave me a shake.

"Tim, wait. Stop. That's not what I said!" I stared at her, confused, numb. Tiffany lifted her hand to my cheek. "I didn't say that's how Caleb is going to be for the rest of his life."

Now I was completely confused.

"Yes, yes, you did, that is what you said."

"Well, that's not what I meant. What I meant was, the doctors are saying that this is how he is right now. This is how he is as a result of the brain damage. He can recover, they said. He can. But he's going to need lots of therapy."

"Where's Dr. Keegan? I need to hear what he has to say."

∽

"The movements you have seen have been reactionary," Dr. Keegan affirmed, "most likely brainstorming," when I began peppering him with incidents of Caleb's movements, determined to convince him otherwise. The doctor was solemn. "We will tell you if we have seen Caleb do any purposeful movement. And up until now, he has not. What we have seen is simply posturing."

"What do you mean by posturing?" I looked down at Caleb who lay in his bed, unmoving.

"Posturing is a term we use to describe movements indicative of brain injury." Dr. Keegan bent down and began rolling his knuckles firmly against Caleb's chest. Caleb arched his back, flexing his arms back against the bed. "When we test Caleb's reaction to pain stimuli, this is what he does. What we want to see, however, is Caleb using his hands to try to deflect the cause of the pain, to push my hand away. But, instead, he's extending his arms and legs away from the pain center, not even acknowledging it." All those movements that we'd been so excited about, prayed for, and thought we'd witnessed had been meaningless. Dr. Keegan looked at me.

"Reacting to pain is a basic human response. When patients don't respond appropriately to pain stimulation, that tells us that the brain has been injured in such a way that the patient isn't even aware of the pain. That means extensive brain damage."

"I told you I'm a terrible liar, that I will always be straightforward with you. I know you want to see Caleb recover and come out of this, and so do we, but the truth is his medication levels are now low enough for us to see his neurological responses. If he were going to exhibit any purposeful movement, we'd have seen it by now."

Seeing the pain on my face, Dr. Keegan added, "Look, this is where we are right now, ok? Just right now. What you're seeing now is not what you'll see a year from now. I do expect to see improvement."

After Dr. Keegan left, I thought about what he had said. Caleb was still in a coma and, on a scale of two to fifteen, two being the deepest comatose state and fifteen being awake, Caleb was registering between a four and a five. Dr. Keegan had said he'd felt Caleb could come out of it, depending on the extent of the damage, and potentially recover, although by how much he didn't know. He did say he believed that Caleb would make a good candidate for rehabilitation. "He is young, Dr. Keegan pointed out, "and it is amazing how children can recover."

Dr. Keegan wanted to transition Caleb from intensive care to rehabilitation. I thought about my beautiful son's face days, hours, moments before the accident, how we had had such fun, me teaching him how to hit a baseball, his delight at his first glimpse of the falls. I wondered now whether I would ever see Caleb back up on his feet, running, moving, playing—living.

When I left Caleb's room, I ran into Tim Frizzell, whom I'd known since I was fourteen years old and living with my grandmother and great-grandmother. My great-grandmother had raised me and, when I was fourteen, she'd had a stroke. For two months, we'd lived in a rehabilitation facility and, for the next six years, all throughout my teens, my grandmother and I took care of her, watching in pain as she slowly deteriorated. She'd passed away when I was twenty. During that period, Tim had been a beloved mentor, the man who had successfully led me to Christ.

"I just can't do this again," I said to him tearfully. Tim gave me a compassionate look.

"Remember, Jesus told us that in this life we will have troubles, but to take heart because He has overcome the world."

"It's not that I don't want the burden of having to care for Caleb the rest of his life," I cried. "I love my son, and I want what's best for him. If I have to take him home and take care of him for the rest of his life, then I will take care of him, just like I did for my granny. It's Caleb I'm thinking about. I don't want that for him, you know? I don't want him to have to live that way."

"Your great-grandmother was much older," Tim pointed out, his hand on my shoulder. "She was too old to recover. But

Caleb's not even three years old. His brain has a much greater ability to heal."

I nodded. The doctors had said as much.

"Let's look at this a different way. Since God allowed you the experience with your great-grandmother, taking care of her and going through rehab, you could say that He's ensured that you are uniquely qualified, in ways that most parents are not, to take care of your son."

I felt a shred of optimism return, as Tim guided me away from my anger and fear.

"It's my belief that it won't be long before you start to see a significant difference in how your elderly great-grandmother responded to therapy and how Caleb responds. I think this is going to be an opportunity for you to see something different."

Yet again, God had sent the right person at the right time with the right message that I needed to hear. It was so much to take in, and more than I could take at the moment as the time for Colby's departure loomed. Jason McKay and his friend, Brian, had come with tickets for the Tennessee Aquarium, and now, with family here to watch Caleb, it seemed a good time to spend the rest of the afternoon there with Colby.

Monday night was quiet. Tiffany sat wading through the comments of four thousand Facebook followers as my father surfed the news stories featuring Caleb. I was sitting thinking about Colby's anguished departure, how he had cried and begged to stay with us. It would be another week before we would see him or Connor. When, I wondered, would we all be back together for good? And would it ever be the same?

As my thoughts turned to whether Caleb might or might

not recover, I felt myself getting upset again.

"I just don't get it," I said to Tiffany. "Why would God allow all this? How can Caleb's suffering possibly be a part of God's plan?"

"Honey, we just have to believe that God will do what He thinks is best for our son. It will be *His* best. God loves Caleb. And, remember, the doctors said Caleb isn't going to be like this forever, that he will recover."

"Yes, and they also said they don't know how much. I mean, for all we know, he could be in a vegetative state for the rest of his life!" I looked at Tiffany and then my father. "It's not that I'm saying I won't accept Caleb the way he is or will be. I just want what's best for my son." Tiffany walked over to me and placed her hand over mine. As I closed my eyes, tears began to fall. Then I heard a voice.

Love is not about what you receive, but about what you give to others freely.

The voice came from inside my heart but it was as clear as if the speaker had been sitting next to me. Far from feeling taken aback, I was offended by the suggestion that I was somehow being selfish. I was, after all, thinking only of Caleb.

"I know!" I shouted.

Tiffany and my father looked up, startled. I, too, was shocked at what had just happened and felt embarrassed. "God," I explained. "God just spoke to me again." And, in those words, God had revealed to me the error of my heart and I'd fired back, in defensiveness. "He said, 'Love is not about what you receive, but about what you give to others freely.'" Instantly I understood what God was saying to me. I covered my face with my hands. "That's it. Wow. I am being so selfish." Tiffany looked confused.

"What do you mean?"

Numerous passages of scripture began flooding my mind, particularly John 3:16: *For God so loved the world that He gave His one and only Son.* The real reason for my lack of faith and not giving over the fate of my son to God was because I wanted Caleb's love for myself. In other words, I wanted those smiles, that bubbling laughter, those beautiful, baby blue eyes, those arms around me when he said, "I love you, Dada!" Yes, I wanted to glorify God, but I wanted this even more. Deep down, I was unwilling to give my son to God, to relinquish control, to trust that He had Caleb's and our best interests in mind. I was unwilling to let the outcome be whatever God wanted it to be, even if we didn't understand the reasoning behind that outcome.

That night, I prayed and finally turned over the fate of our son to God. That night, I came to grips with the fact that, even if we brought Caleb home in a vegetative state or in a wheelchair, his heart was still full of love and he still loved his mommy and daddy. Regardless of what happened with our son, he needed our love and affection. And, even if he could never again display his love to us, that didn't change the fact that we were the examples of God's love to him. The lesson God was teaching me was powerful. Love truly is not about what we receive, but about what we give to others freely, expecting nothing in return. What we receive back truly is a blessing from God, but love does not depend upon it. It is the example and life that we have been given through Christ. It is God's glory, in all things, through love, that reigns supreme.

It also occurred to me that, in accepting God's care of Caleb, I had also decided to love God no matter what, even if my prayers were not answered.

I ended the night with a greater acceptance of the greatest love there is—God's love, for me, for Caleb, and for us as a family. For the first time I felt I had finally experienced what it means to have real faith, deep faith, a faith that is rooted in God's love, faith in His faithfulness.

CHAPTER FOURTEEN

Honk Your Nose

It was now day eleven. The crowd of doctors and nurses was unusually large as we prepared to shift Caleb's care from critical to the rehabilitation phase.

"We are going to try to get Caleb accepted into an intensive rehabilitation facility," one doctor said, "one like Scottish Rite in Atlanta." Scottish Rite was one of the best pediatric rehabilitation facilities in the US. "We feel that Caleb is a strong candidate and, as long as they have beds available, we don't see a problem with him going there." The doctor turned and asked a nurse to schedule physical therapy to start immediately.

"The sooner the better," he said to us. "You really want to try to get back as much as you can within the first year after any traumatic brain injury. The first year is critical. Although we can't predict how far Caleb will go, TBI patients may plateau at certain levels, and only regain a portion of what they have lost. You never really know how far a person with a brain injury will recover."

"Recovery can just stop at any point?"

The doctor nodded. I took a deep breath.

"Just give it up to God," I whispered to myself. "It's in His hands."

These meetings were always a rollercoaster ride, with so much coming at us so quickly, and this one was no different. The doctors agreed they would remove Caleb's trunk line and continue to wean him off the ventilator. A food test was scheduled to gauge whether Caleb could swallow or whether they would need to insert a gastric feeding tube, at least until he could start eating on his own. Things were moving quickly.

The doctors told us that we would likely be in rehabilitation for a few weeks. Weeks certainly sounded better than months, but it suddenly hit me that we were talking about weeks in Atlanta, easily two hundred miles from home. It was difficult enough only seeing Colby and Connor one or two days a week. How would they cope with our absence? Where would we stay? Could we afford it? And what about our jobs? Our finances? I could feel panic rising up within me, as the rollercoaster ratcheted its way to the top. Then the doctor said something that gave me a sliver of hope.

"Caleb is only two years old and, at that age, they are still developing new brain cells, which goes on until the age of six or seven." The doctor gave me a reassuring smile. "Keep doing what you're doing. Keep praying, and stay positive. This is not the time to give up. This is the time to fight."

Tiffany squeezed my hand. When I looked at her, I saw a glimmer of optimism in her eyes. The doctor was right. This was the time to fight. Like a boxer entering the ring for the championship title, we resolved to fight to win back everything Caleb had lost. By God's own strength we would, no matter what or where it took us. Everything—job, money, home, family—it was all in God's hands now.

As an apparent afterthought, a doctor asked how the morning's pain response test had gone.

"Good, actually," a nurse said. "He was not posturing. He pulled his hands in toward the pain for the first time." Tiffany and I gasped. The doctor, studiedly casual, smiled and nodded.

"Good. That's good."

"OK," another doctor said, his gaze sweeping the room, "Would we all agree that Caleb is better today?" Everyone nodded. "OK, then let's get started."

∼

The news agencies were still calling and people were still praying for Caleb all over the world. We were surprised to discover that we had hit five thousand "friends" on Caleb's Facebook page, the maximum number allowed for a personal page, and had to create another "fan" page for all the new requests that continued to pour in. People continued to come by the hospital to visit us and every day we would hear about yet another church that had added Caleb to their prayer list. It was humbling to see the impact Caleb was having, and to feel the love of God's people blanketing us in its warmth.

The news kept coming and, for a change, all of it was positive. Caleb had survived a full twenty-four hours without a ventilator and the doctors had confirmed a breathing tube would not be necessary. The scale of his coma had been downgraded to between six and eight, which meant he was definitely fighting his way back to us. But, it was only when we saw Caleb's face without any of the wires, tubes, and tape that we really allowed ourselves to hope.

"He's so beautiful, Tim," Tiffany whispered.

Caleb was lying in his bed wearing only a diaper. Periodically, an arm or leg twitched. His eyes stayed fixed, still unable to see. Dr. Keegan had said to us, "Remember how it was when you first brought Caleb home as a newborn? How he would lie on his back and randomly move his arms and legs, his eyes and head? Well, that's where you're at now. You've done it before. You just have to do it again."

∼

The first physical therapy session was encouraging. When the therapist propped him up, Caleb winced and she explained he was probably sore from being in bed so long. She pointed out to us how, when seated slightly off balance, he would press his left hand downward, as if to brace himself. One of the most fundamental responses in the human brain, she said, is to react to a sense of falling. He was also able to support his head for three to four seconds at a time, another good sign.

Caleb, as a part of his therapy, would now need to get out of bed regularly, which was music to our ears because it meant we could now hold him in our laps. I resisted the urge to reach for him as Tiffany bundled him into her arms. Sunlight poured through the window, highlighting Caleb's sandy brown hair as he and his mother sat nestled together in a large chair. The moment was stunning in its familiarity, as if I were seeing him in her arms as an infant, curled up asleep, safe and secure. Healthy. Our Caleb.

"It's going to be even harder to leave him at night and sleep across the street now," Tiffany confessed to the nurse, her smile wistful.

"Let me see what I can do."

Shortly thereafter, we were given a private quasi-suite, two adjoining hospital rooms, with Caleb's hospital bed opposite a living area with two foldout chairs on which Tiffany and I would sleep. We were elated to be able to stay with him around the clock now. We would finally be able to rest a little easier, I thought, knowing that our son was only a few feet away.

That night, I prayed over Caleb, asking for the different parts of Caleb's brain to be healed. I prayed that our marriage would be strengthened, that Colby and Connor would remain safe, and that Caleb would be accepted into Scottish Rite. And that all of this would be over soon so we could go home.

∼

Our first night with Caleb was difficult. Even though the doctors had warned us that Caleb's recovery would include what was called neuro storming—fevers and heart rate spikes—and not to be alarmed, it was impossible to relax when monitor alarms kept going off periodically throughout the night, not knowing whether it was normal or if something was wrong.

The next morning, Tiffany and I were exhausted. But when the physical therapist asked if we wanted to start learning how to do Caleb's exercises, all thoughts of tiredness were instantly forgotten. As she began demonstrating some of the range of motion exercises that would help him, memories of my great-grandmother's therapy came flooding back. I pulled out a list I'd made the night before, when I couldn't sleep, of all the exercises I remembered from caring for my great-grandmother for six years. The therapist was delighted that Tiffany and I were willing to be so proactive in Caleb's recovery, saying that the more we engaged with him, the better it would be for Caleb.

"Just be sure not to do too much too soon. If it looks like he's getting tired or starts fussing, take a break."

The goal, we were told, was to get him out of bed three or four times a day, for several hours each time. We wasted no time getting started. At one point, when the therapist came in to check on us, she was excited to see Caleb trying to lift his head.

"Look at that! Look how hard he's trying to keep his head up, to keep himself upright. These are all very good signs!"

We felt proud, as if he had hit the game-winning ball in the bottom of the ninth inning. "Alright Caleb!" we exclaimed, "Good job buddy!"

∽

The second week passed faster than the first. It was now Saturday, fifteen days following the accident. I'd put Caleb down for a nap and Tiffany went to get us some lunch. A nurse came in and flipped on the light above Caleb's bed. Caleb flinched, his eyes squinting. Not wanting to read too much into it, I waited for the nurse to finish checking his vital signs. As she shone her penlight into his eyes, his pupils contracted.

"He's got slight movement in his pupils."

"He does!" I was beside myself with excitement. "When did this start?"

"Sometime yesterday. Look," she said, waving the light left and then right. "His right eye reacts better than his left."

"Do you think he can see anything?"

"It's possible, but I can't say for sure. But his pupils are contracting so he's seeing something."

I thought back to the dream I'd had about Caleb opening his eyes and looking at me, seeing me, and felt hope bathe me in a warm glow.

That afternoon, my dad and I sat with Caleb. I lowered the bedrail and sat next to him on a chair low enough to be where we would be face to face. At home, we played silly games with funny noises and facial expressions, and lately I'd been trying to recreate these familiar activities in an effort to solicit some kind of response. One of his favorites was "Honk Your Nose." I would gently squeeze his nose and say "Got you! Honk, honk!" He would then do the same to me.

"Oh, you got my nose!" I would cry in a comically nasal tone. Caleb would burst into peals of laughter every time. He never tired of it.

I gently pinched Caleb's nose, laughing very animatedly.

"I've got your nose, Caleb!" I squealed, "I've got your

nose!" Caleb gazed vacantly past me. I took his clenched fist, carefully prying open his fingers, and molded his hand over my nose.

"Ow! You've got my nose!" I cried, pressing his fingers against my nose. There was no response. Nothing. I kept doing it. I didn't care. I loved the feeling of his warm fingers against my face, imagining his hysterical laughter when I'd give those nasal grunts. My dad watched us, amused.

As I gently squeezed his nose and then took his hand to pinch mine again. His vacant eyes suddenly brightened. He turned toward me, looking at my nose. He was alert. His mouth curved upward and he let out a giggle.

"Dad! Did you see—?"

"—him smile!" my dad finished. We began to cry and laugh.

"Hey, buddy, it's Daddy. Can you see me?"

Caleb's expression faded and his eyes glazed over again. But I hadn't imagined it. My dad had seen it, too.

I was suddenly hit with an overwhelming sense of déjà vu. The dream, I thought, the third vision. Bits of the dream began streaming back. I had been face to face with Caleb in that dream. I looked around me and then it struck me. *This* was the room I had seen in my dream. *This* was the room in the vision. I had never sat face to face with him in the PICU because the chairs were too tall. Something else occurred to me. In the vision, Caleb wasn't wearing a neck brace and he didn't have the breathing tube that he'd been encumbered with in the PICU. I looked back down at Caleb now, neck bare, face free of tubes and wires. I clapped my hand over my mouth in astonishment.

Then, another thought occurred to me and I found myself rigid, somewhat fearful of the excitement roaring through my veins. The fourth vision, I thought, the one with Caleb walking alongside me, looking up and laughing. I closed my eyes for a moment, afraid to believe. Was God telling me that Caleb would come back to us? That our son was going to be ok?

∼

It was Halloween weekend and that afternoon Todd and Emily arrived with Colby and Connor. It was a joyous reunion. We took turns scooping up each child into our arms, hugging and kissing them.

"I missed you, Dada," Colby whispered as he released his arms from around my neck and looked at me with tears in his eyes.

"I missed you, too, buddy, so much."

Although we hadn't yet heard whether Caleb had been accepted into Scottish Rite, it seemed likely that we would be heading to Georgia the coming week. We had no idea how long it would be before we would be reunited with our boys, family, or friends, so we were determined to make the most of our time together. My dad had volunteered to spend the night with Caleb while we stayed across the street with the boys at the Ronald McDonald House.

As I unlocked the door to our room, my friend Todd nudged me.

"Hey, Tim, look at this." He pointed to a Disney cartoon of Hercules that was hanging on the wall just opposite our door. Hercules was the nickname we'd playfully given to Michael Tagert, the firefighter who had raced up the mountainside with Caleb in his arms. God's fingerprints seemed to be everywhere these days.

"Wow what a 'coincidence!'" I said with a chuckle.

"Yeah, I know, right!"

After the boys were in bed that night, Todd turned to me.

"Hey, you want to talk?"

Todd could tell something had been bothering me all evening. Tiffany was now in deep in conversation with Todd's wife, Emily.

"Sure. Let's go upstairs."

Upstairs was a small chapel; nothing more than a small room. Padded pews lined the sanctuary, which was dark as we entered. Ahead of us lay the only light in the room, a large, illuminated, brightly colored stained glass window. We sat down and, weary, I rested my forehead on the pew in front of me. We began to talk.

We talked about my marriage, the concern we'd had about Colby and how he was handling all this, and about missing baby Connor. Mostly, we talked about Caleb. I told him about the dreams I'd had about Caleb, and the teachings I'd previously done on faith, and all of God's fingerprints that we'd seen, how I felt it was all interconnected somehow.

"I just don't understand why God would allow all this to happen," I said, aware that this was a question I had voiced incessantly, relentlessly, and had yet to find an answer to. "How do I find meaning in all this? I mean, I'd like to think that it's all part of God's plan, but it's frustrating not knowing the reasons behind it."

Todd gave me a sympathetic smile.

"Sometimes we're given what things mean and sometimes not. That's what faith is about. Did God intend this as a means to discipline and grow you and Tiffany? Does God intend to use this as a way to deepen faith or even turn people to faith? We don't know. It might not be any of those things. My guess is it's probably all of those things and more. God always acts with many things in view."

"What about the dreams, though? I mean, it can't be coincidence, can it?" Feeling slightly embarrassed, I explained the first three dreams, and how I'd seen each one of them come to pass.

"What was the fourth dream?" Todd asked. I hesitated.

"Do I sound crazy?"

"Not at all. I firmly believe that God still speaks to us."

I explained the fourth dream as Todd sat, silent next to me. Afterward, I stared at the stained glass window.

"Is it possible that it was God showing me those things—showing me what was going to happen?"

Todd looked thoughtful.

"You know what you saw, and you know what's true in your heart. Not only did the first three come true, but God gave you a witness for the third dream, someone who was there in the room with you—your dad. If it is God showing you these things, then He'll reveal the reasons why. I firmly believe that."

~

The following afternoon, after Sunday services at a nearby church, we had two media interviews scheduled, one with WTVF Channel 5 from back home in Nashville, and another with Allen Morrell, from 180 Degrees Ministries, about a fundraising effort for Caleb's medical expenses. For the first time, we had encouraging news to relate, so the interviews were considerably more relaxed and upbeat.

We also got a call from Jason McKay to meet later in the lobby of the Ronald McDonald House, who said he had a couple of things he wanted to give Colby. When we arrived, we were surprised to find a large group of people assembled. This was no ordinary visit. Jason addressed us.

"Tim, Tiffany, your story has captured the hearts of so many people, not only here in the Chattanooga area but all over. When I first heard about what had happened to Caleb, I knew immediately that I wanted to do something. That's when I came to the hospital and talked to you about our getting the word out about prayer. But that just didn't feel like enough. I wanted to do more." Jason's eyes twinkled as he continued.

"It came to our attention that you don't have a very reliable car back home. So, since you will definitely need one in Atlanta, we wanted to come by here today and give you these."

Jason jangled a set of keys in front of us. I was speechless. Tiffany gasped and burst into tears. I thought of the beat up old '92 Oldsmobile back home that ran on a wing and a prayer. Tiffany and I had wondered how we were going to get around while in Atlanta and had prayed hard for an answer. God had listened. Yet another fingerprint, I thought.

Outside, in the parking lot, a gleaming 1995 Buick Roadmaster with only 43,000 miles on it greeted us. Jason introduced us to Chuck Payne, a friend who had been pivotal in finding and readying the car for us. I struggled for words.

"Thank you both so much. You have no idea what this means to us. Thank you."

As much as we hated to say goodbye, we had pledged to spend as much private time with Colby and Connor as possible that weekend, before Todd and Emily returned to Nashville with our boys. While Todd and Emily went out to eat, Tiffany and I went back to the Ronald McDonald House with the boys. Tiffany focused her attention on Connor, while Colby and I played together on the floor.

"I don't want to go home, Dada."

I bent down to Colby and picked him up, clasping him against my chest. He rested his head on my shoulder.

"I know, buddy. Trust me, I don't want you to go either. I wish you could stay here with Mommy and me." I sat him on the bed and tried to reassure him as he cried, his head in my lap.

When Todd and Emily returned Colby was visibly upset as we gathered his things. As we loaded the van and put Connor in his car seat, Colby clung to me, refusing to let go. Over and over he wailed, "I don't want to go! I don't want to go!" As the door slammed shut, we could hear Colby's muffled voice crying out for us. Tiffany and I hugged as the van pulled out of the parking lot.

"That was hard," I said, as I choked back my tears. "That was really hard. God, please watch over our kids and keep them safe."

Once back in the hospital, I telephoned Todd to see how Colby was doing. He'd cried himself to sleep, Todd said, his voice low.

It had been a good day, but a hard day. I stared at Caleb, his face eerily lit by the yellow and green monitor lights suspended above him. I stretched out my hands over his body and prayed, prayed for our children's safe trip back to Nashville, for Caleb's full healing, and that soon we would able to go home.

Day seventeen was a Monday, marking the start of a new week and a new month. It was the first of November and there had still been no word from Scottish Rite about admitting Caleb to their rehab program. Meanwhile, Caleb was scheduled for an eye exam to ensure he hadn't suffered any physical damage from the injury. There was also still the question of whether a feeding tube needed to be inserted before Caleb could be transferred into a rehab program. I was hoping he wouldn't need it, but the doctor shook his head.

"I think if he were able to eat, we would have seen evidence of it by now." At our concerned looks, he reminded us that it would likely only be temporary. But, he said, he also needed to discuss another surgical procedure, a Nissen fundoplication. I cringed at the thought of subjecting Caleb to another surgical procedure.

"The risk is that, if Caleb is unable to sit up or move his head and he vomits, he might not be able to clear his airway on his own. You don't want him battling another bout of pneumonia again."

We agreed and, reluctantly, gave the doctor permission for the procedure.

∽

"One is working slightly better than the other." We watched anxiously as the narrow beam of light swept back and forth past Caleb's eyes. "But his eyes are fine," the doctor pronounced. "Everything looks the way it should be."

It was his opinion that Caleb's eyesight problems were due to the damage in the vision processing center of the brain. He was responding to light, possibly seeing shadows and differentiating between levels of light, but that might be all. No, he said in response to our questions, there was no guarantee that his sight would improve. Like every other aspect of his rehabilitation, only time would tell.

I had mixed feelings. I was thrilled by the possibility that Caleb might be able to see anything at this point, but what if his real comfort would derive from being able to see us, his mom and dad? What if he could hear us and not understand why he couldn't see us? Would that cause him to panic? I was determined to find hope in the idea that he could at least make out shadows. And I was even more determined that, every time he opened his eyes, the shadows he saw would be his mommy and daddy.

Later that day, when Tiffany and I had left Caleb in the care of my father and my brother Travis while we grabbed something to eat, Caleb smiled a second time.

"I was just playing with him," Travis said, "making funny faces and noises, and then I saw him move his right cheek into a kind of half-smile."

That night, we saw another milestone. I'd been on the phone with a reporter from *The Chattanoogan*, giving them an update on Caleb, when I heard this odd, straining sound. Tears were streaming down Caleb's face and he was struggling to cry out. Tiffany held him close, smiling at how Caleb had made yet another stride, another step further along his journey.

It was with a mixture of trepidation and eagerness that we sat down with the representative from Children's Healthcare of Atlanta at Scottish Rite. It was day nineteen in the PICU at T.C. Thompson. The unspoken question was what would happen to Caleb if Scottish Rite didn't have room for him. Tiffany and I wanted the best possible facility in order to give Caleb the best possible chance of recovery. We'd been praying hard, and now we were about to find out the results of those prayers. As soon as she greeted us, we discovered it wasn't a question of if, but of when, and that when would be in exactly one week, next Wednesday. It was going to be intense, she warned us, with all sorts of therapies from sunup to sundown, with few breaks in between.

"The whole point of going into intensive rehab therapy is to ensure the parents are right there with the child, doing the therapy with them, and being trained to continue once the child goes home."

With Caleb's acceptance into the program now assured and knowing that Tiffany and I would stay and participate intensively in his rehabilitation therapy, we felt blessed. Aside from the practical aspect, I was convinced that Caleb would recover faster if he knew his mommy and daddy were there every step of the way, where he could hear our familiar voices and hopefully soon see us.

Feeling fairly buoyant, we returned to Caleb's room to do some more physical therapy. The improvement in Caleb's muscle strength had been increasingly evident over the past four or five days. He was sitting up straighter and had gone from supporting his head for a few fleeting seconds to almost eight minutes.

I sat on the floor and played with him, taking his hands and moving them over various toys and sensory books to stimulate his brain.

"Do you feel that?" I asked, as I put a Thomas the Train toy in his hand. Turning it on, I let him feel the vibrations of the wheels as they turned. "Choo choo!" Every now and then I would place my hand over his and pick up one of his toys, forcing his fingers to grasp the tiny object. When I let go, the toy would fall to the ground.

"That's okay, buddy," I whispered into his downy hair, "You'll get there. You'll get there."

That night, Caleb lay sleeping while Tiffany and I sat quietly, thinking about all the hurdles we were crossing and how things were finally looking encouraging. I took my cell phone out of my pocket, held it up to Tiffany and pressed the play button. Caleb's voice emerged.

"Hi, Dada. I love you, Dada!" I'd recorded it just a few days before we'd left on our camping trip. Tiffany rested her head on my shoulder.

"I miss hearing his sweet little voice."

∼

I thought back to the previous day, when we'd done some range of motion exercises that, although they were keeping Caleb limber, weren't giving him the weight resistance needed to build up muscle. Any form of resistance training seemed out of the question for someone who could not even grip an object.

At one point, Caleb's arm slipped off the side of the chair and dangled beside him. I watched as Caleb appeared to be trying to pull it back up. After several attempts, Caleb maneuvered his arm back up into his lap. That gave me an idea.

I slid Caleb's other arm off his lap and let it hang beside him. I watched as he struggled to pull it back up.

"Tiffany, come look at this." I slid one of his arms off his lap again and we watched as Caleb tried hard to retrieve it. I repeated the exercise six times, three times on each side. Perfect weight training, I thought. Caleb found it easier to manipulate his right hand more than his left, something Tiffany had noticed several days earlier during one of our many exercise sessions.

After therapy, when we'd laid Caleb back in his bed, he began to fidget, repeatedly trying to turn himself onto his side and kick his feet toward the gap in the side rails. When he managed to catch his feet on the side rail, he would use it to turn himself sideways, his head opposite the gap.

Neuro storming, the nurse said when I asked her about it.

"It's a classic symptom of traumatic brain injury to see someone flail about like this." As much as we were anxious to get our Caleb back, it was unnerving to watch. After having spent the better part of three weeks lying still, often unconscious, he was suddenly very animated.

"Does it ever go away?"

"Yes, it does subside over time. How long it takes depends on the individual and the healing in the brain."

CHAPTER FIFTEEN

The Prayer for Caleb Project

"Tim! Tim! Get up! He's choking!"

I awoke at 4:00 AM to the sound of my wife's screams. Despite the darkness in the room, when I looked toward Caleb, I could just make out the tiny outline of Caleb's feet dangling off the side of the bed. Caleb had somehow maneuvered his body through the narrow gap between the two bed rails. As he slid out of the bed, his neck had lodged on one of the rails. The dead weight of his body hanging off the side of the bed was causing him to strangle.

I leaped up and quickly hoisted him back up on the bed as Tiffany frantically called for a nurse and.

"Baby, are you okay? Caleb? Are you okay?"

I looked down at the hard tile floor, my body trembling. I wasn't sure what was worse, the fact that Caleb had nearly choked to death on the rail that was supposed to prevent him from falling, or the fact that, after already suffering severe brain trauma, he might have smashed his head on the floor.

I heard the pounding of heels and turned to see two nurses and the on call doctor, burst into the room. Caleb was crying, his already irritated vocal cords muffling the sounds. The doctor quickly checked his vitals.

"His lungs sound fine, he looks fine, and there are no signs of any broken bones or anything." Tiffany and I huddled as closely as we could to Caleb to comfort him. "I'm so sorry. In all the years I've been here, this has never happened before."

"It scared us to death," I confessed. "We had no idea that Caleb would be able to move like that. Can we do something? Get a different bed, something with a protective barrier around it?"

"The only thing we have is a crib," one of the nurses offered. "A large crib. Do you want me to see if we can get that?"

"Yes, please. We'll wait with him until you return." I wasn't going to leave Caleb's side for a minute, on the chance he might wiggle out again.

I watched shakily as Caleb drifted off to sleep.

"We'll monitor him closely tonight," the doctor said, as he draped his stethoscope around his neck and stepped away from Caleb's bed. Once everyone had left, I suggested Tiffany go back to bed while I waited for the crib to arrive. By five o'clock, the lights were out and it was quiet again. I whispered a last prayer of thanks to God for waking Tiffany up to save our son's life.

While Caleb was being prepped for his fundoplication and G-tube surgery, Tiffany and I sat in the waiting room. I felt fear flood my soul again, reliving the events that had happened just hours earlier. How could we possibly watch him around the clock to ensure he didn't hurt himself? All the "what ifs" cascaded through me as I contemplated what might have happened had Caleb fallen. What if we made a mistake or let our guard down for one brief moment? What if, in the course of time, he fell again and this time hit his head? How could we possibly safeguard against that? Was it even possible? Tiffany looked up as I tightened my grip on her hand.

"We are just going to have to take one thing at a time," Tiffany said, her soft voice soothing me. "We'll do our best. And we'll pray." I nodded.

Caleb sailed through the surgery.

"He is going to be out for quite some time," the surgeon warned, "and he'll be groggy for a while until the sedation wears off."

It was hard pulling back the covers and seeing the incision across Caleb's abdomen, now sealed with an adhesive patch. I was glad it was over. We spoke to one of the PICU doctors who stopped in to check on Caleb. Out of curiosity, I asked where Caleb was on the coma scale now, as he'd recently been gauged between six and eight.

"Probably somewhere between ten and eleven," the doctor estimated. "He's reacting to light appropriately now, and seems to open and close his eyes when he wants to." I was ecstatic. Caleb had surpassed the scale's halfway point and, to me, it signaled that Caleb was becoming more and more aware of his surroundings. Another good indication, the doctor said, was that Caleb had discovered the insertion site of his earlier brain monitor.

"It's most likely itching," the doctor explained, "and he's trying to scratch it. Movement doesn't get much more purposeful than that."

I grinned.

All the optimistic indications of the day served to distract us from our earlier fears of keeping Caleb safe. We focused instead on the fact that Todd and Emily were arriving the next day with Colby and Connor for one last visit before we left for Atlanta. It would be weeks before we'd see them again.

That night, Tiffany sat in her chair, eyes closed, listening to Christian praise and worship music while I sat reading Caleb's latest Facebook comments and news stories. One story in *The Tennessean* caught my eye. Entitled, "Response to Freak Accident Is a Powerful Expression of Faith," the reporter Rob Payne had written a story unlike all the others, an opinion piece that dealt strictly with faith, quoting some of my comments on why prayer was so important.

Payne had written, "One follow-up newspaper story showed me the father/minister has the right attitude about the freak accident when it quoted him as saying: 'The last two months I've been teaching a series on faith and talking about this very thing,' Brown said, 'that God allows events that seem impossible so we have the opportunity to have faith through them and see the glory of God at work. I totally believe that is what this is about, too. Everything is still possible, which is why prayer is so important.'"

As I read my own words, affirmed by the writer, it was another reminder of how faith had played a large role in everything that had happened over the past three weeks. It was as if God was saying: *See? Everything I have been teaching you about faith is true; and now part of the reason I have allowed you to experience what you have over the last few weeks is so that you can know it is true, not just in your head, but in your heart as well, through experience.*

The lessons I had taught on faith were being played out before me like a blueprint. God had allowed a seemingly impossible event from any human standpoint and now, through a lot of prayer combined with good decisions on the part of doctors and nurses, Caleb was healing and on the road to recovery. Woven through it all was one thread, the voice of praise from literally tens if not hundreds of thousands all across the world who were now giving glory to God for all that He had done, all that He was doing, and all they expected Him to do.

I had two ideas. The first was that I would talk to Jason McKay about the HelpCaleb.com website and see whether I could turn it into a blog. I felt compelled to chronicle the progress I hoped we would experience at Scottish Rite, as I was convinced that God was going to somehow use our story to bring glory to Himself. I had always enjoyed writing as a way for me to record all the things that I felt God stir within me. Now I would use it publicly to share the events of our lives, to provide a record of the ongoing miracle that was continuing to unfold in front of us. With that in mind, I roughly sketched out what I would later call "The Prayer for Caleb Project," a way for people to get involved and spread the word about prayer for Caleb's healing and ongoing progress. Prayer had played the central role in getting us this far, and I was sure it would be prayer that would see us safely home.

CHAPTER SIXTEEN

Scottish Rite

"Watch this!"

Tiffany and I had just arrived at the hospital Monday morning to find my dad nearly beside himself in anticipation of our return. Dad turned toward Caleb and, in one quick motion, whipped Caleb's blue blanket up into the air. Caleb's eyes shot open, moving as if trying to track where his grandfather "Poppy" was. Dad dropped the blanket back on top of Caleb. Tiffany and I glanced at each other, curious to see what Caleb would do next.

"I'm gonna get you!" Poppy playfully growled. All of a sudden my Dad swooped back down and grabbed the blanket, tickling Caleb as he did so. Caleb's mouth curved into a huge smile. Caleb was having fun. He was reacting, feeling emotion. He was actually having fun! I lunged for my camera, reminded of my third dream, where he and I had been face to face, his eyes radiant, his smile joyous. I was ecstatic.

"Hey, Colby, come here for a second," I said. "Watch this!" As Caleb beamed at his poppy's antics, I hoisted Colby into my arms. "Did you see that?"

"He smiled," Colby said. "Is he all better now?"

I chuckled and gave Colby a squeeze.

"Not yet, buddy, but he is better. He can smile now." We could all smile now, I thought.

∽

The next twenty-four hours were difficult. Not only did we have to say goodbye to our two boys again for another two weeks, but after nearly a month of sharing our trials with family, everyone was now preparing to leave. Tiffany and I would be on our own until it was time to leave for Atlanta. It was a sobering prospect. Up until now, at least one family member or friend had been in the hospital with us every waking minute. Their presence had been a reassurance, a gift from God. One by one they left, starting with Todd, Emily, and our boys. Colby was in tears.

"This just rips my heart out," Tiffany lamented.

"Me, too. I wish we could just go home." Our old life seemed so distant, so long ago, and it would be at least another month before we could even contemplate returning to Nashville, depending on how well Caleb did at rehab.

My dad, who had been with us for virtually the entire time we'd been at the hospital, was leaving that night. Tiffany's parents had also said their goodbyes. My mom and brother volunteered to stay overnight with Caleb to give Tiffany and I one night alone for hopefully a good night's rest back at the Ronald McDonald House before they left the next day. And Tiffany's sister, Misty, was coming to help us prepare for our trip to Atlanta.

The air was crisp and cool as we made our way back to the hospital the next morning.

"It's hard to believe that we're actually leaving this place." Tiffany's words were slightly muffled as she huddled close to my side. We'd spent the past three and a half weeks at T.C. Thompson Children's Hospital.

"I know. It seems like yesterday we were running through those doors to the emergency room, not knowing whether Caleb was going to live or die. And now here he is doing so well that he's ready to start rehab."

"It's scary," Tiffany said. "There's a certain comfort in being here. Like, if anything happened, they would know what to do. The doctors and nurses have all been so amazing."

"God has worked through them a miracle."

As Tiffany began packing, I turned my attention to Caleb's first therapy session since his surgery. I sat him up in bed and he immediately began to cry. I was eager to get him started on the road to recovery, but Caleb clearly wasn't up to it. The doctors had warned us there would be days when Caleb would need a break and to accept that and not push him. There would be plenty of rehab, I told myself, once we got to Atlanta. I took him in my arms and sat, holding him, rocking slightly. He quieted. Evidently, this was one of those days, a day where the most important thing was to simply love him, and the way Caleb wanted to be loved was to be held. Moments later, he was fast asleep.

"It's just a different kind of therapy," Tiffany said, as she stood in the doorway, her emerald eyes warm as she watched Caleb sleep. "But it is therapy."

As we packed the very last of our stuff and said goodbye to Misty, we took a last look around. It felt strange seeing the room empty; every trace of our being at the Ronald McDonald House for nearly four weeks had been erased. There was so much emotion connected to this space that it felt almost like leaving home. I put an arm around Tiffany. We stood at the close of what had been a very intense chapter of our lives and were now heading off to start another. Tiffany was right—it was scary. We were once again setting off into the unknown, although at a more measured pace than when we'd first been hurtled in this life-changing direction. I tightened my arm around Tiffany's shoulder.

"You ready?"

She sighed. "Yes."

Pat Pearson stuck her head through the doorway. She and

another nurse, Lori Atchley, had been particularly devoted to Caleb and always reminding us to work together as a team, and to never let ourselves become divided.

"You are going to need each other," she advised. "The statistics are against you. Studies show that eighty-five percent of all marriages that undergo trauma like this end in divorce. The pressure on your marriage is going to be phenomenal. But," she added, "we worship a phenomenal God. If you stick with Him and cling to each other, you'll get through it together."

Another messenger from God, I thought. The message was clear: *Stick together. This isn't going to be easy. You're going to need each other.* Pat affirmed what so many had said to us. We knew God was telling us something, that He was calling us to pay attention, to remember our marriage vows, to make every effort to walk through this as one. We were grateful.

∽

Wednesday morning we awoke to the sound of nurses unhooking Caleb's heart monitor and blood pressure cuff.

Lori Atchley stopped by to wish us well one last time.

"Hey, little man," she said, sitting down and settling him comfortably in her lap. "You're looking so good." Caleb laid his head on her chest and relaxed. "Oh, yes," she said, rocking him slightly, "you are going to do just fine."

Tiffany hugged Lori before she left.

"Hopefully, one day soon, we'll come back and he'll come running down the hall and through those double doors himself."

"That's what we're all praying for." Lori smiled at Caleb. "And you go down there to Scottish Rite and show them what it's all about, okay, little man?"

As the EMTs arrived to take Caleb to Atlanta, Pat Pearson returned and gave us both a big hug, reminding us yet again to stay close together. As we walked out the door, Pat put her hand on my arm.

"You make sure you two get out and spend some time together, you hear me?"

"You've got it, Pat," I promised, smiling.

We walked out through the double doors and down the hallway toward the elevators. Everyone paused to watch as we left. It felt strange, knowing we wouldn't be returning. Walking out of the final set of double doors into the cool November air felt like a dream. Caleb had not seen the light of day or felt the breeze in nearly an entire month.

I climbed into the back of the ambulance with Caleb. Tiffany pulled in behind the ambulance in our new car. I looked at it and thought back to the day when our group of friends and supporters had surprised us with it. Everyone had been astonishingly generous and supportive, I thought, everyone we'd crossed paths with, from Fall Creek Falls and the campground to the hospital and emergency staffs, to the complete strangers everywhere who continued to pray for Caleb. It was humbling and uplifting. I looked down at Caleb, who lay asleep on his stretcher as we headed down I-75, cars barreling past us at death-defying speeds. I was reminded yet again of the frailty of life and how we were so dependent upon God for every moment. I prayed for God's divine guidance and protection as we made our way south to Atlanta. And, as we went, I relaxed, sensing that God was indeed with us.

∽

Scottish Rite was large, much larger than T.C. Thompson, the hospital at Erlanger. Everything was foreign, from the layout and appearance of the buildings to the medical staff. We were assigned to room 355. For the next few hours, we met several nurses and staff members who had us fill out paperwork. Everyone was warm and caring and responded to Caleb as we related the journey that had brought us to their door. Already it was starting to feel less foreign.

Dr. Sholas, of whom we'd heard good things, entered the room in the boisterous manner we'd been told to expect, with a team of doctors in his wake. We vigorously shook hands. He immediately set to work examining Caleb, sitting him up, moving his arms and legs, and testing his reflexes.

"He's very limber," Dr. Sholas observed, looking pleased. I told him we had been doing range of motion exercises with Caleb. He gave us an appraising look.

"Not many parents work with their children like that. And I can tell you that it's made a distinct difference. You have given him a good head start." Dr. Sholas continued his examination of Caleb. "He looks great. He has elasticity in his arms and legs, and looks to be trying to hold himself upright when you sit him up. He has some prominent deficiencies in his eyesight, but those should improve over time. He should do very well here, very well indeed."

His words were the answer to our prayers.

"There are three overall therapy approaches we'll be taking here," Dr. Sholas explained. "Occupational therapy, which focuses on fine motor skills, like walking, picking up things, and sitting up; physical therapy, which focuses on the big picture, the building of muscle tone in order to hold yourself erect and develop sufficient strength to use your arms and legs; and speech therapy, which focuses not just on speaking but the use of the tongue, swallowing properly, etc. The speech therapy should help Caleb learn to eat so he doesn't require a feeding tube much longer.

"So," Dr. Sholas said as he finished up, "the plan of action is to have Caleb's therapists evaluate him over the course of today and tomorrow. They will tailor a therapy plan and review it with you tomorrow. Right now, we doctors are merely here on standby, in case you need us. We'll make sure he gets his vitals checked and that he gets his g-tube feedings, but, all in all, the majority of his care is going to be up to you. Things are different now. You are no longer in an intensive care unit. Caleb is no longer unstable. And because Caleb is now stable, he no longer needs around the clock care." He gave us a reassuring smile. "I know this is going to be scary at first, but this is the next part of Caleb's journey. He has progressed to get to this stage. So, wonderful to meet you all and I look forward to seeing this little guy get better, and start eating, talking, and walking again."

Tiffany and I gave each other hopeful looks as the parade of doctors exited.

As we met a few therapists and each performed their own evaluations, we saw a lot more movement out of Caleb, most importantly tangible purposeful movements. We also saw him giggle a lot as he responded to them. Tiffany and I were riding a crest of exuberant optimism as we watched him react and listened to the positive observations of each therapist. I'd been afraid Caleb might resist, finding all the attention and examinations exhausting, but he seemed to enjoy the attention. Not surprisingly, he fell asleep well before bedtime.

Tiffany and I unpacked our things and began settling in, talking softly. The word that kept coming up as we talked to each other was hope.

"I just feel so much hope now," Tiffany said. "I really feel that this is the place God wants us to be."

"It's strange," I said. "At T.C. Thompson, it was such a rollercoaster ride. "Every day I felt like my faith was being challenged in some new way. At times I even feared that my faith was gone, like all hope was lost. But then, it came back. We saw

Caleb get better, and now, being here, I can't help but feel optimistic. With this new phase we're in—this second part of our journey—I really feel a tremendous sense of hope."

That, I decided, would be the theme as I began blogging about Caleb.

Hope.

PART TWO

Hope

"Those who hope in the LORD will renew their strength. They will soar on wings like eagles; they will run and not grow weary, they will walk and not be faint."

–Isaiah 40:31

CHAPTER SEVENTEEN

A New Phase

The next day marked the beginning of Caleb's journey into rehab. It was November 11th. The morning began with a long series of orientations as physical, occupational, speech, and every other kind of therapist we could imagine came in, introduced themselves, and did a short routine with Caleb to see where he was developmentally. The feedback was encouraging. Each was impressed with how well Caleb could move his body, and the indications were that Caleb could hear us and, to some extent, understand. He seemed to be able to move on command and sometimes grew very emotional when Tiffany or I spoke to him. They concluded that Caleb could differentiate between light and dark, and perhaps even discern shapes. He might, they said, have already begun experiencing moments of greater visual clarity. We had seen some evidence of that ourselves. When Tiffany or I stood in front of him, Caleb sometimes tracked our movements with his eyes.

The speech therapist told us that speech therapy and eating went hand in hand, so part of the strategy would involve helping Caleb engage in the familiar process of eating. The therapist spooned a few drops of ice water into Caleb's mouth. We watched anxiously as Caleb rolled his tongue around it. The goal was to see if he could swallow. After a few moments, he did. We were jubilant.

The therapist then pulled out a small cherry lollipop and

rolled it across Caleb's tongue. He responded immediately, leaning forward to get another lick. Tiffany and I grinned at each other.

The initial physical therapy evaluation was equally encouraging. All the therapy we had done up to this point, with the range of motion and stretching, meant that Caleb was considerably more limber than his condition had led the therapist to expect. He could sit cross-legged and bear his weight somewhat when the therapist stood him up, and held him with his knees locked in place.

All in all, it was going to be a rigorous schedule, beginning at eight o'clock each morning and ending at three o'clock in the afternoon. Tiffany and I decided we would also work with Caleb during the evenings to continue what he had worked on earlier in the day. Prior to the accident, our habit after dinner was to get down on the floor and play with the kids for a while. We decided to incorporate that familiar routine into our nighttime therapy reinforcement sessions.

That evening Caleb was understandably tired but still in good spirits. Our son was returning to us, becoming more and more interactive, and we watched him smile and laugh as we held and played with him. I took out a book my father had bought, one that lit up, made sounds, and narrated as the pages were turned. I asked Caleb to turn the page and watched as he tried to lift his hand. When I supported his elbow, he managed to turn the page four times.

That night, we all fell asleep, exhausted and happy.

∼

Every activity from now on would be seen through the lens of therapy. In an effort to engage Caleb in normal daily routines we would begin with grooming—combing his hair, bathing, and brushing his teeth, as if he were back at home.

"Hey Caleb, want to walk to Daddy?"

During Caleb's physical therapy session, the therapist said he appeared to have retained his muscle memory for walking. She gently set him down on his feet, holding onto each hand.

"Okay, Caleb, kick your foot out. C'mon, let's walk to Daddy. Show Daddy how you can walk."

I held my breath as I watched Caleb take his first steps.

"Hooray!" Tiffany and I clapped our hands. Everyone, including Caleb, sported huge smiles. Caleb's legs were still too weak to support his weight, but he was determined to put one foot in front of the other. Sometimes one leg would swing across the other, twisting him off balance, but the therapist kept him upright and encouraged him to keep moving forward. When he reached me, tired and triumphant, I swept him up into my arms and gave him a great big bear hug.

"One thing that helps children get their legs and feet moving to walk," the therapist explained, "is having them ride a tricycle." She fitted a small helmet on Caleb and strapped his feet to the pedals.

"C'mon, Caleb, let's go for a ride!" With that, we began wheeling him all around the third floor of the hospital, his legs pumping up and down with the pedals, his face beaming. His hands were left free. I nudged Tiffany.

"Look! He knows what to do. He's holding onto the handlebars by himself."

At speech therapy, we were excited and nervous because, as the therapist explained, we were going to start with eating. So much was riding on Caleb being able to regain his ability to eat, including his ability to speak. I sent off a swift prayer and watched as Caleb progressed from swallowing drops of water and juice from a spoon to sipping juice and swallowing dribbles of yogurt. The therapist was impressed, and said his ability to relearn to swallow so quickly was a very good sign that he might be able to eat by himself in the future—no more feeding tube, in that case.

Near the end of the session, the therapist encouraged Caleb to try sucking juice from a straw, something that required considerably more skill because he would have to create the suction. She placed the straw in Caleb's mouth and began encouraging him to try to drink through it. I was skeptical, afraid we might be asking too much too soon. The therapist, however, wanted to push him a little. My jaw sagged as the liquid in the straw began rising hesitantly, up and down, up and down. He remembered! He wanted that juice!

"He'll get it eventually," the speech therapist said with a smile.

"I think speech therapy is going to be his favorite," Tiffany said, eyes sparkling.

Caleb's occupational therapist confirmed what we had suspected, that Caleb's tendency to look to the right meant that it was likely the vision in his left eye was worse than his right. That correlated with the fact that his overall muscle strength was weaker on his left side—he had to strain to use any of the muscles on his left side. We played with various toys designed to stimulate his senses: toys that made sounds or played music, toys that lit up, vibrated, and those that generated a cause and effect, such as pulling a string to make a noise. Caleb loved them. Armed with a better understanding of what his strengths and weaknesses were, Tiffany and I decided to focus more of our personal therapy activities on his left side.

Our second full day at Scottish Rite was equally productive. One of the philosophies there was goal setting. It was very important, they told us, to set and update our therapy goals, keeping them realistic yet always ahead of us, giving us something to strive for. The therapists pronounced that Caleb had managed to meet every single one of the first week's goals they'd set for him by his second day. The focus for the remainder of the week would be to improve Caleb's sense of balance to get him to sit upright on his own, and continue to strengthen all the muscle groups on his left side. After three weeks of clinging to each other for support every time we faced yet another challenge or setback, Tiffany and I were now hugging each other in delight over the miraculous headway Caleb was making.

That afternoon, while Caleb napped, Tiffany and I discussed the most exhilarating of the day's revelations: Caleb was progressing so well and so quickly that it was possible he might only need to stay in Atlanta for four weeks instead of the customary six or eight. Three goals they wanted to see Caleb achieve before going home, they said, was to clap his hands, place objects into other people's hands, and to cross over his midline, that is, to reach with one hand to the opposite side of his body to pick up or put something down. I did a quick calculation. At the rate Caleb was going, we might make it home in time for Christmas. What a blessing that would be I thought, all five of us back together again, in our own home! It was clear to us that all the prayers being offered on Caleb's behalf by family, friends, and complete strangers were making a difference.

Saturday and Sunday would be less intense than our first three days, we were told. The weekends were reserved more for group activities to improve social interactions among the children. Saturday began with music therapy. A young woman sat down with a guitar, and the children sat in a circle about her, as she sang a number of familiar children's songs. Parents looked on as she tweaked the lyrics to incorporate each child's name, singing personalized stanzas to every child, and interacting with them as much as possible. Tiffany and I watched as other therapists encouraged individual children to move to the music in ways that aligned with their occupational and physical therapies. It was impossible not to be impressed by the holistic approach and the clear dedication and devotion these therapists had to the kids.

As the woman sang and strummed her guitar, a therapist stood Caleb up, supporting his weight and moving him in time to the music. He began swaying to the beat, and I felt Tiffany's hand tighten on mine. The therapist placed various items in Caleb's hands as she worked with him, letting him explore them. I studied everything she did, determined to reinforce these activities later on.

After the music session Caleb went across the hall to the main gym for some physical therapy. The therapist worked Caleb's arms and legs and engaged him in various play activities to help him learn how to focus on objects and build his strength. As she worked with him, she explained the whys of Caleb's movements.

"You see how, when he sits in his wheelchair, he constantly moves his head from side to side?"

We nodded. It was impossible not to notice.

"Well, it could be an indication of his brain injury, but I don't think so in his case. I think it's just because of his poor eyesight. It's as if he's feeling his way forward with his head, with his body, to see if he bumps into anything. He doesn't do it when he's not in motion." Sure enough, when she laid him down on the mat, he relaxed and stopped moving his head from side to side and, instead, focused on their play activities.

"When he's sitting on the floor," the therapist explained, "he knows he's not moving. He feels the mat beneath him so he feels secure, knowing he's not likely to bump into anything."

I thought back to those first few days when we began moving him from his bed to his chair and back, and how he would cry. We feared we were hurting him. Now I wondered whether he might have just been frightened because he couldn't see where he was going, who was holding him, or gauge whether or not he was safe.

"Don't worry about it for now," the therapist advised. "This movement can actually be part of the healing process, and, as you know, his sight has improved in just the few days since he arrived here. It may very well continue to get better."

I believed her. Within just the last two weeks, Caleb had gone from being virtually blind, not reacting to light at all, to fixing his eyes on us, tracking our movements, and apparently discerning shadows and shapes.

That evening, I found myself reflecting on how life had changed for us in so many ways. Thinking back to when I had been wholly immersed in the normal hustle and bustle of life, I had congratulated myself on being a pretty good dad by coming home each evening, sitting down to dinner with my family, and then getting down on the floor and spending time with my kids, no matter what other responsibilities or worries I had. Yet, even in those intimate moments I was often miles away, anxious about our bills or thinking about taking on that extra job to make ends meet. I wasn't in the moment, not wholly present. I thought back to when we'd been struggling so hard and I was working three jobs. I had thought then that, if I sacrificed a little time and worked really hard to pay off our debts, then I could do all the home repairs, replace our unreliable car with the minivan we had been dreaming about, and go on the vacation we had always hoped to share. Eventually, I thought, once I got "there," I would finally be able relax and spend more time with Tiffany and the kids without worry, and be more present.

In keeping my eyes fixed forward on the future, on that fuzzy image in the distance, I'd been missing a lot of what was important, precious, and fleeting right in front of me—the things I was seeing at this moment, the beauty of Caleb's darkly fringed eyes as he smiled, the sweet smell of his breath as I tickled his face with my nose, our faces so close that his lips would brush my cheek, the hands so small that I could fit both of his into one of mine. It was through this tragedy that I had been given a chance to start over, to see things differently, to be reminded of what truly mattered. In addition to everything else we were learning, God, I felt, was showing me not to let worldly pursuits cloud my vision of what was important, even if those worldly pursuits were intended to accomplish more important things down the road for our family. I'd been so focused on working really hard to get to some elusive place that I'd forgotten to live in the place I was in, to be content and enjoy the blessings that God had already given us.

"Thank you, God," I prayed, "for reminding me of who You are in the midst of what we are going through, and for demonstrating to us the beauty of what it means to live in relationship with You and each other."

∼

"There will be good days and not so good days. Some days you'll take two steps forward, and other days you'll find yourselves taking a step or two back."

I'd been given that advice by several people before leaving for Atlanta, not to let the occasional, inevitable speed bumps derail us. Caleb had been soaring like an eagle his first three days, taking our spirits with him. It was now time to return to earth. It was a bit of a hard landing.

Caleb had had a rough night, repeatedly coughing, and I had been up until four in the morning, worried he might choke. Despite our fatigue, we made our way down to our morning physical therapy session.

This time, the therapist really pushed him to strengthen his upper body. She laid out a thick foam mat and had him lie face down with his shoulders and head extended beyond the mat so that he would have to support himself on his arms, like doing a pushup, in order to remain level and keep his head up. The position was difficult and he immediately began to cry. I fought the urge to rush forward and pick him up to kiss his tears away. A glance at Tiffany revealed she was also struggling. This was his journey and we were there as coaches, to praise and encourage him to keep trying, not to impede his progress. He was such a trouper, laboring for several moments, before collapsing his arms and resting his head for a moment before starting again.

Since it was Sunday, we had a lighter therapy regimen. We headed down to the hospital chapel where they held a weekly children's service. We sang, "Jesus Loves Me" and "This Little Light of Mine," and I looked around the congregation. All about us were children recovering from various injuries and diseases. The scene reminded me of those who had surrounded Jesus. Here before us were the lame, the blind, the deaf, and the suffering, from every imaginable background, all under one roof, singing songs of praise to God. All of us were there for one sole purpose, united with one goal, to love God and let Him love us. I thought about what Jesus had said: "Let the little children come unto me and do not hinder them, for it is such as these that make up the kingdom of heaven" (Luke 18:16).

That afternoon, Caleb's exhaustion got the better of him. He became emotional and resisted doing any more therapy. He didn't appear to be seeing well either, unable to focus even on what was directly in front of him. He needed to rest and recharge, so we gave him the afternoon off. Grateful, he slept.

I replayed the day in my head. It really hadn't been a bad day but, nevertheless, I had been feeling a bit dejected and apprehensive. Mindful of the warning they'd given us back at the hospital that brain injury patients can level off and stop recovering at any moment, we were understandably nervous that any apparent setback or plateau might mark the end of Caleb's recovery. I had to remind myself of just how far he had come in a mere four weeks, from a comatose toddler who might never regain consciousness, see, speak, walk, or even eat again to the now determined little guy who had emerged from his coma to swallow, walk with assistance, and even giggle and laugh.

That night we prayed with hands outstretched over Caleb, asking God to heal him completely, thanking God for the healing that had already taken place, and thanking God for allowing us the grace to keep our son.

∼

During that first week, things had been intense. Our lives became immersed in various therapies. Every activity became a teaching opportunity, a strength-building opportunity, a skills-building opportunity.

As Caleb underwent more and more challenging therapies, it was heartbreaking to watch him sometimes weep out of frustration or fear. He was becoming increasingly more self-aware, and appeared to realize that something was wrong. His muscle memory was apparent, such as when he gripped the tricycle handlebars or tried to push off his feet to stand. The therapists agreed that he probably was remembering the things he once knew how to do but could no longer do, at least not without difficulty. When Caleb became frustrated to the point of crying uncontrollably, the therapy would abruptly end and Tiffany would wrap her arms around him and cuddle him until he stopped.

Caleb had also progressed from walking with the help of two therapists supporting his limp body to now one who did not always have to bear Caleb's weight as he fought to take steps on his own. He also now sported braces on his feet to keep him from dragging his feet and tripping. The braces were necessary, we were told, because he lacked the strength to sufficiently control his legs. Each day he walked slightly further, the goal always to reach either his mommy or daddy, as his path progressed from a simple, straight line to a wide circle spanning the entire room.

It struck me that, whether it was learning to eat, walk, sit up on his own, or play, we had celebrated these very same milestones with Caleb two years earlier, when he was about six months old, and here we were celebrating them again. Somehow, it felt even more exciting the second time around.

With his increased muscle strength and control, Caleb had begun exhibiting behaviors similar to those he had displayed as an infant. Everything we placed in his hands he invariably stuck into his mouth. When I asked one of the therapists about this, he confirmed that this was a natural behavior exhibited by babies who were beginning to interact with the world around them. I recalled a post by one of Caleb's now nine thousand blog followers, whose child had gone through a similar situation. Her child, she wrote, had regressed at first, only to later fast-forward through all the stages of a growing baby again.

Caleb was also doing very well with his speech and swallowing therapy. He had made excellent progress sipping juice, including from a straw, before moving on to a Sippy cup with no difficulty. Applesauce had proved no problem and Caleb was given the green light to start sampling pureed foods. We were ecstatic as the therapist lifted spoonfuls of pureed chicken, mashed potatoes and corn. Caleb's eyes gleamed each time the spoon was raised. Tiffany and I took turns feeding Caleb as the therapist watched. At one point, Caleb fixed his gaze on Tiffany for about eight seconds, before turning and staring at me, which did not go unnoticed by the therapist.

"I'm going to push the envelope here a bit," the therapist said, eyes twinkling, "and see if Caleb will tolerate a little chewing." She picked up a macaroni elbow coated with cheese and squished it between Caleb's teeth. Caleb's jaw began to move. He knew exactly what to do. We watched as he chewed it up and swallowed it down, without any coughing or choking. The therapist leaned back in her chair and looked at us.

"This kid's ready to eat."

∼

When it was nearly bedtime, Tiffany and I made our nightly telephone call to Colby to tell him goodnight. Colby's voice chattered excitedly over the speakerphone about all the fun things he had done that day.

"I miss you, Dada. I love you, Dada," Colby said. I glanced at Caleb and felt my heart wrench. Caleb had started to cry at the familiar sound of Colby's voice.

"Would you like to speak with your brother?" I asked Colby. "Even though he can't talk, he can hear you."

I held the phone up to Caleb's ear as Colby said, "Hi, Caleb, it's Colby. I miss you. I love you, Caleb." Tears continued to slide down Caleb's face. I pressed the phone back up against my ear as I drew Caleb into my arms and held him tightly.

"Hey, Dada," Colby chirped, "did you know I'm coming

to see you soon?" Colby's aunts were bringing him down for Thanksgiving in just over a week, along with some other family and friends, and he would be staying with us for about five days. Needless to say, Tiffany and I were thrilled at the prospect of reuniting with our other two boys.

"I can't wait!"

"Me either!" There was a pause. "Hey, Dada? I don't wanna go to Fall Creek Falls again." His comment came out of nowhere. I swallowed hard. "But, I do wanna go camping again, Dada."

"You do?"

"Yeah, I like camping, but I wanna go someplace with no rocks. Can we go to the beach?"

CHAPTER EIGHTEEN

I...Love...You!

"On a scale of two to fifteen, I'd say Caleb's a fifteen."

When I heard those words, I wanted to shout with joy. The media had been periodically checking in for updates on Caleb and it was during a conversation with Scott Arnold, a news reporter from Channel Five WTVF in Nashville who had asked about Caleb's coma, that I realized I didn't know where he currently stood in terms of the coma scale. No one here had made mention of it at all. Caleb had started out in Tennessee between a four and a five, with two being the deepest comatose state, and had progressed to somewhere between ten and eleven before we left for Atlanta. I asked Dr. Sholas, who gave me the good news.

"Now, you must understand," Dr. Sholas added, when he saw my elation, "just because Caleb is out of his coma doesn't mean we're not still facing significant difficulties. Caleb's got a lot of good things going for him, but he also has some things going against him. One good thing is that he's making a lot of progress very quickly. One not so good thing is that a large part of his injury is located in the visual center of his brain, so there may be some long-term or even permanent vision loss. And that vision loss could have a negative impact on how well he recovers."

Dr. Sholas went on to list other potential challenges, including learning disabilities, the inability to behave normally in his interactions with other people, being unable to function completely in society, and possibly even later issues with his brain that could worsen his condition or overall mental capabilities. There was no way to predict, he said. We would just have to wait and see.

The road to recovery, I thought, really was a road versus and not a destination. And it was going to be a long road, one with a question mark that seemed to loom over our heads. I was grateful to have God as our compass, even if I wasn't sure the path would lead to where we hoped to go. It had already taken us places we thought we'd never go, and we had learned some valuable life lessons along the way.

How many times, I wondered, had I been in the mall, the grocery store, a park, or some other public place, and seen a special needs child, eyes fixed vacantly on one spot, mouth hanging open, drooling slightly, body twitching uncontrollably, hands or feet drawn up, being wheeled by a parent. How many times had I seen their inability to talk, move, or interact in a way that was deemed socially acceptable and thought, "That's so sad" and then quickly averted my eyes lest the parent think I was staring.

Now I knew what it felt like, seeing that same uneasy look in people's eyes as I pushed my son in his wheelchair. Now I shared that disconcerting feeling that my child was pitied by strangers. My reaction to kids with special needs and the parents who cared for them had become markedly different. Now, instead of looking away, I found myself bending down, trying to make eye contact even when they couldn't see me, and saying, "Hello. How are you today? Aren't you beautiful?" I could tell the parents didn't hear comments like that very often. They should, I thought to myself. They should.

I wheeled Caleb outside to a somewhat secluded waterfall-style fountain I'd spotted from a third floor window. Tucked between two buildings, it was the focal point of a small garden. There was no one there when we arrived. I sat on a granite slab adjacent to small frogs, lily pads, and sculptures of dancing children, all made of stone, and unbuckled Caleb's seatbelt. Caleb perked up as the wind blew through his hair and the smell of damp, decaying autumn leaves hit his nose. The sun was displaying its last glorious rays to greet the approaching evening. It had been a long, therapy-packed day and he was tired. I picked him up and held him against my chest.

He snuggled into my neck, one hand caressing my cheek. I talked to him softly and told him how much I loved him. Unable to resist, I tickled his tummy and was rewarded with a bright smile and a giggle. He cuddled closer, gave a sigh, and went quiet. We sat in silence and I thought about that sigh. That and his giggles were the closest we'd come to hearing his voice so far. I prayed that soon we would hear more, that this was just the beginning.

∼

The end of that first week at Scottish Rite was marked by another visit, one from a neuropsychologist who wanted to educate us about possible learning disabilities in children with traumatic brain injuries and on what our options would be regarding Caleb's future education, particularly when it came time to start school. Children like Caleb, we'd been warned, who had suffered brain injuries often also suffered various learning or behavioral disabilities later on, and special programs existed to aid these children through school.

"I'm particularly impressed with Caleb's emotional well-being," the neuropsychologist commented. "Often, children in these circumstances are not in touch with their emotions or are unable to regulate them." They might stay angry or sad and often cry, she explained, incapable of being consoled. Caleb, however, was doing very well. "He laughs when he's supposed to laugh, cries when he's supposed to cry, and, when he does cry, hugs and attention are enough to calm him." I tried to keep her comments in perspective, but I could not suppress the delight and relief I felt at hearing her words.

In week two, we turned our attention toward teaching Caleb how to make vocal sounds. The therapist was very encouraged by how Tiffany and I interacted with Caleb, because, she said, we were already doing much of what she recommended parents do when their children were learning to speak. We had sung his favorite songs, like, "Itsy Bitsy Spider" and "Twinkle, Twinkle, Little Star," pausing occasionally for Caleb to try to blurt out the next word. We also played silly games, like I've Got Your Nose, or the Wa Wa Yell, where you put your hand over your mouth and shout, "Wa, wa, wa!" Every time we played these games, Caleb would giggle, and then let out an, "aahhh," sound before laughing again. The therapist told us that we would see a progression toward talking, with Caleb making initial sounds like the ones we were hearing, and then moving through the various stages of speech, just as a baby does.

All of these things, the therapist said, helped foster language in children, and were more effective than any therapy a stranger might perform.

Later, after Caleb's nap and dinner, a nurse popped in to let us know that they wanted us to begin charting precisely how much Caleb was eating on his own, now that he was on pureed food, so the staff could better calculate how much needed to be administered through his feeding tube overnight. The rule of thumb, she said, was that if he could eat more than half his food by mouth, then no overnight feeding would be necessary. Caleb, we assured her, was definitely eating more than half of his diet on his own, and, in some cases it was nearer ninety percent.

"I think we can safely skip tonight then," the nurse said. "Keep a record and we'll see how he does." We already knew that if he could go three months without needing to be fed through his g-tube, they'd take it out. Two days later, it seemed an even more likely reality. The speech therapist began experimenting with chopped food and pronounced Caleb capable of graduating to soft toddler meals, including chicken nuggets, mashed potatoes, and macaroni and cheese, his favorite. As a result, one of Caleb's doctors ordered the nurses to cease tube feeding. It was time to start marking off the anticipated three months until Caleb's g-tube could be removed for good.

"You're on your own now, little man," the doctor said. "Eat whatever you want."

An even bigger goal was to have Caleb released in three weeks, which meant we might be home before Christmas. Despite Caleb progressing by what seemed to us like leaps and bounds, we were initially skeptical. These timeframes, we already knew, were very fluid and changed from week to week. But, when we queried the doctors, they said that it was important with younger children to ensure they got as much of the basics down as possible, building a strong foundation to work from, and then hurry and get them on home into a familiar environment. It was what they referred to as the third stage, the first being the PICU and the second being the intensive therapy Caleb was undergoing now. Home was, without question, the best place for Caleb to recover, they said, as his brain would be stimulated in familiar ways as he played with his own toys, slept in his own bed, and was surrounded by family.

The prospect of going home really gave me pause. I felt a mixture of fear and excitement, fear because I knew that we would be returning forever changed, and excitement because we would all finally be reunited, and begin moving forward with our lives together.

During our second week at Scottish Rite, Caleb continued to make reasonably steady progress. By now, we were really starting to see the overlapping effects all the therapies were having. At first, they seemed quite independent of each other—muscle strength versus fine motor skills versus eating and talking—however, as Caleb developed further, we could see how interdependent they were. At the core of it all was purposeful movement, intent, and ability.

Caleb's walk was becoming steadier and he had less difficulty lifting his feet and putting one foot in front of the other. His left ankle, in particular, appeared to be getting stronger, so he was no longer crossing his feet when he tried to walk. And, although he still needed help, he was starting to bear more and more of his own weight. The therapy was definitely making him stronger. This strength was evident in his passion for the tricycle, as he was now pushing down on the pedals and moving around the third floor by himself, with us hovering nearby, sometimes a little faster than I would have liked.

"I think I know what Caleb might be getting from Santa this year," I whispered to Tiffany, as I watched him pedal. In the words of one of his therapists, Caleb was "blazing the trail."

Some of the most rewarding moments that we had that week belonged to Tiffany. Caleb's speech therapist had also been engaging him in all sorts of action/reaction kinds of activities when Tiffany impulsively blurted, "Caleb, give Mommy a kiss." Up to this point, Caleb hadn't reacted or reached for us when we asked for kisses.

But this time Caleb didn't hesitate. He instantly turned and grabbed her cheek with his hand, pulling her in for a big, sloppy, wet baby kiss. Tiffany was ecstatic. Later, when it was time to go, Tiffany stepped in front of Caleb.

"Come on, Caleb, let's go," she said, clapping her hands and holding them out in front of her. Caleb did another first—he reached his arms out for her to pick him up, and was rewarded by an exuberant hug that left him giggling.

We extended his reactive exercises to singing. A speech therapist sang some familiar songs to him, including "Itsy Bitsy Spider." As she reached the end, she sang, "…and the itsy bitsy—", pausing before the word, "spider." Caleb's mouth opened when he realized she was waiting for him to say the next word. He exhaled heavily, making an "ahhhh" sound. The therapist grinned.

"He knows there's supposed to be a word there. He wants to finish the song."

"You think he knows the song still, but just can't vocalize it?"

"I think it's possible."

This was the first time we had heard him really vocalize on cue. It was working. It was really working.

"Hey, Caleb, look! Do you see the bubbles? Come on, little buddy, let's pop 'em!"

We were back in therapy and the therapist had taken out a soap bottle and begun blowing bubbles towards Caleb, in an effort to combine both vision and eye-hand coordination exercises. At the sound of my words, Caleb's eyes lit up. He began slapping his right hand up and down, smacking the surface of the bench, his left hand struggling to do the same. I propped up his left arm and he tried to pull it away in his eagerness to pop the bubbles between his hands.

"Come on, Caleb, let's pop the bubbles!" Caleb moved his arms wildly, trying to pop as many as he could. All the while, he kept making excited little gasps, as if trying to talk.

"Did he just say 'pop'?" Tiffany exclaimed, her eyes wide in astonishment.

"It sure sounded like it."

Every time, before she blew more bubbles, the therapist asked, "OK, Caleb, do you want more bubbles or are you all done?" After a few times, Caleb grunted.

"Did he just say, 'more'?"

"He's really trying to talk today," the therapist chuckled.

As the next set of bubbles slowly drifted down in front of Caleb's face, he reached up with his hands, popping one right in front of him, bucking in his chair in excitement when he did so. Not only was he struggling to form answers to our questions, but he also appeared able to make out the bubbles, something I wasn't sure he'd be able to see.

It really was a week of things to celebrate. We'd seen Caleb start to turn pages of a book when a therapist reading to him prompted him to do so. I thought back to our first night here at Scottish Rite, nearly two weeks before, trying to get Caleb to do the same thing. He couldn't. He could barely even lift his arms up, let alone turn pages. Now, he was doing it with each hand. And, in musical therapy, while the therapist played and sang upbeat songs, like "If You're Happy and You Know It," and "Five Little Monkeys," Caleb began to sway back and forth to the music.

I had been propping him up on his feet so he could stand during the session when I felt his hips sway. I looked down in concern, gripping his safety belt more tightly with my hand, thinking he was losing his footing. He wasn't. His stance was fine. Instead, he was moving his body back and forth. I elbowed Tiffany.

"He's dancing!" We stood and watched our little boy swing

and sway to the music, arms moving alongside, not once losing his balance, comfortably in control of his movements.

～

After dinner one evening, we strolled over to the hospital's boutique that was now ablaze in Christmas decorations. I felt a heaviness settle into my heart upon seeing all the red and green garland, the fancy gold-trimmed ornaments, and boxes wrapped up like presents ready to be placed under a Christmas tree. I thought back to our last Christmas. Tiffany had been pregnant with Connor, and Colby and Caleb were just old enough that the thought of what Santa had brought them had them leaping around in anticipation. Colby, not yet four years old, bounced down the steps leading into the living room first. Not far behind, Caleb, two years younger, came crawling down the stairs feet first, with his mother hovering over him. When the boys came around the corner into the living room and saw our Christmas tree ablaze with strings of multicolored lights, their eyes gleamed.

I wondered what Christmas would be like this year. Would we still be here? Would we be home? Would Caleb even be able to see the Christmas tree with all the pretty lights? Would he be able to play with his brothers and enjoy the sights and sounds of tearing open a Christmas present? I hoped so, but there was no way to be sure. Still, I reminded myself, there was much to be thankful for and Thanksgiving was now practically upon us. We were going to be reunited with Connor and Colby on Wednesday for five whole days.

I sat down with Caleb while Tiffany browsed the shop. I'd been thinking of all we'd seen over the past few days and recalled a bedtime game that he and I always did at home right before he'd go to sleep, after we'd said our prayers. I would hold his cheeks between my hands and whisper, pausing after each word, "I...love—" at which point Caleb would excitedly shout "You!"

I looked at Caleb wiggling in his seat and put my hands on his cheeks and leaned in.

"I..."

Caleb smiled at me expectantly.

"Love..."

Caleb wiggled in excitement and opened his mouth, but nothing came out.

"You!" I cried, as he giggled. He definitely remembered. "Good job, buddy."

"Hey, Caleb, can Daddy have a kiss?" He stretched out his hand, grabbed my cheek, and gave me a big, open-mouthed, wet kiss. My heart went to the races and I kissed him back.

CHAPTER NINETEEN

Rocky Balboa

"Caleb is graduating today," Kristen, the physical therapist, announced, as she entered our room, pushing a new wheelchair. The previous chair, she explained, contained body and head supports, designed for patients who could not sit up on their own. "Caleb is beyond all that now. He needs a big boy chair!"

The new chair was decidedly smaller, and possessed no restraints other than a seatbelt to keep Caleb from climbing out of it. Caleb had gone from needing to be propped up to needing to be prevented from climbing out of his seat. Tiffany and I grinned at each other.

That Saturday night, thanks to Tiffany's mother who had come down for a visit, Tiffany and I had our second night out alone since the accident a month and a half earlier. We'd been in Atlanta almost two weeks at this point and, although we were excited about Caleb's relatively steady progress, we were both tired and a bit quiet as we sat in our corner booth at the local Chili's. I would catch snippets of the conversations buzzing all around us when I wasn't lost in my own thoughts. I glanced around at the many carefree faces, all of whom were chatting about work, football, what had happened that day, what they planned to do the next day, and all the mundane things one typically shares with loved ones when life goes on as expected. Just a few weeks ago, that would have been us, living life with the certainty that life was good, confident that nothing bad was going to happen. It was amazing just how quickly life could change. While a part of me was grateful for the wakeup call, I wouldn't hesitate to turn back the clock and spare Caleb all of this.

I rested my hand on Tiffany's across the table. She looked up and smiled. I felt her fingers grip mine. We spent most of our time talking about how we were thankful for having Caleb, for him still being alive, what he was doing in therapy and all that he was accomplishing, and what we still had yet to do in the weeks ahead. We talked about Colby and Connor and about how excited we were to be seeing them again in a couple of days. Despite the challenges ahead, we had never been more aware of just how many blessings we had to be thankful for.

Tiffany's sisters and their husbands arrived late Tuesday night. Not only were we thrilled to see the boys; Caleb's therapists were delighted to see the boys as well. Part of therapy, they explained, was getting the children back into a normal routine and, for Caleb, his normal routine had been playtime with his brothers. It was when they were engaged in playtime and meaningful interactions with brothers and sisters that patients often became more interactive, playing, standing, walking and talking more.

On Wednesday morning, John the occupational therapist, stood and watched as Colby picked up a Thomas the Train toy, one that made chugging noises when pulled by its string.

"Hey, Colby, let's show Thomas the Train to Caleb," I suggested.

"No, he can't play with it. He doesn't know how."

"Try," I urged.

Colby turned to Caleb.

"Here, Caleb. Look, it's Thomas." Caleb turned toward the

sound of his brother's voice. Colby pulled the string and the train made a *choo-choo* sound. Caleb got excited. It had always been one of his favorite toys. As Colby pulled the train around Caleb's body, Caleb appeared to track the blue engine with his eyes. He reached out and grabbed it, and tried to put it in his mouth.

"Hey!" Colby exclaimed. "I was playing with that!"

The therapists agreed that having Colby and Connor there had energized Caleb. As we were leaving, Colby asked if he could push his brother in the wheelchair. I felt a well of emotion surge through me: sadness that Caleb needed to be pushed, yet overwhelming love for Colby, who wanted nothing more than to spend time with his brother.

∼

It was time to decorate the Christmas tree.

The idea of even having a Christmas tree in our hospital room was one that hadn't occurred to either of us. But Jason McKay had called to say he'd driven all the way from Chattanooga to come and visit Caleb and to bring a three-foot Christmas tree and a box of decorations for our room. Everyone pitched in to decorate. Even Caleb managed to hang one or two decorations on the tree, while we sang "Jingle Bells."

A woman who lived nearby had stopped by to offer us her house to use over the Thanksgiving holiday while she was away. We were astounded by her thoughtfulness and generosity, a real Good Samaritan. Tiffany bundled up the boys and headed over there for the night while I remained with Caleb.

It felt a bit strange waking up alone on Thanksgiving in a rehab facility instead of at home. It didn't feel like a holiday, particularly because there were still daily therapy sessions to attend. Caleb wasn't terribly engaged, as if he, too, sensed it was a holiday and expected a day of rest.

After therapy we made our way to the gym. Thanksgiving dinner was being catered and served by students from a nearby college. As I looked around at all the kids we had come to know by name, I saw many new faces, family members who had come to celebrate Thanksgiving with them. So many children from so many walks of life, I thought. There were kids there who had suffered car wrecks, brain aneurysms, severe burns, and even one who had been shot in the head. Yet, it was a day to give thanks and celebrate God, celebrate recovery, and celebrate our love for each other. As we bowed our heads to pray, there was much to be thankful for.

Back in our room, we Skyped with my family who were at my grandmother's house. It was a longstanding Thanksgiving tradition to gather there every year. A lot of the family had not seen Caleb since he'd been comatose in the hospital. A chorus of "Hi, Caleb!" greeted him.

"Hi!" Caleb delightedly shouted back.

Everyone, including me, nearly fell out of their chairs. They cheered, which only excited Caleb more. Later, I thought about how poetic it had been that Caleb had spoken his first real word on the day our entire country gave thanks for its blessings. Still on an emotional high, I headed up to the playroom to where my sister-in-law sat watching Colby and Connor.

"Hey, Tim, look at this," Chassi said, placing baby Connor at my feet. He started rocking himself back and forth until he was on his hands and knees. I watched as he began crawling. It hit me. It hit me hard. We had been gone so long that we had missed one of Connor's first milestones, learning how to crawl. I had mixed feelings. I felt joy at seeing him progress, yet I was pierced by the realization of just how much our lives had changed in just a matter of weeks. By the time we returned home with Caleb, two months may have passed, two months during which time might feel suspended, but in actuality it had not. I was grateful we would have the next five days with our kids. We were determined to make the most of our time together.

The days that followed were full of other firsts for Caleb, possibly stimulated, as the therapists said, by the presence of his brothers. He'd learned to throw a ball (and now wanted to throw everything he got his hands on) and how to kick one. The therapists were working hard to get him to indicate yes and no, either verbally or through movement. Beyond the occasional sigh or grunt, Caleb still, for the most part, wasn't forming words, but when one therapist offered him a book in one hand and a ball in the other and asked him to choose which one he'd like, Caleb reached up with his right hand and patted the book. She began reading the book to him. Halfway through, Caleb tired of it and reached out to close it. The therapist offered him a choice between the book and ball again. Without hesitation, Caleb patted the ball.

Later that day, when he was in his bed, he lay down on his side and tucked himself into a fetal position. Turning onto his tummy, with his knees tucked up to his belly, he pushed himself upright. This was the first time we had seen him sit up completely on his own in bed. I thought back to the incident where he'd wiggled through the hospital bed rails and almost choked himself, almost falling to the tile floor. I wasted no time. We requested and received a hospital crib that same day.

That evening, I sat Caleb in his high chair and fed him his dinner. Once he was finished, I pulled off the tray.

"Down!" Caleb demanded. My eyes shot open and I stared at Caleb.

"Whoa! Did you just say 'down?'"

"Down!"

"Well, I guess so!" I said, chuckling, as I swooped him up

out of the chair and set him down.

When bedtime rolled around, I gave Caleb his nightly tuck-tuck. I leaned down close and said, "I…" Caleb lay there silently, his eyes glued to mine, with a glimmer of a smile. "Love…" I added, and paused again.

"Uuu," Caleb finished.

"YOU!" I repeated, and kissed him vigorously. He giggled.

∽

That weekend, I was reminded of the Sylvester Stallone movie, Rocky. In particular, I thought of the iconic scene where he'd been training, running before dawn, and had climbed an impossibly high stretch of granite steps. He'd pumped his fists over his head in victory. That weekend, Caleb was Rocky.

One of Caleb's occupational therapists asked whether Caleb had done any stair climbing. I winced. He'd tried it the previous week and it hadn't gone too well. We followed her out into a nearby stairwell. She pushed the door open to reveal a long flight of stairs leading up to the next floor. I raised my eyebrows and she smiled.

"I'm not expecting Caleb to go all the way up. All I want to see is whether he understands the concept, to see if he's willing to go up a step or two." She positioned Caleb in front of the first step while I went up five or six steps ahead to encourage him from above.

"Caleb, honey," she said, "you're in front of some stairs now. Let's go upstairs and see Daddy." As I began coaxing him to come to me, Caleb slowly lifted his right foot up and planted it on the first step. As the therapist held him from behind, Caleb shifted his weight to his right, lifted his left foot, and placed it squarely next to the other. I braced myself for the tears we'd experienced the previous time. There were none. Instead, he looked inordinately proud of himself and eager to continue. Slowly and steadily, right then left, sometimes alternating, he made it all the way up to the fourth floor, the entire flight of stairs. I scooped him up and swung him into my arms, kissing him all over his face. He was my own little Rocky. I put him down and he began to cheer, making excited sounds, but what really caught me was that he clapped his hands together. This was one of the coordination goals he needed to reach before being allowed to go home. Even the therapist was rocking her fists in the air, cheering for Caleb. Then came the moment when he really blew me away.

"Down!" Caleb demanded, looking at the bottom of the stairs.

"Did he just say 'down?'" Caleb's therapist asked. I grinned.

"I think so."

"Down!" Caleb kept repeating as we slowly made our way back down the steps. Clearly, he meant what he said, that he wanted to go down the stairs.

That evening I grabbed a few needed moments alone. As overwhelmed as I'd felt at the Chattanooga hospital, where every moment was a rollercoaster ride, another complication in the tenuous path to recovery, I was now feeling a bit overwhelmed by the hurdles Caleb was clearing in his daily struggle to regain what he had lost. The hand of God was definitely making itself felt, I thought, supporting Caleb along every inch of this climb, supporting all of us. I thought of a saying I'd always felt was a bit cliché.

I don't know what tomorrow holds, but I know Who holds tomorrow.

Now it seemed to take on a much more profound meaning. Not that I hadn't always known, always believed, that God holds our tomorrows but now I was experiencing Christ on a far more intimate level, as my Comforter, as the Deliverer of my entire family, as our Rock in the midst of this turmoil. I had been living in a world where I had convinced myself that I held some form of control. Only now was I truly starting to understand that, in reality, I had no control whatsoever. Most of us, I knew, planned ahead, taking whatever course in life we felt was important, but I was discovering that the Christian life was tentative, one of fluidity, of being amenable and pliable to the moves of God and the directions of His grace. In fact, one of the things I believe God has shown us is that it's when we insist on exerting control, trying to force things to be the way we think they should be, that's when we run into life's real difficulties. It is only when we learn how to surrender to God's love and grace and move within the flow of His will that we start to appreciate the sovereignty of God and just how much God is intimately involved in our lives.

I thought back to that telephone call I'd received from my dad just before we'd left on that fateful trip. Dad had been apprehensive, not knowing the reason why, but sure that something was going to happen to someone close to him. His apprehension had transferred to me and I had felt panicked by the fact that Tiffany was going out that evening with the children. I had felt compelled to get on my knees and pray for their safety. I thought of Psalm 91:11, and asked God to give His angels charge over my family, to protect them always, and not to let anything happen to any of them.

The truth was God had answered my prayer, though not in the way I would have ever imaged. He did give his angels charge over us, and He did not let anything come against our tent, our family. He saved both my wife and my son that day. He carried our son up on high in that firefighter's strong arms, and never let his foot be dashed against a stone. Michael had run all the way to the top without stumbling, without once falling. And now, it appeared, Caleb was being borne up on angels' wings along the road to recovery. And the end of the Psalm? A promise I would now pray for every day, that Caleb would be blessed with a long life, and that he would see Christ's salvation.

∽

Saying goodbye to our other two boys at the end of the long weekend wasn't any easier than it had been the previous times. Watching our boys sob as they left really tore at our hearts.

"I hate this, Tiffany. I just want for all of us to be back together again in our own home."

"Me too," Tiffany whispered into my chest as we clung to each other. "Me, too."

Our official discharge date was set for December 7th but, although I knew Caleb was on schedule with his progress so far, we had known other families who'd had their discharge dates delayed. Feeling a bit anxious after having promised Colby we'd be going home soon, I sought out our social worker the next morning to find out what the general consensus was about us going home. As it turned out, my anxiety had been for nothing. Caleb was not only meeting his weekly goals, she said, but exceeding them, and was well on his way to going home and having outpatient therapy instead. It was my turn to behave like Rocky, pumping my fists in the air in delight. In just eight more days, we'd be heading home.

Sure enough, Caleb kept making tangible progress, including with his speech. Tiffany was a bit disappointed that Caleb had said, "Dada" twice now and she'd yet to hear, "Mama." Unlike Colby, whose first word had been "Dada," Caleb's first word as a baby had been "Mama." Still, she was thrilled just to hear him trying to sound out any words at all.

The night before, Tiffany had been brushing Caleb's teeth, an activity he'd never been all that enthusiastic about. It was classic Caleb behavior for him to wiggle away and proclaim, "All done!" Sure enough, as Tiffany maneuvered the toothbrush, Caleb pushed it away.

"Aw duh."

Tiffany and I both burst out laughing.

Tiffany had now begun walking Caleb to his therapy sessions instead of pushing him in his wheelchair, giving him more practice, as she scooted behind him in a small rolling swivel chair, supporting him from behind. One afternoon, after music therapy, Tiffany walked Caleb all the way down one hall, turned left, came all the way down a second hall, past the main nurse's station, and, after a short rest, began walking back to our room. As I heard them coming down the hall, I came out and watched Caleb working hard, putting one foot right next to the other.

"Hey little man. Look at you. You are doing so good!"

"Are you coming to see Daddy? Come on! Come and see Daddy!"

I threw up my hands and Caleb beamed. He began to laugh and jostle about as Tiffany struggled to keep a grip on him. Faster and faster he went, putting one foot in front of the other, until almost stumbling, as he tried to run.

"Whoa! Slow down, little man," Tiffany said, chuckling.

He walked valiantly, even with a snap in his step, as he came close and fell into my arms. I hugged him tightly, telling him how proud I was of him. He too was quite proud, clapping his hands together with joy.

Caleb's eagerness to walk had us wondering whether he might even need a wheelchair when we went home. We ran our question by Kristin, Caleb's senior physical therapist.

"That's a good question. We're not yet sure whether he'll need a wheelchair or whether we can send him home in just a stroller. Every week, he's doing better and better, meeting all of his goals, often exceeding them." She smiled and shook her head in disbelief. "It's quite possible he won't need the wheelchair."

I mustered the nerve to ask the real question I wanted answered.

"So, do you think, based on what you've seen, that Caleb might walk again someday?"

"Oh," she cried, "absolutely! Of that I have no doubt." Tiffany and I looked at each other with a smile of relief. "He's already getting good at walking and I don't see any end in sight."

Wow, I thought, we really were going home in a week.

That night I took Tiffany out for her birthday, thanks to a visit from her Uncle John, who came to spend the evening with Caleb. We headed to a nearby Cheesecake Factory. What a difference from the last time we'd had a night out, when we were fighting to remain positive, still so worried that we'd barely tasted our meals. Now, it seemed, we had much to celebrate. We talked about our successes, we talked about the challenges ahead, we talked about Colby and Connor, and about our own relationship, our thoughts and feelings. Most of all, we talked about going home.

"I get to make homemade Christmas cookies with my boys this year!" Tiffany said, her eyes sparkling.

A week before, Tiffany had mentioned how disappointed she felt that she wasn't going to get to indulge in her favorite Christmas tradition, baking cookies with the kids. When Colby and Caleb were old enough they had joined in. We would gather in the kitchen and take orders from Mommy, sometimes throwing flour at each other, tickling and playing, and making sure that there was enough leftover cookie dough batter to snack on.

I thought back to the other family traditions we had always enjoyed together: decorating the Christmas tree, sitting down at Christmas Eve to talk about the true meaning of Christmas, about

Jesus being born, about His life and what He meant to us, reading the kids *'Twas the Night before Christmas* at bedtime, and, after they'd fallen asleep, Tiffany and I turning off all the lights and sitting in the living room in front of the tree and drinking hot chocolate while Christmas music played softly on the radio. I'd open up the Bible and read the story of the birth of Christ. We'd talk, hug and kiss, and before our final preparations for Santa's visit, we would share how special our greatest gifts were, our children and each other.

It seemed surreal now that, a mere six weeks earlier, we'd been faced with the very real possibility that we might be spending the rest of our Christmases with just two children instead of three. Tiffany and I gripped hands and sent up a prayer of thanks that this Christmas would be as joyful, if not more, than any other we'd ever had. No one would have to ask us what we wanted for Christmas. We already had it.

∼

As we neared our final week, time seemed to fly by. We had several meetings concerning Caleb's prognosis and how best to transition him once we got him home. We had a list of things we needed to prepare for, including Caleb's overall safety, including how to move him from room to room and properly transport him in the car.

We asked about Caleb's eyesight, which they assured us had already improved significantly. They couldn't predict with certainty but agreed that there were no indications of anything preventing him from regaining most, if not all, of his sight at some point. We asked again whether Caleb would require a wheelchair, because his walking had improved dramatically over the past few days, from barely being able to stand to taking steps with very little assistance. Their answer was exhilarating. Caleb would not need a wheelchair.

That night, before bed, I watched Tiffany playing with Caleb on the couch. For the first time in nearly two months, it was as if life had returned to normal, like Caleb had never been anything but his original self. He giggled, laughed, played, and, for the first time since the accident, revealed his sense of humor. He was making funny little snorting sounds and then laughing at himself. I thought of the little plaque hanging by our living room back home that read, "Live Well, Laugh Often, Love Much." I looked at Tiffany and Caleb laughing together, and couldn't resist joining in. What a great motto to live by. I couldn't wait to see it again.

CHAPTER TWENTY

The Necklace

Wednesday, the first of December, dawned clear and cold. We would be ticking off our final seven days in Atlanta, starting today. I was feeling quite positive. Sure enough, that morning's therapy yielded more good news.

"I've been watching him closely over the last three weeks," John, Caleb's occupational therapist, said, "and he has really progressed rapidly. Developmentally speaking, in these past three weeks, he's gained about nine months."

Amazed, I thought back to Caleb's initial evaluation with Dr. Sholas, who'd told us that, developmentally, Caleb was operating at about a nine-month-old level, comparable to his little brother, Connor. I'd felt devastated when I'd first heard that, not knowing whether Caleb would ever improve.

At the end of therapy, Tiffany bent toward Caleb and said, "Okay, Caleb, say, 'Bye, bye.'"

"Bye," Caleb said, clear as a bell.

John smiled and winked at him.

"Bye, Caleb."

The following morning, Caleb gave his mother her long-awaited, belated birthday gift. Caleb was all ready to go, dressed, washed and sitting in his wheelchair by the door, anxious to get moving. Tiffany ducked into the bathroom to give her hair a quick brushing. Caleb began fidgeting.

"Ma!" he bellowed. He'd finally called her by name.

Caleb had good cause to be impatient. We were headed out of the rehab facility for a formal outing with one of Caleb's therapists, and our destination was a place called The Sensory Gym, a learning/activity center for kids that focuses on their sense of touch.

"It's really good for Caleb to be exposed to all kinds of different sensory stimulations," the therapist explained. "The more sensory input he has, the more it will encourage his brain to heal."

This outing, as they told us, was the last step in preparing Caleb to go home. It would be a learning experience for us as well as Caleb. The therapist planned to take us through what would become routine activities, things we wouldn't even think about, like maneuvering safely outside and transporting Caleb safely in our car.

As things stood now, Caleb would be discharged the following Tuesday and we would begin our drive back to Tennessee. We planned to spend the night at the Chattanooga home of Paige and Kevin Thompson, who'd been hiking just ahead of us when Caleb had been struck. We'd been wanting to connect with them ever since the accident. Now would be our chance. From there, it would be home, sweet home.

By the time we returned to Scottish Rite, Caleb was more than ready for a nap. Donna Wood, one of Tiffany's dear friends, stopped by to see us and to celebrate Tiffany's birthday by taking her out to dinner. As Caleb slept and I waited for Tiffany and Donna to return, I waded through the posts on Caleb's Facebook page. It never ceased to amaze me the staggering number of strangers who had taken up the banner in support of Caleb and took the time to send such heartwarming messages of hope. One was Bobbie Ford who, in addition to putting together various fundraisers, including Caleb's Run and Caleb's Concert, had recently shared with me that the town of Alexandria in Tennessee had voted Caleb to be that year's honorary Grand Marshall for Alexandria's Christmas Parade. Bobbie had just posted pictures of the parade's lead car, with Caleb's image pasted on its side.

"We would have loved to have had Caleb at the head of the parade," Bobbie wrote, "But since he couldn't be here, we put his picture on the lead car."

I took pause again at all God had shown us over the last two months, the many fingerprints and unmistakable ways in which God had revealed Himself to us. I remembered how, before coming to Scottish Rite, I had felt compelled to keep a diary of both the events as they unfolded, and our reactions—what we thought, what we felt we were learning from these often harrowing experiences, and what we thought God wanted us to learn. Why? What was God doing behind the scenes, I wondered. Over the last couple of weeks, as I had been writing, I had noticed a theme developing.

"You know," I'd said to Tiffany, "before Caleb's accident, I felt God leading me to write those lessons on faith. He has taught us so much about having faith in Him. And when we were at T.C. Thompson, we found our faith being tested, and then strengthened.

"Then, when we came here to Scottish Rite, Caleb started healing dramatically, and I found myself—we found ourselves—placing our hope in Him above all else to see us through." Tiffany grinned at me, eyes twinkling. She already knew where I was going with this.

"I just feel that, when we get home, our focus is going to be more on—"

"Love," she said, squeezing my hand. "It's faith, hope, and love!"

"Exactly! It's 1 Corinthians 13. The most important lesson

of all: loving God, loving each other, and loving others."

I looked up as Tiffany and Donna returned.

"Hey Tim. Look at what Donna got me for my birthday," she said, holding up a dainty silver chain that Donna had bought at Caleb's Run, on which hung a pendant. Etched on it were the words, "Faith, Hope, Love."

"Oh, wow."

"I know!"

∽

Our final few days at Scottish Rite passed with the same increasing rate of progress. There were moments when not only Tiffany and I were blown away but the therapists were too. Caleb was getting decidedly more vocal. He would excitedly blurt out, "Bye!" every time we left a room and, of course, my favorite, when he'd get all excited and shout, "Dada!"

The therapists continued to reinforce the importance of Caleb making conscious choices about things. That afternoon in speech therapy, as the therapist began singing "If You're Happy And You Know It," Caleb apparently wasn't happy. He interrupted by singing somewhat tunelessly over her and began motioning wheels turning with his hands. She stopped and chuckled.

"Oh, you want 'The Wheels On The Bus,' do you?" He tried hard to sing and motion along with her. Afterward, she turned to us.

"Did you see that? He wanted to choose another song and he let us know. That is exactly what we want to see."

Caleb also continued to exert his independence in other ways. When it was time for his nap, he didn't want to go to sleep. At first, he resisted by playing quietly in bed. I looked up when I heard him grunt. Across the dimly lit room, Caleb was pulling up on the rails of the crib, trying to stand up.

"Tiffany," I whispered, "look!"

Caleb began walking around the perimeter of his crib, wobbling at first, his right hand running along the rails. As his confidence grew, his step grew heavier and he became excited. He bounced, and then stopped. He bounced again. And then again. Delighted with himself, he began bouncing as if on a trampoline, shrieking, "Mama, mama, mama!" in time to his bouncing. Tiffany and I burst out laughing, each of us ready to sprint forward should Caleb suddenly lose his balance. He never did. Steady on his feet, he bounced and bounced and bounced.

"Oh, boy, there'll be no stopping him now!"

The following day, as we began our final evaluations before getting ready to be discharged, one of Caleb's occupational therapists confirmed that his improvement was continuing to progress.

"Developmentally speaking," she said, "I'm grading Caleb somewhere between twelve and eighteen months. It's hard though to evaluate him accurately, because his eyesight might be causing him to appear to be operating at a lower level than he actually is." She smiled at us. "He's doing great, though, really. I don't think you need me to tell you that. And I'm positive that, when he gets home, he's going to do even better."

All the therapists we met with that day told us essentially the same thing, that once Caleb returned to his home environment, he'd start improving even more dramatically, making huge strides developmentally, and relearning a lot of what he had lost. I bit my lip. Could we, I wondered, keep up this same level of care and attention once we got home? Or would everyday life slow us down? Might we inadvertently hold him back somehow? I shook off my fears. We'd get through this, I thought, thinking back on how much we'd overcome already. We'd get through this together, with God's love and guidance.

We spent the rest of the day meeting therapist after therapist, going over developmental achievements and goals, safety tips and procedures, and plans for what to do in the weeks and months ahead.

Against all odds, Caleb had definitely shown his tenacity while at Scottish Rite, particularly over the last two days. Ever since Caleb had learned how to stand up in his crib and cruise around its perimeter, he hadn't stopped. He was determined, now more than ever, to walk everywhere.

That evening, we kept Caleb up past his bedtime because Scott Arnold from Channel 5 WTVF in Nashville had requested a live interview via Skype to get an update on Caleb for their eleven o'clock nightly news program. Just as Scott Arnold was wrapping up the interview, Caleb waved his hand at the screen.

"Bye!"

We couldn't have asked for a better demonstration of Caleb's improvement.

As we sat quietly before bed, Tiffany and I spent our last night holding each other for a while. We couldn't help but cry as we talked about our blessings, that our family was still together, that Caleb was getting better and just the fact that he was still with us, and that the following day—because of the prayers of tens of thousands of people all over the world—we would finally be going home.

CHAPTER TWENTY-ONE

Extreme Makeover: Caleb Edition

Tuesday, December 7th, had finally arrived. Tiffany and I bounded out of bed in our haste to start packing. Looking around, I couldn't believe how much stuff we had accumulated. Lots of it consisted of gifts from both friends and strangers. Christmas cards had been arriving by the hundreds for Caleb from Facebook friends. Fortunately, Misty and Ryan had volunteered to drive the two hundred and fifty miles from Nashville to Atlanta to help us pack up and transport our belongings. Sometimes I found myself just shaking my head at the extraordinary lengths people were going to—family, friends, and strangers alike—in order to help us. Ken Raetz, one of my closest friends, had brought together a team to renovate our home over the past few weeks with Caleb's arrival in mind, including repairs that had been put off because we hadn't had the money. Tiffany and I never ceased to be amazed at the outpouring of generosity that continued to come our way.

Our caseworker and several nurses stopped in to review our discharge papers. All the information, especially concerning Caleb's nine medications, all with different dosages and administration times, was dizzying. In two days, we had an appointment scheduled at Vanderbilt Children's Rehabilitation Center, our caseworker said, and we would need to follow up with our primary care physician and see an ophthalmologist, a neurologist, and a gastroenterologist. And that was just the beginning.

Caleb would also need physical, occupational, and speech therapy at least three times per week. She was pleased to hear that one of Caleb's Facebook friends revealed that The Music Class in Nashville was offering Caleb one free season of music therapy, which he had loved while at Scottish Rite.

We reviewed all of the goals and milestones that Caleb's therapists had set for him, and the nurses reiterated all the medical-related concerns: medicines, wound care, g-tube care, etc. I was relieved to see all these instructions presented to us in a large take-home packet because the sheer volume of things to remember and coordinate was overwhelming. Between this, doctors, staff, and therapists dropping by with last minute ideas, suggestions, and advice, a stream of well-wishers, the WSMV Channel 4 news team from Nashville showing up to tape another interview, and trying to pack, our last day was a little crazy.

John, Caleb's favorite occupational therapist, stopped by one more time to see Caleb and give us some last-minute tips.

"You're going to do just fine," John said as he picked Caleb up for a hug. "He really is," he added, looking at us. "Caleb is going to do great when he gets home. You'll see."

A break in the mid-afternoon whirlwind signaled it was time to leave. The news crew filmed us making our way down the hall lined with staff waving and hugging us goodbye. Outside, the December air was cold. We packed up the car and Misty's van. She and her husband were going straight back to Nashville, while we stopped overnight in Chattanooga. After a quick stop to fill Caleb's prescriptions, we would be on our way to Tennessee.

The solemnity of how we were now off life support, so to speak, and fully responsible for Caleb suddenly hit me. We drove at a very measured, moderate pace. Tiffany and I talked almost continually over the following two hours, discussing our fears and concerns. We needed to create an entirely new "normal" for our family. We would not only be caring for two healthy, vigorously active little boys, but we would also be caring for Caleb, who was now a special needs child. It would require a hard look at our finances and mapping out some sort of plan, juggling a regular life and its demands with the added pressure of almost daily multiple therapies, around the clock medicines, and the need to watch Caleb every minute so he didn't fall. Caleb, on the other hand, sat in the car, relaxed and happy, even giddy at times, bouncing his feet off the seat in front of him.

It was after dark when we approached the Thompsons' house. Since they lived on the top of a mountain we had to navigate steep inclines complete with hairpin curves in pitch-black darkness. Our hearts were in our throats as we crept up the tortuous, unlit mountain road, flanked by sheer rock cliffs looming on our left and steep drops into the invisible blackness on our right. I felt uneasy.

"This reminds me of Fall Creek Falls," Tiffany muttered, gripping the steering wheel with white knuckles. "I don't like being around rocks anymore." She glanced anxiously out the window, looking up the cliff face. I felt the same fear, as if another rock might be tumbling toward us and we wouldn't know it until it was too late. We exhaled in relief when we finally reached the top of the mountain. Caleb was sleeping peacefully when we pulled up at about nine o'clock.

We ate dinner, talked, and watched the kids play together. It felt wonderful being in a real home, sitting around someone's dining room table and having a meal that hadn't been served by strangers or come out of a takeout container.

"It's amazing the things we take for granted," I mused. The Thompsons had been just steps ahead of us when Caleb had been struck. No doubt they had often pondered how things might have turned out differently for them had they been just a few paces slower.

As bedtime approached, I felt nervous. It was time to give Caleb his medicine. Up until now, it had always been administered by hospital professionals, but now we were going to have to open the g-tube, drop the medicines in, and flush the tube with water ourselves. Tense, I studied the instructions for several moments before attempting to do it, but everything went well. After we got Caleb tucked to sleep in a playpen in our room, I went outside to retrieve a few more things from the car.

The night was very cold and crisp, the sky carpeted with stars. For a moment I was in awe of the beauty but, without warning, a wave of sadness swept over me. I rubbed my damp eyes, as I was suddenly transported back to that night at the campground. The stars overhead had been just as bright, just as plentiful, just as breathtaking. It had been just a few hours before dawn when Colby and I had gone to collect firewood. I stared at the sky and thought back to how I'd promised Colby that the very next night we'd camp out under the stars, the four of us. Instead, we'd spent the following night in a hospital, convinced that Caleb was going to die. I shook myself. Picking up our suitcases, I headed back inside, intent on focusing on the positives.

"Lord, thank you for bringing us here, for keeping us safe thus far, and continue to watch over us on our journey home."

∼

There was a tangible excitement in the air when we woke up early Wednesday morning. We were heading home. Tiffany and I started gathering our things together. Jason McKay had arranged a one o'clock press conference at the nearby Spring Creek Road Baptist Church in East Ridge and had asked us to arrive two hours beforehand to meet some of the people who were coming to see Caleb. By the time we'd loaded the car, eaten breakfast, and spent a few moments with the Thompsons, it was time to leave. We waved goodbye as we pulled out of the driveway. In the daylight, the drive was scenic and we were considerably more relaxed.

When we reached the church, we were greeted by a number of familiar faces from our anxious days at T.C. Thompson. Christine Weller stepped forward to introduce herself. Local to Chattanooga, she was a photographer who had e-mailed me a few days before we'd left Atlanta. When I'd told her we were stopping in Chattanooga, she jumped at the chance to photograph the press conference as well as drive up to Nashville to record our homecoming.

We spent the two hours before the press conference talking, sharing stories, hugging, taking pictures, and praying. Virtually every news outlet in Chattanooga and many from Nashville were there to cover it, thanks to Jason's efforts.

The news crews positioned their cameras in a row facing the front of the room, where a white podium and table stood. Caleb was especially animated due to all the attention he was getting. As we entered, cameras snapped on every side. It was a little surreal. We were about to have our message heard by many thousands of people. Tiffany took a seat at the table as I stepped up to the podium and began to speak.

I started by thanking everyone who'd helped arrange the gathering and all those who had prayed for Caleb, sent gifts and cards, and had helped us weather the past nearly eight weeks in one form or another. I leaned toward the microphone.

"On an October weekend nearly two months ago, my wife and I and two of our sons, Colby and Caleb, went on our very first weekend camping trip. That weekend, on October 16th, 2010, our lives changed forever. The story that you all know is the story about a rock falling some two hundred and fifty feet from above, and hitting our son Caleb in the head as he was being carried by his mother. And though it was that rock that made the news, that spread Caleb's story to the entire nation, it was another Rock that has brought all of us here today. And that Rock is God himself."

I went on to talk about prayer and how it had played such an integral role in Caleb's recovery, from the first prayers spoken over him immediately after the accident to the many tens of thousands all over the world who continued to pray for him.

"And now," I said, looking into the cameras, "as we begin this third and final part of the journey, we believe that just as prayer has gotten us this far, it will be prayer that will get us through this as well."

I updated everyone on all the latest news about how Caleb was doing and how quickly he had progressed in his rehabilitation in the last 4 weeks, meeting and exceeding all the goals that had been laid out in front of him. Remarkably, I noted, Caleb had regained about thirteen months of development he'd initially lost.

"Caleb still faces lots of challenges," I continued. "His eyesight, though better, is still intermittent. He still has a lot of work ahead of him with things like his fine motor skills and his speech. Caleb also has a long way to go before he can learn to walk on his own, although we are very encouraged that we may see him do that pretty soon as he is very motivated to walk again, as you've seen today; he loves it."

I looked around the room at everyone listening, slight smiles on their faces. I explained what our plans were over the next couple of days and began our final thanks, before opening up the floor to questions.

"From the bottom of our hearts, we want to say thank you, to all the people who were there that day at Fall Creek Falls, who worked to help save our son's life, to Michael Tagert and all the people at the top of the trail, to the people who prayed with us and for us as we waited for help to arrive. And to everyone afterward, people like Jamie Walling, to all the people who worked on our son as he was flown to Erlanger. To all the staff at T.C. Thompson who saved our son's life more times than I will ever know as he struggled to survive those first couple of weeks. To the amazing staff and therapists at Scottish Rite, who lovingly worked with and adapted all of their techniques to fit Caleb's needs, to the now nearly nine thousand people who follow Caleb's progress daily, to the hundreds of churches and the countless thousands of people across the world who continue to pray for Caleb. We want to say God bless all of you, and thank you again, from the bottom of our hearts.

"As I said earlier, this journey is not yet over. We still have a long way to go. And, as we begin this third and final leg of our journey of faith, I would ask you to please continue to pray for Caleb and for his progress. Thank you."

I glanced at Tiffany who was holding a wiggling Caleb in her lap. Normally, if I spoke at church or an event somewhere, we tried to keep our children calm and quiet, but this time it was different. Caleb's rolling his toy car back and forth across the table, trying to get out of his mommy's lap, and pulling at the microphone and my notes, were all testaments to his improvement, proof positive of the miracle we were there to celebrate. At the end, after we'd mingled with the crowd and were preparing to leave, cameramen reached for their cameras to film Caleb one last time as he waved and shouted, "Bye, bye!" With one final handshake and a hug from Jason McKay, we were back on the road.

It was time to leave. It was time to go home.

∽

When we pulled off the interstate in Nashville, our excitement grew. When we pulled onto our street, we could barely breathe. We pulled over to the side of the road to gather ourselves for a moment.

"Caleb, are you ready to go home, buddy? We're here! You ready, honey?" I asked Tiffany. She smiled.

"Yes. Let's go."

We drove off slowly toward the far end of the street. As we rounded a curve, our house came into view. Tiffany gasped at the bright flashing lights of a fire engine.

"Is that a fire truck?" Tiffany cried. "At our house?"

As we drew closer, in the dark cold of the night, we saw people, hundreds of people, family, friends, and neighbors, carrying "Welcome Home!" signs. Someone spotted us and cheers erupted. Our front lawn was awash in the bright lights of a WTVF Channel 5 camera. As we pulled into our driveway, Colby fought his way to the car, screaming, "Dada!" Tears were streaming down his face. I could barely get the car door open against the waving, cheering crowd.

Tiffany and I wedged ourselves out and clutched Colby and Connor, before unstrapping Caleb from his car seat. Tiffany hoisted Caleb into her arms and held him up before the crowd. More cheers erupted. We began making our way through the crowd, pausing every few steps to hug familiar faces and to let people see Caleb. As we neared the front door, I saw a sign tacked to it: "Extreme Makeover: Caleb Edition." I grinned, realizing this was undoubtedly the work of my friend, Ken Raetz, who'd recruited volunteers to come in and renovate our home. When I opened the door, I stopped dead in my tracks. It was like walking into a new home. Stretching from the entry into the kitchen and throughout the living room was a new beautiful wood floor. The walls had been freshly painted in warm, inviting colors. New carpet had been laid throughout the second story and down over the stairs to help protect Caleb. The kitchen was stocked with food. Ken was beaming at our stunned reactions.

"We wanted you to be able to come back home and not have to worry about anything—no repairs, no food, nothing. All you have to do is take care of little Caleb." We stood and stared, speechless. Family and friends had even decorated the house with all of our Christmas decorations. Our Christmas tree sat in the corner, lights twinkling.

"People have volunteered to provide food for you for the next two months," Chassi announced, bouncing Caleb in her arms, "including some folks from Caleb's Facebook page."

Amid all the chaos, the Channel 5 reporter asked for a quick interview. Chassi set Caleb down on his feet, holding his hands. As the camera rolled, Caleb began stomping his feet vigorously, walking in place. As everyone cheered and shouted encouragement. Caleb became more excited and stomped faster, delighted with the attention he was getting. At the end of the interview, I looked down at Caleb and said, "OK, Caleb, say 'Bye, bye.'"

"Bye, bye!" Caleb chirped, his face lighting up at the shouts and applause.

We spent the next few hours with family and friends as the crowd dissipated. Caleb became overwhelmed by all the excitement and began crying. The therapists had warned us that too much stimulation could be more than he could handle, and that at times he might need breaks. As I explained this to everyone, Tiffany took Caleb upstairs to our bedroom. At one point, I, too, felt overloaded. I sat on the couch and propped my feet up on the coffee table, trying to process it all. I had so many emotions running through me I feared I was going to lose it in front of everyone. I bit the inside of my cheek hard to keep the tears in check. Tiffany appeared at the top of the stairs.

"Tim, would you give me a hand putting Caleb to bed? He needs his medicine." We laid Caleb gently in his crib, which had been moved into our bedroom. Baby Connor would now switch places and sleep in Colby's room. Caleb lay surrounded by all the stuffed animals he had grown to love in Atlanta. Tiffany and I prayed over him as we had done every night since the accident.

After everyone had left and Tiffany and I were in bed, Colby came in and snuggled in between us, unwilling to let us out of his sight now that we were finally home. The familiar smell of the sheets and Tiffany's head on the pillow next to mine convinced me that we really were home again. I couldn't get over how comfortable our mattress was after two months of sleeping in strange beds and hospital chairs. Tonight had been unquestionably the most joyous night of our lives since the birth of each of our children. As I lay there listening to the soft sounds of Caleb's breathing as he slept peacefully just a few feet away, I swelled with pride thinking of all that he'd done tonight, how he'd smiled, laughed, clapped his hands, stomped his feet, tried to walk, and said goodbye to everyone. Over the past two months, I thought I would never feel such joy again. I cried silently, tears soaking my pillow, as I sent up prayers of thanks to God.

After Tiffany and Colby fell asleep, I was exhausted, but my mind was whirling. I thought back to all the events leading up to the accident, all through that fateful day when we'd feared the worst, of all the fingerprints that God had shown us, all the miracles He had performed, the events at T.C. Thompson and at Scottish Rite, our trip home, and all the surprises that had taken place this evening. I kept returning to one question—why? Why had God allowed all of this to happen? Why did He speak to me a year and a half earlier to warn me that I would need my whole heart? And what did that phrase mean anyway? What was His purpose in all the extraordinary occurrences that had followed? And what about the dreams—the visions? The first three had happened just as I had seen them, but what about the fourth? What exactly was God doing behind the scenes? Lord, please don't let us miss the lessons You're teaching us, I prayed.

Little did I know, as I contemplated the next stage of our journey, God had more in store for us than we could ever have imagined.

PART THREE

Love

"And now these three remain: faith, hope and love. But the greatest of these is love.
—1 Corinthians 13:13

CHAPTER TWENTY-TWO

Reality Hits Hard

The following morning, Tiffany and I woke to find ourselves in our own bed, our three boys within reach. It hadn't been a dream. It was real. We were home. We were all back together again.

It didn't take long for reality to hit. Connor's cries bellowed from the next room.

"I bet he's hungry," Tiffany sighed, rolling over to check the time.

"We'll have to wake Caleb up pretty soon," I said. "He'll need his medications." Colby, tucked between us, began to stir. "How are we going to manage all this by ourselves?"

"I know. In the hospital we had tons of help and now it's just us."

I wanted nothing more than to close my eyes and sink back into blissful sleep. Colby, however, was now fully awake and had other ideas.

"Hey, buddy," I said, giving him a squeeze, "how does it feel to be home now?"

"Good, Dada. I'm hungry." I chuckled and squeezed him tightly in a big bear hug. Giggling, Colby fought to escape. I found myself not wanting to let go.

No sooner were we all downstairs, with Connor nursing, Colby demanding breakfast, and Caleb trying to roam everywhere, did we admit that we truly couldn't do this all by ourselves. We needed help. We were terrified that Caleb would fall and hit his head on the wood floor, or smack the corner of the coffee table as he struggled to get to his feet, or try to climb up on a chair or couch and fall off. Unlike normal children, we had been warned that a bump on the head for Caleb could have dire consequences.

Colby was understandably possessive of our attention and, now that we were back at home, he had regressed a bit in his behavior, openly displeased by Caleb receiving the lion's share of our attention. As Tiffany hurried to nurse Connor and get him situated, and I was occupied doing everything to keep Caleb from falling down, Colby began to whine.

"Mommy, I want some cereal!"

I maneuvered Caleb close enough to permit me to pour Colby his cereal. I glanced at my watch and sighed audibly. Caleb should have had his medications half an hour ago.

"And just think," Tiffany said, coming into the kitchen and giving me a wry smile, "this is only the first day."

Tiffany held Caleb as I prepared his g-tube for his meds.

"I'm not sure how we're going to do this, Tiff. I've got to find work soon, and we won't have enough money if you aren't working, too. Even if you're not, how can I go off to work and leave you with all three boys when Caleb needs all of your attention just to keep him safe? Plus, you're going to have to take Caleb back and forth to therapy." Tiffany looked at me, her expression grim. Like me, she had no answers.

That afternoon, my mother showed up as planned to watch Connor and Colby while we took Caleb to Vanderbilt for his outpatient evaluation.

"You're going to stay with Nanni while we take Caleb to therapy," I said to Colby. He burst into tears. Clearly, he was convinced that we were going away again, and that we weren't coming back.

"Hey, buddy, come here," I said, and wrapped my arms around him. "This isn't like last time. Caleb's much better now, remember? We're home now, and Mommy and Daddy are not going to leave you ever again. Nanni is just going to stay and play with you for a couple of hours until we come back, okay?" Colby wiped his eyes and walked toward his Nanni and into her arms.

Walking into the Vanderbilt Children's Rehabilitation Center, I was struck once again by fear of the unknown, not knowing what the days and weeks ahead would bring. We looked around at the different families coming and going, each with children suffering various disabilities.

Caleb's physical therapy evaluation went very well. Oddly, it seemed as if he had learned to do even more since his final days at Scottish Rite. He appeared to be more aware of his surroundings, was trying to talk a lot more, was better at playing with his toys, and changed positions with only minimum assistance.

Kelley, the physical therapist, was very nice and knowledgeable, answering all of our questions, and seemed very pleased with Caleb's progress.

"From this point on," she said, "I'd like us to focus on strengthening his body, especially the upper body and legs, improve his balance, and get him started walking. I'll start preparing a list of goals for Caleb and give it to you at our first therapy session."

When the occupational therapist arrived to evaluate Caleb, she walked him through a variety of activities, from reaching and grasping, and playing with balls and blocks, to scribbling with a marker in either hand. And while he struggled a bit with self-care skills like taking off his shirt, he excelled at feeding himself with his hands or a spoon. Caleb was visibly delighted with himself, clapping his hands and giggling. The therapist was impressed.

Caleb's vision was about the only area lacking improvement: he could see objects on his right side but, once they crossed over his midline and into his left field of vision, he lost them, a sign of a significant deficit that still needed attention. Again, we would receive a list of goals for Caleb at our first session later in the week. We were given the name of a local vision therapist who specialized in helping children with head traumas regain their sight. But, until Caleb learned to express himself, it would be very difficult to assess what he actually could and could not see.

We hurried home, anxious about how we were going to tackle the rest of our day. Colby rushed into our arms while Connor, happily sitting on the floor, burst into tears at the sight of his mommy, and raised his arms to be held. I had hoped that Caleb would be so tired after his various evaluations that he might be content to sit quietly in his portable playpen while Tiffany and I got a few things done. That was not to be. He was ready to play.

Holding my hand, he walked toward his Buzz Lightyear riding toy and, with my help, climbed on. In no time, he was off, pedaling furiously, with me in hot pursuit. Caleb tried to chase Colby a few times, as I supported his hands in mine. We had a blast. But, while I didn't want to cut into his fun, we still had about two or three hours' worth of therapy activities to tackle before the day was out, not to mention the administrative stuff I needed to tend to.

I needed to assess where we stood with our health insurance and make sure everything between our insurance company, Scottish Rite, and Vanderbilt Rehabilitation Center was in order. I also needed to draft a schedule to accommodate all the various therapy and medical appointments we were going to have to juggle in the coming days, weeks, and months. Equally important was reviewing the safety standards that Scottish Rite had provided us to ensure we did everything we could to safeguard Caleb from harm. In addition to supervising him constantly, we had been advised to place child safety locks on all cabinets, remove all doormats, set our water heater to no more than 120 degrees Fahrenheit, install safety gates at the top and bottom of our stairs, provide a safe, padded play area, and place bumpers and pads on the edges of all of our hard furniture. Arguably, one of the most challenging tasks would be to make sure toys were never left on the floor for Caleb to fall over, not an easy thing to maintain with a lively four-year-old and a ten-month-old.

I eyed the to-do list of occupational and physical therapy safety standards—forty-eight different items. How on earth would we ever manage it all? We hadn't even been home a full twenty-four hours yet and already I found myself so pressed by all the things I had to do that it was hard to focus on Colby, who was now pleading for attention. He resisted our efforts to try to get him involved in his brother's therapy, protesting that what we needed to do with Caleb was "for babies." Unfortunately, despite his pleas, Colby was left to entertain himself as Tiffany cared for Connor and I turned my attention to Caleb's therapy activities.

The next few hours were far from easy. Every so often, I would need to halt the therapy and put Caleb into his playpen while I tended to Colby, helped Tiffany in the kitchen, or ran upstairs to look for something. Caleb did not like this at all and made his unhappiness readily known, screaming every time I plopped him into his playpen.

The days that first week consisted of an endless litany of demands: Caleb's therapies and medications, and having to watch him around the clock while caring for a baby and an increasingly resentful four-year-old. While Colby relentlessly demanded our attention, Caleb, on the other hand, was anxious to throw off his reins and do his own thing. It was virtually impossible to even hold a conversation while keeping an eye on our roving three-year-old, knowing that one wobbly step could have potentially devastating consequences. Tiffany and I were starting to feel more tightly strung than piano wire.

I sketched out an approximate schedule of appointments that spanned the coming six months. Just looking at it made me queasy. There were physical and occupational therapies three times each week, appointments with ophthalmologists, neurologists, gastroenterologists, speech therapists, and vision therapists, and that was just in the first few weeks, not to mention our hoping to enroll Caleb in the musical therapy he loved so much.

The way things were going, not only did we not have time to get back on track jobwise, but we also had zero time to focus on each other, falling into bed exhausted at the end of every day and waking up tired and stressed in anticipation of yet another day of nonstop driving at breakneck speed. It wasn't surprising that we were abrupt with each other; what little patience we had left was reserved for the kids. We could afford to ignore each other's needs for now, we figured, in order to meet all the needs of the kids.

At least that's what we thought.

CHAPTER TWENTY-THREE

The Heart of the Matter

Caleb continued to achieve daily milestones. It was not quite two months since the accident and he'd recently taken three or four steps up and down the stairs with little assistance, while holding the handrail. As we watched, ecstatically, he'd even walked five complete steps all by himself. Rather than clinging to us for support and our having to watch his every move, we were now more like gymnastic spotters, there to provide stability when necessary. Things that we took for granted, such as jumping or moving around while holding an object in our hands, were tasks that Caleb still had yet to master, but overall he was showing real progress.

Our therapy to-do list continued to change, reflecting Caleb's progress. Now, instead of holding his hands to help him walk, we were encouraged to hold onto an item like a broom handle and have Caleb hold onto the other end. More and more exercises were geared toward making Caleb's movements more independent. Standing on his own and maintaining balance was one, and Caleb's new therapist suggested we do this while singing or playing songs he liked and clapping our hands—anything to keep him occupied and distracted while his muscles continued to do their work.

Caleb received a stellar assessment when he had his hearing checked, much to our relief. Perfect hearing, Tiffany proclaimed, when they returned from his appointment. His speech assessment wasn't quite as encouraging, but then we'd had a pretty good idea of what to expect, based on the few words that Caleb infrequently spoke. Essentially, he was about a year behind developmentally in his speech. Still, the therapists were encouraging and suggested that Caleb might begin to form phrases and sentences within another year. We were scheduled to formally start Caleb's speech therapy sessions the week after Christmas.

Caleb's informal home therapy sessions were eating up three or more hours of our time a day, longer when he became distracted by his brothers. As much as I hesitated separating him, particularly from Colby who continued to resent all the attention Caleb was receiving, it became necessary for one of us to take Caleb upstairs and work with him privately, while the other stayed downstairs with Colby and Connor.

Christmas was bearing down on us with incredible speed and, with all the activities that controlled our waking moments, we were feeling completely overwhelmed at times. Autumn had barely begun when we'd been abruptly uprooted from our lives and found ourselves inside a hospital. Thanksgiving had been celebrated at the rehab center, and although we'd been excited about being able to celebrate it all together, we had still spent it inside a hospital. With all our attention focused on Caleb's progress, there had been no time yet to even think about Christmas. But, two weeks before Christmas, we received a gift of sorts that helped us make that mental transition—it snowed. It snowed a lot.

Snow wasn't something we saw a lot of in Middle Tennessee. So, although it made driving conditions nearly impossible for several days, it also meant we had some time to catch our breath, to slow down and spend a little more time with the boys.

Tiffany and I were still functioning somewhat on autopilot, reactive to the needs of our children without any spare moments to relax and consider each other, beyond the occasional fleeting kiss as one of us flew out the door. Communication between us was starting to break down as frayed nerves and tempers began to exhibit themselves in abrupt, argumentative bursts. Something had to be done. I thought back to all the people, hospital staff and friends, who'd warned us not to put our relationship on the back burner; that, above all, we had to consciously and intentionally connect with each other because the strength of our family was built on the core strength of our marriage, our commitment to each other.

I thought of the horrific statistic I'd been given on how few marriages survived a trauma like this one and remained intact, how couples, if not careful, could grow apart, letting adversity divide instead of unite them. It was so easy to take a marriage for granted when we felt the need to put our kids first. It was our job to weather an attention drought and still survive. Or at least that's what we told ourselves, silently, internally, me with my thoughts and Tiffany with hers, independent, unconnected.

One night, after the kids were finally asleep, we dropped down on the couch exhausted, sitting slightly apart, and closed our eyes.

"I know God is with us and that we've seen His activity everywhere with all He's done with Caleb," Tiffany said, her voice faltering slightly in the darkness, "but I feel like I've pushed Him into the background."

I nodded, thinking that we'd also done the same with each other. We sat silently a moment, each lost in thought.

"Perhaps the reason why we're not hearing from God is because we're not spending much time with Him," she added.

I too had felt that I had not seen God's activity as much, not since the days we'd been at T.C. Thompson. I opened my eyes as Tiffany reached out her hand and gently stroked mine. There was such love and affection in her expression as she looked at me. I hadn't seen that look in weeks. I certainly hadn't given it myself, I realized. I felt a rush of gratitude and guilt wash over me.

We began to talk, and it was as if a dam inside each of us had broken and raw emotion began to spill forth. There was so much we had not yet grieved and processed yet. Both of us, it turned out, was feeling the same. We had been trying so hard to be strong for each other as well as for the boys that we hadn't seen how our resolve was making us appear unemotional toward each other. Or how we'd viewed each other's resolve as an emotional distance, as having withdrawn, retreated—disconnected.

As we held each other, crying, Tiffany said, "This is what we need, right here."

I was suddenly struck by something that had happened right before Caleb's accident. Tiffany and I had been struggling then, too, with not communicating enough with each other. I had heard God's voice inside me back then, saying, *The problem is you are not seeing each other's hearts. You need to listen and speak to each other's hearts.*

That revelation had hit me hard back then. But, with everything we were now facing, we had forgotten that truth. We both now sensed that God was reminding us. We had to look beyond each other's behavior and words—what the other person was doing or saying—to the *why*, the root cause of why the other person was feeling the way they were.

"The truth is that I'm so afraid. Ever since we got back home, I've felt outside of myself, like I'm not normal. I walk around and I keep having these flashbacks of our camping trip. I see you crying, holding Caleb in your arms after the rock hit him. I see his face turn blue. I hear you screaming. I see myself trying to run back up the trail…" I was crying so hard, I could barely get the words out. "I see it all the time. Just the other day, I picked up a tiny toy soldier that was lying on the ground and suddenly I remembered Colby, Caleb and me playing with those toy soldiers just a couple of nights before we left for our trip. We'd sat on this floor right over there and we played with them, without any idea of what was about to happen.

"There's this incredible sense of loss that I feel every time I think of how Caleb was before the accident. It hurts so much. Don't get me wrong," I said, clasping her hands. "I'm so thankful for where he is now, and I know that God is with us and that He continues performing miracles for us, but I'm still so afraid. I constantly fear for Caleb's safety, every minute of every day. I fear for his future. I hate not knowing what life is going to be like for him when he turns five or fifteen or twenty-five."

"I feel the same way," Tiffany whispered. "I hurt for what Caleb has lost, and often I find myself feeling shame, thinking, 'If only I had done this or that...' I know I shouldn't, that it's letting the Enemy in. But we have to remember that we have our son back and he's getting better every day. That has to be our focus. We can't think about a year from now or even a week from now. We have to take one day at a time. God has shown us that we can trust Him, and that's what we need to do. We need to have trust and faith."

I thought of one of the promises we'd made to each other before Caleb's accident, how we would always try to see each other as Christ sees us, to know that, although we'd inevitably live our marriage imperfectly, in Christ we were beautiful, holy, and a reflection of God's love. Choosing to see each other as Christ sees us while also being transparent about the issues of our hearts that drove our moods, thoughts, and words had been very healing for us in the past. It certainly had been tonight. One thing we both agreed on was that we wanted—we needed—more time with each other.

"I can't see how anyone who does not know God, who does not have a relationship with Him, could ever get through something like this," Tiffany said, shaking her head. "It's just too much."

∼

The Monday before Christmas I was working on the house, Tiffany was in the kitchen, and the boys were playing in the living room. Tiffany turned to see Caleb crawling into the kitchen, having made his way from the living room and down the hallway. She watched as he crawled toward the pantry, sat back on his heels and pushed himself up onto his knees. Reaching up, he grabbed the pantry door handle and pulled himself to his feet. He looked at Tiffany and, using sign language, said he was hungry. Tiffany swooped down and gave him a huge hug.

"You're hungry? Let's get you something to eat."

"Tim, you're not going to believe this!"

Just two days earlier, in physical therapy, as Caleb had been working on walking, he'd surprised everyone when he took about sixteen steps without assistance. Caleb, it seemed, was determined now more than ever to walk again.

CHAPTER TWENTY-FOUR

A New Kind of "Normal"

Christmas came and went in a flurry of freshly fallen snow and torn wrapping paper. The night before, we'd sat down together as a family and I read aloud about the birth of Jesus from the gospels of Matthew and Luke, explaining to the boys the gift of love that God had given the entire world through the birth of His Son. The birth of Jesus had brought joy to many different people, I explained, from impoverished shepherds who had witnessed the jubilance of the angels giving glory to the wealthy wise men who had traveled hundreds of miles to give homage to the newborn King.

"For God so loved the world that he gave his one and only Son, that whoever believes in him shall not perish but have eternal life," I read from John 3:16, as the boys huddled about me. "We celebrate Christmas because we all needed a Savior," I added, looking down at them. "We needed a way out of the mess that we had made for ourselves in this world. And Jesus is that way. Jesus is our Savior."

For a fleeting moment, I thought back to a few nights earlier when I'd waded through two large bags of mail and sorted out the bills we owed. Caleb's medical expenses had passed the $300,000 mark and at first I'd felt the familiar panic of not having a way to pay for it all. But, after Tiffany and I discussed our finances, we reminded ourselves of how we'd agreed to trust in God to provide a way through such difficulties and how important it was to keep our focus on what really mattered—our love for each other and for our family. The fact was evident, God did provide. My family alone was proof of that. We were all still here, together, celebrating the birth of Christ. Celebrating God's love for us all.

∽

Caleb was literally blowing through the goals set by his therapists, accomplishing in weeks what they had hoped to see him achieve within the first three months after we returned home. He was walking farther and farther and crawling less as well as eating and drinking so well now that he no longer needed his g-tube. Overall Caleb was making even greater improvements for us at home than he was in front of his therapists at Vanderbilt. We were quite excited.

Tiffany and I worked hard to keep our promises to have faith in each other as well as God, but it wasn't always easy. The strain of our routine wore on us daily, testing our resolve. By the end of our third week at home, we were trying to spend more time with each other, getting the kids down to bed earlier and spending quiet time talking and praying together. But, even with all of our efforts to draw closer to one another, something still didn't feel right. As each day passed, frustration and irritation thickened the air between us. By the time New Year's Eve arrived, those frustrations and irritations came bubbling to the surface. Instead of ringing in the New Year with joy and a heartfelt kiss, we were barely speaking to one another. I thought ahead to the following day. We had arranged for someone to watch the boys so we could go out on a date. I found myself dreading the time alone together instead of looking forward to it.

New Year's Day 2011, a Saturday, dawned cold and stayed chilly, both outside and in. The strain between us persisted. We bickered about everything it seemed, second-guessing each other right and left. With the three boys and the relentless extra demands that Caleb's care made on us, we didn't even have time to vent, to clear the air. There was just too much to do. When the time for our date rolled around, we weren't sure we even wanted to go. There was a chasm between us and I couldn't understand why I was feeling so resentful and off-balance, especially in light of all that we had recently recommitted to.

We drove in silence. When I pulled in to park the car, I glanced at Tiffany who was staring straight ahead and saw tears rolling down her cheeks. I felt my eyes begin to prickle.

"Everything just feels hopeless," Tiffany whispered. "So big and so impossible." She took a deep breath and let it out slowly. "I just don't know what to do. I have never felt under so much pressure in my life. With everything that's going on with Caleb and the rest of us, it just seems like there's no hope, no end in sight." We both sat in silence, but the ice between us was melting.

"It seems like there's something else here," Tiffany added, "an emptiness, a darkness." I thought back again to all of the people who had warned us to honor and protect our marriage no matter what. *You are going to go through a lot. You are going to need each other. You are going to have to make sure that you set aside time with each other. You need to be strong for each other. Don't be tempted to let this divide you.* We had agreed with these truths wholeheartedly but somehow we had still let things slide. Juggling all the changes in our lives and all our new responsibilities felt overwhelming. All we wanted was to get through each day without dropping any of the numerous things we were juggling.

"It's this sense of hopelessness, I think, that's so difficult to deal with. We've gone through some pretty tough times before, but never once have I ever felt hopelessness, not like this. It feels like something foreign, like something is trying to drive us apart, you know?" I paused, bit my lip for a moment and began listening for the Spirit to possibly give me some clarity. He'd spoken to us before, I thought, so why not now? Then, in a moment, I felt I was given insight, like a curtain had been pulled back to let me see behind the veil. I chose my words carefully. "I think we're under attack from the Enemy. I can't think of any other reason for it. I mean, we know what we're supposed to do. We know the truth. We know how to speak to each other's hearts and see Christ in each other. I can't think of any other reason why we'd be experiencing this kind of hopelessness."

Tiffany reached over and took my hand, her worried expression lessening slightly.

"You're right. I know your heart. And I know that you love me and you love our family."

"And I know your heart, that you love me and the kids."

Tiffany gripped my hand harder. "I believe the Enemy is doing all he can to tear us apart, to destroy our family."

It made sense in light of the fact that we had, again, taken our focus away from God and listening for His voice and instead had been focusing more on our personal struggles and circumstances.

We sat and talked and cried and prayed, returning to our goal of talking and listening to each other's hearts, pushing past the emotions on the surface toward the core issues of why we were feeling and reacting the way we were. I felt a new sense of anger this time, not for my wife and not for the difficulties between us, but for the continued assault on our marriage from the Enemy. We resolved that night that we would no longer stand for anything to come against or between us. Our family and God's glory were too important for us to become simply another statistic. If God was for us, and we knew He was, then nothing could come against us, we reasoned.

As I pulled the car out of the parking lot and headed for home, I felt a renewed sense of hope. We were a team. We would pull together and get through this. And, all the while, we would continue to open our hearts to God, making special time for Him and each other. That was the path we wanted to take. Together.

～

The day arrived for Caleb's eye evaluation. Dr. Durocher, reputed to be a leading vision therapist in Nashville, led Caleb through a battery of evaluations as we anxiously watched and waited. From what we had witnessed in the rehab center, we were convinced that Caleb suffered blind spots and that his left eye was much worse than his right. We were startled to learn that, according to Dr. Durocher, Caleb didn't have a single blind spot at all and was perfectly capable of seeing well in both eyes. The problem, we were told, was that Caleb's brain was unable to interpret correctly the information his eyes were sending. He was suffering from a form of tunnel vision, seeing quite well what was in front of him, but his peripheral vision was blurry. The doctor also told us that Caleb's depth perception was off, that it was hard for him to discern distance between objects before him.

Dr. Durocher felt that, with enough therapy, Caleb could regain most of his vision. For now, we were told to return weekly, as well as do exercises with him at home. I sighed inwardly. We would of course do everything we could but we were already averaging about three hours a day doing physical, occupational, and speech therapies at home, and now we had to add more daily exercises. It was excellent news, I reminded myself, and it was likely just temporary. Once Caleb regained his sight, we'd be able to stop. I sent up a silent prayer of thanks to God for the encouraging news.

That night, after tucking the boys in and kissing my wife goodnight, I made my way downstairs to spend some time alone with God. As I closed my eyes and exhaled, I felt my mind inexorably return to the same questions that had been nagging me for months. Why had God allowed the accident to happen? Had it really been God's will for Caleb to be struck by the rock?

I wasn't feeling angry toward God, not anymore. I just desperately wanted to find some answers, to discover some meaning behind it all.

"Father," I prayed, "I know You are Sovereign, that You are in control of all things. I know that all things work together for the good of those who love You, Lord, and that nothing happens to us that does not first come before You and Your wisdom. I know that you either cause, allow, or deny all things according to Your will. I know that You love Caleb. And I know that You allowed that rock to hit our son. But what I don't understand, Lord, is why?"

As I sat quietly in my living room, I thought about the age old questions about good vs. evil, light vs. darkness. I knew that Christ had won the victory over the Enemy, Satan. Nonetheless, I recalled the admonition in Scripture to be on guard, that the Devil roams about like a roaring lion seeking whom he can devour. Was this the work of the Enemy, I wondered? I thought again about the conversation my wife and I had the night God made it clear that the Enemy had been trying to thwart our marriage. Had the Enemy been behind the accident too? I sat for the better part of an hour, pondering and praying.

Then all of a sudden I could literally feel God's presence around me. A thought entered my mind, and then a whole series of thoughts. It was as if in one moment I was given a sense of the bigger picture. It was startling. I could feel the adrenaline as it ran through my veins. My mind flooded with words, pictures, and ideas, which seemed to connect, one by one, as if some of my questions were starting to be answered. I quickly grabbed a pen and began writing down everything I was hearing in my spirit. It was a complete jumble and I couldn't piece it all together conclusively, at least not yet. Looking down at the page, I decided not to worry about it. I figured that if these were indeed things I was hearing from God, then over time He would certainly confirm them and reveal them to me more fully and clearly.

~

The following day was Caleb's neurological evaluation. The staff was very encouraged by Caleb's progress, especially since arriving home, but did have a few cautions for us in terms of how Caleb might develop socially. Children who suffer brain injury, especially frontal lobe injuries, have an increased chance of developing inhibitive issues over the course of their lifetimes, they said. This could include an inability to comprehend and respect the personal space of others, such as talking too close to people's faces, or not grasping certain social or cultural norms. There could also be impairment in the development of the higher learning centers of his brain later on, affecting critical thinking, problem solving, or higher learning in general. The news was disheartening but, when Tiffany and I discussed it later, we agreed that it was something over which we had no control and we would simply have to take a wait and see approach. In the meantime there was certainly no shortage of things to work on to help Caleb.

Less than forty-eight hours later we received confirmation that our efforts were indeed paying off. Just a few weeks earlier, Kelley, Caleb's physical therapist, had listed half a dozen goals that she wanted to see Caleb achieve, ideally by mid-March, giving him three months to accomplish them. We were still in the first week of January when Kelley admitted that she was going to have to devise a new set of goals for Caleb because he had already mastered the entire list.

"Now that he's starting to walk, let's go ahead and start mixing it up a little bit. Get him to do some other things," Kelley said, handing me a list. Scanning it, I saw we'd be focusing on teaching him how to stand on his tiptoes, and squat to pick up objects. The plan sounded great to me since Caleb was starting to walk a lot more. Later that same day, Caleb, who'd been sitting on the floor, suddenly got to his feet without a word and walked away. I watched amazed. It was so casual, so effortless, so natural. I cheered and clapped my hands. Caleb turned and beamed, and began clapping his hands too, although he clearly had no idea why I was so excited. I was already plotting how to encourage Caleb to get up on his tiptoes. Reaching for a piece of chocolate candy on the countertop should do the trick, I thought. Caleb adored chocolate.

The New Year is traditionally a time of new, positive resolutions for making changes and better choices. After my first sit down meeting with the elders where I was serving as a part-time minister before the accident, I knew that the first of many changes was about to take place. At first they were eager for me to resume my duties at the church, but after hearing our story and particularly about me hearing from God and about the visions, I was swiftly told that I was no longer welcome to serve as their minister. The news was heartbreaking. I'd been nervous to even bring up the subject knowing that our church tradition by and large rejected the idea of God speaking today or of modern-day miracles. I'd promised God that if He allowed Caleb to live I would never cease to tell His story, no matter what the consequences. Here was my first test.

I'd also received a call from Simplex Healthcare, who'd been my main employer for the seven months leading up to Caleb's accident. Although I was ineligible for unpaid leave because I'd worked less than twelve months, Simplex supported us in other ways, including donating to Caleb's medical bills fund, sponsoring Caleb's Run event in nearby Alexandria, and, with the help of generous coworkers, gifting me two weeks' salary while Caleb was in the hospital. They had called to see how we were doing. I would have leaped at the chance to start working again but I knew that it just wasn't possible, not yet. There was no way Tiffany could cope with three boys and all the therapy appointments by herself. Our primary focus now had to be on Caleb's recovery and doing everything possible to facilitate it. We had received gratifying responses on Caleb's Facebook page from people who pitched in periodically, but it still wasn't enough to offset my absence. So in the meantime, I started a business from home in order to supplement the family income, and remain closely involved in Caleb's therapies and to help Tiffany.

It came as an enormous relief when Chassi, Tiffany's sister, pledged to start helping us four days a week, starting the following week. That would allow us to adjust our responsibilities considerably. Chassi would watch Colby and Connor so that Tiffany could take over for me in ferrying Caleb to his various daily therapies. This would free me up to begin putting more hours into my home business.

Another cause for celebration was the news that Michael Tagert, the young firefighter who had raced Caleb up to the top of the trail the day of the accident, had accepted our invitation to visit on the coming Sunday. Caleb would finally get to meet his hero.

On Sunday, the house was overflowing with friends and family, all awaiting Michael's arrival. News crews from both WTVF Channel 5 and WZTV Channel 17 were in place to record the reunion.

"He's here!" shouted someone looking out the kitchen window. Michael walked in, followed by his parents and several family members. Seeing his face brought forth a flood of vivid memories. Michael had been just steps behind us, near the bottom of the trail, when Caleb was struck by the falling rock. He had sprinted off with Caleb, leaping over rocks like an Olympic hurdler and disappearing within seconds. The trail that had taken us forty minutes to descend had taken him only fifteen minutes to run back up, all while holding Caleb's dead weight.

As Michael stepped inside, I grabbed him and hugged him. Tiffany, with Caleb in her arms, was right on my heels.

"Hey, there!" Michael grinned, reaching out to touch Caleb's hand. Caleb smiled back without his customary shyness and, fascinated, reached out and tentatively touched Michael's beard. "He looks great!" Michael exclaimed. He took Caleb in his arms and laughed. "Wow! You've gotten heavier since the last time I held you."

When we sat down and began talking about the events of that day, Michael confessed that he had almost not gone to Fall Creek Falls.

"I really didn't want to, but my family kept insisting I go with them."

"God knew you were needed that day. Do you remember when we got near the bottom, how we stopped right before that final turn to the falls to take a picture, and one of you offered to take it for us?"

"That was me," Michael's sister, Shelby, interjected. "That was the picture that was all over the news." There was a long pause.

"You know, I thought it was going to be a lot worse," Michael confessed. "When we all heard that thundering crash coming down the trail, I thought it was a rock slide at first. I thought everyone at the bottom was going to be crushed."

The conversation was punctuated with numerous thoughtful silences as we relived the details of that day. I asked the question I'd long wanted to ask.

"At what point did he stop breathing?"

Michael turned toward his Uncle Robert, who'd also helped that day.

"It was near the top, wasn't it?" At his uncle's nod, Michael added, "All the way up I just kept looking to see if he was still breathing. His face was so blue. I remember at one point near the top hearing this gurgling sound. His lungs were filling up with fluid. He was still breathing but barely. So I just ran as fast as I could. Once we got to the top and turned him over so he could vomit, that's when he started to breathe a little better and some color returned to his face." Michael shook his head. "I was so sure there would be an ambulance there, waiting for us. It'd been, like, twenty minutes since Caleb got hit, and I couldn't believe there was no one there. I mean, there were all kinds of people there—a pediatric nurse, a doctor, and all these people saying he needed CPR, and that we needed to drive him to the hospital. But I knew we couldn't move him, that if we did, that would be it."

"Well, it was your quick thinking that saved my son's life," I said, feeling my emotions well up inside me. "I want you to know that I am eternally grateful for what you did for our son. You knew exactly what to do. And, really, you saved my son twice, you know. You saved him once when you ran with him up to the top of the trail, making sure he didn't bleed to death, and then again at the top when you kept him from choking on his own blood. And now you get to see him playing, smiling, and laughing. It's because of you. You're a hero. You're our hero."

As Michael and his family readied to leave we hugged everyone and then hugged them all again. Michael kissed Caleb goodbye. I wondered how Michael must have felt, knowing that he'd saved someone's life, that he had saved our little boy's life. He displayed great affection for Caleb and was thrilled that Caleb was doing so well. I didn't have to promise myself to make sure Michael became a part of our lives. He already had.

That night when dinnertime rolled around Colby led us in prayer. When he finished, he asked us if he could help Caleb say his prayer. I was reminded of how they had prayed before the accident. Invariably, Caleb would wait until Colby had begun to speak his prayer and trump him by finishing it. At first, it had irritated Colby, but soon it became a family joke. I thought about how they'd done the same thing the night I suggested to Tiffany that we take that camping trip. I shook off the memory as Colby turned to Caleb.

"OK, Caleb, say 'God is great.'" We all looked expectantly at Caleb, who sat there in silence, looking quizzically at his brother.

"Say 'God is great,' Caleb." Caleb opened his mouth hesitantly.

"God … gate." Tiffany's eyes met mine as Colby's face lit up.

"He said it! Mommy, he said it!"

"You're doing a wonderful job teaching him, Colby."

Colby slowly recited more words for Caleb to repeat but Caleb sat there, silently watching him. I winked at Colby.

"Good job, buddy. I know God loved it."

Colby nestled in against me as I turned the pages of a storybook that featured talking dinosaurs. He wore a worried expression.

"Dada, there are no dinosaurs now, are there?"

I smiled and shook my head.

"No, Colby, there aren't any dinosaurs left today."

"That's because they all died." His voice quivered.

"Yes, that's right, they did." I looked down and saw tears in his eyes.

"Dada, I don't want to die."

"Hey, hey," I said, taken aback, and pulled him tightly against me. "Where did that come from? What made you think of dying?" Colby started crying. "Are you thinking about what happened to Caleb?" He nodded.

"Colby, I know you're scared. When Caleb got hit that day, we were all scared, even Mommy and me. But just because people die, that doesn't have to be a scary thing. You know why?" His eyes met mine. "Because we love Jesus. And when we grow old and when we die, we get to go and be with God in heaven. One day, we will all be together in heaven as a family." I squeezed his shoulders. "But that's not something you need to think about right now. That's something that won't happen until a very, very long time from now."

"But I don't want to go to heaven," Colby sobbed, his face pressed against me. His words were muffled. "I don't want to be with God. I want to be with you!" I felt my heart swell to its bursting point as I wrapped both of my arms around him.

"Colby, I know you don't understand right now, but you will one day. But right now, you don't have to worry, OK? You're not going to die. You're going to live a long life and grow up and have kids of your own one day. And Mommy and Daddy are not going anywhere. Caleb is fine. He's okay. And we're all going to continue to be a very happy and loving family." I crooked one finger beneath his chin and coaxed his face up. Our eyes met. "We love you so much."

"Will I always be yours?"

I broke into a grin and hugged him to my chest.

"Oh, Colby, no matter what, you will always be mine. You are my son and I love you with all of my heart."

At that moment, I realized that we needed to make a change. I had to stop separating Colby and Connor from Caleb when we did his nightly therapy sessions. Evidently, Colby was feeling left out, perhaps even left behind, and he needed to feel more a part of the family. It would take increased effort and more creativity on our part to figure out how to involve Colby without boring him while still getting all of Caleb's therapies in, but it had to be done, and done right away.

∼

All our hard work with Caleb was really paying dividends. Every day seemed to bring the "old" Caleb closer and closer to us. By this point, he was barely two months shy of his third birthday and had begun exhibiting the rebellious tendencies that newly found independence invariably brings. One afternoon, after Caleb had finished at the rehab center, Tiffany stood near the door talking to someone. Caleb wanted to leave. So he did. As Caleb carefully stepped into the hallway, Tiffany called out to him.

"Caleb, no, sweetheart, don't go outside. You need to wait for Mommy. Come here, please." In response, Caleb thrust his outstretched palm in her direction.

"No!"

Tiffany did a double take and then walked over to Caleb,

bent down, and talked to him at eye level.

"Caleb, don't tell Mommy no. That's not nice. Now, come here, please." She stepped back toward the doorway. Caleb planted his feet and stared at her, defiantly. She raised her eyebrows and met his stare.

"Caleb, come here, now." Caleb gave her a long look and then, resigned, trudged back to the doorway. It was all Tiffany could do to keep from laughing and swooping him up for a hug.

"Just like old times, eh?" I chuckled.

∽

As Caleb's physical, occupational, and communication skills continued to improve, so had his overall demeanor. More and more he would spontaneously clap, laugh, and make loud, excited noises. That was the real Caleb. Before the accident, whether he was playing with his toys, walking down the hallway, or riding in his stroller at the grocery store, he had this charming habit of suddenly clapping, laughing and exclaiming, "Yay!" as if disarmingly in love with life, which never failed to bring a smile to the faces of whomever might be nearby.

Caleb had recently achieved his previous three-month goals within the first month and Kelley, Caleb's physical therapist, had handed Tiffany another list of goals for Caleb at the start of a session. At the session's end, Kelley shook her head in wonderment.

"I can't believe it. I just put together a new list of goals for the next three months, and he's already met half of them today! Well, it's back to the drawing board," she grinned. "I'll have a new list for you next week."

That night, for occupational therapy at home, I had the boys sit at the kitchen table with me to draw and color pictures. For several weeks, Tiffany and I had been integrating therapy and playtime, trying to get the boys to play together while working on Caleb's therapy goals. It took a lot of creativity and hard work to find ways to integrate therapy and make it a fun part of our lives, but it was worth it. Our prayers, it seemed, were being answered, as we began to find balance in our home again, a new kind of normal.

CHAPTER TWENTY-FIVE

Miracle on 3rd St.

"There it is," I said to Todd and Travis. "We're here."

As the tires crunched over gravel, I gazed at the sign up ahead and felt my stomach heave. I wanted nothing more than to turn the car around and return home. But I couldn't. I glanced at the sign again.

You are now entering Fall Creek Falls National Park

My heart pounded as I recognized side roads, parking areas, and nature trails. It was Saturday, the 29th of January, and although it was colder and the deciduous trees had lost the last of their leaves, everything else was just as it had been back in October. I looked at my brother and my best friend, who were eyeing me carefully. They had agreed to accompany me on this trip so I wouldn't have to make it alone. For the past three weeks, ever since I'd had that encounter with God while praying in my living room, asking Him why He had allowed Caleb's accident to happen, I'd felt a growing compulsion to return to Fall Creek Falls and relive the events, to record everything that had happened. Why, I didn't know. I had a sense that God wanted me here for a reason. I wanted to be open to whatever God might show me. However, right now all I could think about was not throwing up.

We'd arrived earlier that morning at the Sunrise Campground roughly the same time that Tiffany, the boys and I had awoken there last October. As I drove down the long gravel road to the campground, it was as if I were reliving a long forgotten dream, as if I had stuffed all the emotions and memories of that day in a closet somewhere in the back of my mind, having pushed the door closed with all of my might against what threatened to spill out and overpower me. We approached our campsite, number 44, at which point the precariously latched closet door burst open, flooding my mind with unwanted memories. I felt perilously close to weeping and fought furiously to contain it, less because I didn't want to cry in front of Todd and Travis and more because I was afraid that, once I started, I might not be able to stop.

I stopped the car where we'd camped. We sat there for several moments in silence.

"Are you ready?" Todd asked, his hand on my shoulder. I breathed in so deeply it hurt.

"Yes…uh, no." Taking another deep breath, I opened the door, got out and looked around. Nervously, I began recounting out loud all that had happened the night we'd arrived and the next morning.

I went on and on, Travis and Todd following in silence, just listening. In my hand was a voice recorder, so I didn't have to write everything down. The recorder was a welcome distraction from the emotions threatening to drown me. I felt disconnected from the past for a welcome moment.

"Do you want us to step away for a little while so you can gather your thoughts better?" Todd asked. I nodded and flashed him a grateful smile.

I spent an hour on my own, talking into the recorder, retracing our steps from when we'd first arrived through the numerous frustrations of setting up our campsite, my firewood walk with Colby where we'd paused to gaze at the blanket of stars in the midnight sky, where Colby and I had lit his first campfire with the help of Jason's hairdryer, where we'd had breakfast and played baseball with the boys, on up to when we left that afternoon for Fall Creek Falls. It replayed vividly in my mind, as if it had been just days instead of months that had passed. I rejoined Travis and Todd and we climbed back into the car to head for the falls.

Up ahead I could see the parking lot for the main falls where we'd originally parked. We turned in and got out of the car, making our way to the trail's entrance. My legs were shaking and my stomach was churning like a whirlpool. I sent up a quick, silent prayer begging for the strength I knew I was going to need in the coming hours. This was going to be even more difficult than I had imagined.

At the very start of the trail was the park's welcome sign. It was there that Michael Tagert had laid Caleb when he'd reached the top of the trail, trying to restore Caleb's breathing. I pointed down to the ground to indicate the spot. I opened my mouth but no words came out. I began to weep uncontrollably. I felt myself crumpling inside as I relived those moments, my whole body shaking with sobs.

"Is this where it happened?" Todd asked gently, his arm around my shoulder. I nodded.

In my mind's eye, I could see Caleb lying there at our feet. I saw myself weeping and holding his hand. I saw everyone who'd gathered around. I turned my head back and saw Tiffany and Colby as they'd sat and wept in fear.

"Yes," I whispered, "but that came later. I need to focus on our trek down to the bottom of the falls first."

I turned on my voice recorder and willed myself to choke out the words. Todd and Travis stepped away, keeping a discreet eye on me. When I'd finished, I waved them back over and we walked toward the lookout above the two hundred and fifty-six feet down to the gorge. The view was stunning. Just for a moment the memories faded, as I drank in the sheer majesty. I had always loved nature's wonders, which is why I had chosen this spot for our camping trip in the first place. But such untamed beauty is just that—untamed. No longer was I swept away with a sense of joyous, adventurous innocence. Instead I felt stark fear. I thought back to Caleb standing on the safety rail, excitedly looking out at the falling water, reaching out his hand as if to touch it.

Before we made our way down the trail, there was one place I wanted to see, one place that we hadn't gone to that day. We walked to our right, onto a trail that led across the top of the gorge. As we rounded a corner, we were given another glimpse of the falls below.

"I bet it was right here," my brother mused, as he studied the terrain. There were only a couple of places from which that rock could have fallen. The place where we were standing was almost certainly the place where it had previously rested. "Did they ever find out what happened? Why the rock fell that day?"

I shook my head.

"The police suspected that it might have been teenagers, but there was no way for sure to know whether they'd pushed it deliberately, accidentally, or whether the rock just fell by itself. But the ground wasn't muddy, like it is now—we came here before the rains. Everything was bone dry. I can't think of any reason for that rock to have fallen on its own. But, I don't know."

We turned back and began making our way to the trail that led to the bottom of the falls. That forty-minute leisurely hike down to the bottom was now a fearful descent into the thickest, darkest place of emotional and spiritual pain, the worst I'd ever experienced. I had to stop repeatedly, my breath erratic and shallow, my heart racing to keep up with the flood of emotion and fear. My legs felt like Jell-O and I was reminded of how they'd threatened to give way the last time when I'd tried to run with my son's body up to the top of the trail and failed. Every tree, every rock, every turn in the trail, every foothold—they were all painfully evocative.

The roar of the water crashed in my ears. Fear mixed with adrenaline. I looked up and saw scores of jagged rocks protruding from the gorge wall. I had never noticed them before. Now they loomed ominously and I couldn't stop myself from scanning the bottom for unsuspecting victims. I didn't want to be there. And, yet, I knew I had to be. I felt called. Summoned.

As we rounded the final corner, a panorama of wetted sandstone, limestone, and siltstone, ice-capped from the wintry mountain cold, spread out before us. Where the water struck the rocks below it seemed to freeze almost instantly. The entire area around the base of the waterfall was white with ice. I stopped at the end, where the trail met the jagged rocks that led down to the water's edge, unable to take another step. This was it. This was where the footing had become treacherous, where I'd handed Caleb off to Tiffany and taken Colby's hand as we began feeling our way down through the rocks. Todd came up behind me.

"Are you okay, man?"

"Yeah. It's just…it's a lot harder than I thought it would be."

I looked around, replaying the events in my mind as best I could. But here, at this very spot, moments before the rock had struck, I hit a wall. My mind was a blank.

"I'm having a hard time remembering exactly what happened here."

"I don't think you really want to go through all this again."

Todd was right. I took a few steps, carefully making my way down past the rocks toward the water, Todd and Travis on my heels. I studied the ground, determined to figure out where we'd been standing when the rock struck. I couldn't find it. I looked up, hoping I'd recognize where the rock had first appeared.

"Nothing looks the same as I remember. I guess everything happened so fast."

I continued making my way across the rocks. Up ahead, a large flat rock lay like a platform between the end of the trail and the water below. I crossed it and stepped past. And stopped.

"This is it! It was right here."

Todd and Travis looked up. I looked around again and then at my feet.

"I was standing here, right here, with Colby there to my left." I pivoted and pointed to the flat rock behind me. "Tiffany was there, holding Caleb. And then we heard…we heard…"

Suddenly I was back there. I could hear it—the thundering sound of the boulder as it came crashing down. I could see it. I watched as it shot past me like a cannonball. I turned to see Tiffany grab hold of Caleb as the force of the rock nearly blew him out of her arms, my son rapidly turning blue. I felt the certainty in that moment that I had just witnessed the death of my son.

I collapsed against a large rock and began to weep. Todd and Travis rushed to my side, their own tears falling at the sight of my pain. I cried and cried and cried, for what had happened, for the loss of the Caleb we'd known, and at the fear for my family's safety that never left me now, that might never leave me. As I emptied my soul, I felt rage and frustration fill the void.

"Why couldn't the rock have just hit me?" I shouted. "I was right here! It flew right past me! Why did it have to hit my son?" After a couple of minutes of regaining my composure, I felt my anger recede and exhaustion take its place.

"Okay, I can do this now." I lifted the voice recorder to my lips and pressed the record button. Taking a deep breath, I spent the next twenty minutes narrating in vivid detail everything that had happened that day. Afterward I was totally and utterly drained. I collapsed against the large rock again. I began to pray, handing over to God the entire weight of all the emotions I was feeling, listening desperately in the silence that surrounded my sobs for God's voice.

At that moment, I could sense God's presence all around me and even in me, filling up those painful places in my heart with His love. I knew immediately that He was speaking to me, but this time I didn't hear words. What I was experiencing was too deep for words, as they were words that were being spoken to the deepest recesses of my spirit. I became oblivious to everything around me. Tears came and went. I felt that God was doing something with the pain residing within me, replacing it with understanding, context, meaning, and, above all, hope. While I couldn't put anything into words, I sensed that this was part of the reason I was there, that God wanted to meet me in the place of my deepest pain and offer me healing and hope.

When I felt my strength return, I called out to Todd and Travis. As we retraced our steps it was easy to see the path that the rock had taken as it had tumbled past us. A large piece of surface rock was broken off where Tiffany had stood, most likely the spot where the boulder had struck before bouncing up to hit Caleb in the back of his head.

The sun had begun to set. We took a last long look around. Oddly the place felt almost holy to me now, a place of great tragedy but also of a great miracle. As we made our way back up the winding trail over slippery rocks and rough terrain, we marveled at how Michael Tagert could have run full speed up the trail with Caleb dangling in his arms.

"Coming back up really makes it hit home what an incredible feat that was," Todd puffed.

"I'm feeling it at this pace," Travis admitted.

"God was with him for sure," I said. "It's just like Psalm

91:11, 12 says: 'For he will command his angels concerning you to guard you in all your ways; they will lift you up in their hands, so that you will not strike your foot against a stone.'" We climbed the rest of the way in silence, sweating despite the chilly air.

I paused again at the entrance where Caleb had lain for over an hour. I again relived every moment, recording it as tears spilled. We didn't stay long. I had accomplished what I had come to do. The final part of our journey still lay ahead.

We set off on the nearly two-hour drive to Jason McKay's, where we would spend the night. Tomorrow we would return to the hospital at Chattanooga.

Jason, whom I'd first met over a reluctant fire at the campground that October weekend, had used his background in media relations and as a local Christian radio personality not only to raise awareness of Caleb but also to stimulate the ongoing investigation into what had happened that day at Fall Creek Falls. No single person had done more to encourage prayers for Caleb than he had. The next morning, we sat and talked, reliving everything that had happened.

"When I came to visit you all in the hospital that Sunday, the night after the accident, I remember you taking me to see Caleb. I remember when I saw him how I just felt certain that this little guy was going to pull through. There was just something about Caleb. I couldn't put my finger on it, but I just couldn't stop thinking that he was going to come out of this OK." He smiled at the recollection. "It was so amazing to see how involved other people became with Caleb, how many people who had never known him before yet felt a connection with him."

"The whole city of Chattanooga hung on every text, every phone call, and each and every Facebook update for what little bit of news there might be. Every time we read a post about him waking up, or starting to show some signs with this or that, we cheered. I mean, for weeks, that's all people wanted to know or talk about. Caleb's story was plastered across the front pages of all the local newspapers. It was on all the radio stations here. It was the lead story out of the gate at six and eleven every night on all three stations. That's big news."

I thought back to something I'd read a number of times from comments on Caleb's Facebook page, that God was using Caleb's story to help others. Jason agreed.

"It inspired people. This situation, this story—it strengthened, it renewed, and in some cases I know, it gave birth to faith. I truly believe that one day we'll be celebrating in heaven, in awe of the impact that Caleb's little life had. But I don't think we'll have to wait until heaven, though," he added. "It'll be interesting to watch your son grow up and see what he's going to become. A lot of people here think he must have something very special ahead of him. It was nothing short of a miracle."

I thought about the odds of our tent having been right next to Jason's that weekend. The odds of how many medical and emergency personnel that just happened to be in that same place when Caleb was struck. The odds of the dozens of other fingerprints we'd seen. It couldn't be coincidence. It truly was miraculous.

∾

It felt strange pulling into the parking lot of Erlanger Hospital. As we walked down the hallway toward the elevators, something caught my eye.

"Guys, look at this!" I stared at a photograph of my family hanging on the wall. Back when Caleb was first in the hospital, we had noticed one of the hospital's walls covered with photos and articles, entitled "Miracles on 3rd Street." Each year, T.C. Thompson Children's Hospital featured a story on that year's most startling miracle recovery. This year's "Miracles on 3rd Street" article featured Caleb.

As we entered the elevator and pushed the button for the fourth floor, I felt both nervous and happy. We emerged from the elevator and turned the corner. There was the familiar red phone, the large double doors, and the sign that read "Pediatric Intensive Care Unit."

After chatting with some staff, we headed down the hall to the waiting room. It was here that we had spent countless hours in an endless sea of waiting. I punched in the password out of habit, much to Todd and Travis's amusement. I sat down on a green-grey-patterned chair, closed my eyes and breathed, blowing back open the door to let the next batch of memories pour out.

We talked at length, laughing, crying, and sharing memories of everything that happened, from the first moments when they had learned of Caleb's accident to the family meetings, the initial frightening news of Caleb's brain swelling, the litany of medical problems that threatened to swamp us, and the daily ups and downs, all the media stories, and the clamor of visitors. We spoke of God's many fingerprints—the miraculous things that had happened, such as how I had heard God's voice telling me I would need my whole heart for what was coming, my dad calling before our trip fearing something bad was about to happen, how Michael Tagert had been at the right place at the right time to rescue Caleb, the other medical professionals at Fall Creek Falls who had "happened" to be there that day, how Tiffany had heard God's voice telling her to turn away just seconds before the rock had struck, the multiple appearances of Psalm 91, the lessons on faith and how God used them to prepare our faith, the four visions I had experienced, one of which had still not happened yet, Steve Austin touching my face when I was struggling with my faith and what that had personified for me, and how God had orchestrated the many thousands across the world to enthusiastically pray for Caleb. We relived it all.

After two hours, we lapsed into a companionable silence. It was very evident that God had been in the midst of everything that had happened, and that He was still in the midst. When another family entered the waiting room, we got up and headed down to the cafeteria. As we sat down, Todd spoke.

"You know, one thing I keep thinking about is what you said yesterday, 'Why not me? Why didn't the rock just hit me?' I can't help but wonder what would have been the media's and the public's response if it had been you instead of Caleb. It would have made the news," he added, "but, like Jason was saying yesterday, so many of these stories flare up and rapidly die out. Caleb's didn't do that. But, if it had been you, it's more likely that they'd have said, 'Here's a poor family whose father was killed by a rock or who was in a coma, or whatever. What a shame.' And that would be that."

I hadn't really thought of it that way. But Todd was right.

"Here's the thing, Tim—you wouldn't have been here to lead the charge. Maybe we'd all have been so busy helping Tiffany cope that no one would have had the opportunity to rally so many people to pray, to come together, to seek a miracle. Who would have written all the stuff you wrote on Facebook and on Caleb's blog, all the people you inspired? And what about us being here now? Surely God is having you record all of this for a reason." I glanced at Travis and was taken aback at how emotional his reaction was to Todd's words.

"I was just thinking about the effect this miracle has had on my own life," my brother explained. "Caleb showed me the power of God, that you can't just rely on doctors; you have to rely on Him. God used Caleb to reveal a miracle, and to show us all that miracles still do happen. I needed that."

Todd sat there, nodding at Travis' words as he continued.

"You know, from the moment you set foot in T.C. Thompson, everything was vying for your attention—Caleb, the doctors, your other children, family, friends, media, and on and on. It left no time for you and Tiffany to connect and communicate with each other. There were so many opportunities for your love and commitment and grace for one another to be tested. I wanted to bring that up because I love you both, and I know that stress, and all the issues that have been coming up between you two, has been present with you guys since the beginning, and it has threatened to derail your relationship. The bottom line truth is that the Enemy would like nothing more than to use all this to thwart the efforts of your marriage and your ability to be parents together, for all of your children, and especially for Caleb in the midst of this. The Enemy wants to destroy your marriage."

Todd's next words were choked by a flood of emotion.

"You want to give hope? You want to give hope to people who will one day walk in your shoes? Then be an example of what it looks like to trust in God through the storm, to stay obedient and come out on the other side. You can give hope to people who feel that there is no hope in situations like this, to show them that it's not possible to get through these things alone, but that you can get through anything if you do it together, and do it with God. That's what will give God glory in the midst of this."

I shared how Tiffany and I came to realize that the hopelessness we'd been feeling was, as Todd had suggested, an attack by the Enemy, and that we had resolved to not be a statistic, to stand together, to stand on faith, to love and see each other the way Christ sees us. I said we'd recommitted ourselves to spend more time with each other and God, and to speak to each other's hearts.

"How's it been?"

"Beautiful. This last month has been absolutely beautiful."

∽

I was exhausted. I had just relived twenty-six days of the hardest days of my life these past two days and had examined them under a microscope. But one thing was certain; I had felt God right beside me during those two days. And I knew that I had finally begun to the process of healing.

As we left Chattanooga, it felt like a very difficult chapter in my life had closed. I had dreaded the very idea of ever returning, but now, having faced my fears, I could look past the tragedy to the miracle behind it and to the hope ahead.

"Dada!" Caleb's excited shriek greeted me as I opened our front door. It was so good to be home. I had missed my family terribly. After spending some time with the kids, Tiffany and I collapsed onto the living room couch.

"Tell me about your weekend first," I said, wanting to hear the sweet sound of her voice instead of my own. I'd been talking nonstop for two days.

"I had a nice conversation with Ryan Kennedy at church this morning," she began.

Ryan was a good friend of ours, a minister at 180 Degrees Ministries. He had helped organize one of the fundraisers for Caleb after the accident.

"He asked how you and I were doing. I said that we were doing great, but that we had had to come to realize a few things over the last month. I told him some of the things we've been talking about, how that it had been tough with all the challenges, and how we'd been feeling hopeless, and about how strange and unusual that was, like something was trying to drive us apart."

"'You know why,' he said, 'don't you? Because your story,

everything that has happened with Caleb, with all these people who have been called to pray for you all over the world—the miracle itself—it would take away God's glory if you two didn't stay together. It would absolutely take away God's glory.'"

I thought back to Todd's words.

"What?" Tiffany asked, seeing my expression. "Was that a fingerprint?"

"Well, as it happens, we did talk about God's glory this weekend, about how an important part of our testimony to others is not only Caleb and everything God has done with him, but also us—our marriage and how our staying together and remaining faithful through all the challenges and difficulties would give God glory. It's like when we talked about faith, hope, and love, and how the most important part of our journey is where we are now –

love. I believe that is what will give God glory in all of this—loving God and loving each other, no matter what."

Tiffany leaned over and hugged me.

"Tiff, remember what I said back in the hospital, when all the media attention started and people all over the world were praying for Caleb, that I wondered if maybe God was doing something behind the scenes to get people's attention, to bring glory to Himself?"

"I remember."

"I think all of it ties back into those lessons on faith God led me to write before any of this ever happened. Remember the first one? Faith is believing that what God says is true, no matter what, and believing that God will provide whatever is needed for His will to be accomplished. The second lesson was that God grows our faith by challenging it. And the third lesson is that sometimes the challenges He allows—"

"… are impossible for us to deal with," Tiffany finished.

She leaned over and gripped my hand.

"That's right, which leads then to the next lesson—the purpose of faith, which is ultimately *to glorify God*. The point in all the lessons is to remind us that God allows difficulties and challenges in order to grow our faith, not weaken it. When others see us as Christians go through the impossible and, instead of faltering, come through stronger than ever, our faith shows the evidence of God in our world; because only God could give us the strength to get through something like this. And when other people see how our faith enables us to survive, when they see God at work in our lives through faith, their faith begins to grow. And in some cases it creates brand new faith. So, when you think about it, what better way for the Enemy to destroy faith in God than to destroy those who are faithful to Him? Like our family?" Tiffany's expression grew thoughtful.

"But we know his lies, don't we? We know the schemes of the Enemy. I think that, as long as we look to God, keep our vows, and never let divorce even be in our vocabulary, we'll make it through to the end, no matter what."

We sat in silence a few moments.

"Tim, did God show you anything this weekend?"

Immediately my mood shifted within me. As I began to speak, it was like a fog in my mind lifted and the things God had spoken to me in my living room a few weeks earlier, the things that I hadn't fully understood at the time, and then again at the bottom of Fall Creek Falls—the groanings in my heart that were too deep for words —they were all now coming to the surface. Like dots that were beginning to connect, I felt the questions I'd had about Caleb's accident, about why God had allowed it to happen, were starting to be answered.

"I remember, one night just after Caleb's accident, Ken Raetz said something I'll never forget. He said, 'Tim, you've been entrusted with a sacred pain.' At the time I didn't know what he meant by that statement, but I think I know now. God knew the rock was going to fall that day. And yes, for whatever reason, He allowed it to hit Caleb. But it wasn't out of vengeance or some kind of punishment against us. And God felt our pain when it happened. In fact it hurt God's heart to allow it to happen. But He allowed it because somehow Caleb's story fits within the scope of His bigger plan that He is continuing to fulfill throughout all history. Caleb's story—our story—is just one of many stories, of all the lives, of all the people that God is using to touch people in this world, and bring others to Himself."

"It's as if God said, 'I know this is going to hurt, but I want you to entrust to Me your son, because there are some things that I am going to do through him to touch the lives of a lot of people.'"

"Tiffany here's what I sense God is saying to us in all this. God never wanted Caleb to get hurt. But the truth is, we live in a fallen world where bad things happen to people every day. We live in a sinful world where there is an Enemy, where people do horrible things, and where bad things just happen. But I think God is calling us to look at things from a different perspective—not on the world with all of its pain and suffering, but on Christ who overcame pain and suffering. And because Jesus died and was raised from the dead, defeating death, we get to have the blessing of seeing the bigger picture, to know that God is moving us and all believers toward a new world where there is no pain, no suffering, no tears, no sin, and no death.

But we are not there yet. And so while we live in this world, in this life, we can expect that bad things will sometimes happen. But because we are God's children, we can have the confidence of knowing that we don't have to face them alone. And concerning Caleb, our son, it was like God said, 'The rock will fall, and it will hit him. But I am not going to leave you in the midst of this feeling as though I am absent.'"

I felt the familiar prickle of tears as my voice became thick.

"And honey, this is where all the fingerprints come in. Again it's as if God said to us, 'Here is what I am going to do: A year before it happens I am going to tell you well beforehand that something is coming. I will set you on a path to understand faith, to prepare you and your wife, because right now you are not yet ready. I will give you a blueprint to teach you and show you how faith works, so that, when you walk through this difficult time, you will have exactly what you will need and know that I am with you.'"

"And Tiffany, that's exactly what God did. He revealed His presence all around us through all these fingerprints. He put people in our lives—brothers and sisters in Christ—to be there for us right when we needed them. He showed me visions of our son, to show us ahead of time how He planned to heal him, how Caleb was going to get better. And there were so many more fingerprints. And in all of it, it's as if God has been saying to us 'I am here, I am in control, I have this whole thing planned out—and I am using your son for a very special reason as a part of my plan. I am going to use his life to touch others. You can trust Me. Your pain will not last forever. My promises will never fail you.'"

I leaned my head back against the couch as I considered the words that had poured out of me so spontaneously.

"Tiffany, one thing I think I've come to understand now more than ever is what the Sovereignty of God really means. If God is Sovereign, then He causes, allows, or denies all things. If God did not cause an event, and He didn't deny it, then He certainly allowed it, because He could have prevented it. I keep thinking about Romans 8:28, where it says, "And we know that in all things God works for the good of those who love Him, who have been called according to His purpose." In other words, all things, no matter what, happen for a reason. What's interesting about that verse is that the 'good' that is talked about there isn't defined the way we think of it. It is a specific kind of good that God has in mind. Paul says in the very next verse, in verse 29 'For those God foreknew, He also predestined to be conformed to the likeness of his Son.' That's it! God's purpose for our lives in this world is twofold—for those who don't know Him to come to know Him through Christ, and for those who are already in Christ, His will is for them to be 'conformed to the image of his Son'"—that is, to know Him even more. I exhaled heavily.

"So in other words, for us as believers, all of our life's events, whether good or bad, God causes, allows, or denies, and He has committed Himself to making sure that they all work together, like pieces of a puzzle, so that, in the end, our lives are shaped to look like Christ's own life. And somehow, Caleb's story, our story, fits into that plan."

Tiffany and I clung to each other, in awe and speechless over the things God had shown us. Indeed, the pieces had begun tumbling into place. In the days ahead I would soon realize that this was just the beginning of God connecting the dots for us. What came next would change our lives forever.

CHAPTER TWENTY-SIX

Missed Warnings

It was the second week of February and Caleb continued to progress by leaps and bounds. He had accomplished months of development over the last six weeks. We were delighted to be invited to participate in a televised Ronald McDonald House fundraiser in Chattanooga. Throughout the numerous photo shoots, interviews, and the television crew filming, Caleb was eager and willing to show off all he could do.

One evening later that week I had been spending some quiet time alone with God, thinking about everything He had shown us recently. I thought back to those first words He'd spoken to me: *You are going to need your whole heart for what is coming,* and how that first encounter with Him had set us on a course of learning, of preparing our faith for what was coming. The question that had been burdening me ever since was why had God told me something was coming without telling me what it was, so I could have just not gone on the camping trip at all? Why did you let us go in the first place? Why didn't You warn us, I asked. It was then I heard the voice, that same voice, inside my heart.

I did.

I was thunderstruck. I racked my brain thinking back to everything I could remember that had happened before our camping trip, searching for anything I might have forgotten. And then it came to me. My father's phone call earlier that week. How apprehensive I'd felt the night before our trip when Tiffany was going out with the children, how I felt that something might happen to one of them. The countless obstacles we'd encountered just trying to get ready and leave on our trip—the incredible difficulty finding a rental car and a campsite, losing most of the day before getting on the road, and then getting lost. I thought back to all the subsequent hurdles when we finally reached the campsite in the middle of the night. And Tiffany, I thought, with a pang, how she had tried to gently persuade me that perhaps we should just stay home or camp someplace other than Fall Creek Falls, someplace closer to home perhaps, and how, when we couldn't find the falls at first, she suggested we return to the campsite. I refused to even listen. How many more indications did I need before I was willing to say, hey, maybe we should go another time? But no, the obstacles had just infuriated me and I was determined to control the situation and make things happen the way I felt they should happen. I was too attached to the outcome to consider altering our plans. I didn't listen. Not to anyone. Not even God.

"I didn't listen," I whispered. A landslide of guilt threatened to bury me. If I had listened, perhaps I would have realized that something wasn't right. Maybe I would have prayed to God for guidance. Maybe we wouldn't have gone, and maybe Caleb would have never been hurt. But, at the time of our camping trip, Tiffany and I had just emerged from a very difficult time in our marriage. We were distracted mentally, emotionally, and spiritually. We were simply not listening. Or, more correctly, I was not listening.

It was then that God began to pour healing into the fresh open wounds of my heart. I felt a warmth flow through my body as if I were being bathed in love. Instead of hearing words this time, again, I simply gained a sense of meaning, of perspective. It was then I realized what was happening within me. God was revealing to me for the first time what He meant when He said "You are going to need your whole heart for what is coming." He was answering my prayer. I sat down in front of my computer, and began to journal the thoughts and words that began to light upon my mind.

> *Words cannot describe my feelings tonight. I think God is finally helping me to understand what He meant when He said, "You are going to need your whole heart for what is coming."*
>
> *Just a few moments ago, I had this scripture from Ezekiel suddenly come to mind: "I will give you a new heart and put a new spirit in you; I will remove from you your heart of stone and give you a heart of flesh. And I will put my Spirit in you and move you to follow my decrees and be careful to keep my laws." (Ezekiel 36:26-27).*
>
> *I realized when God brought that passage to my mind that He was telling me that the "whole heart" that I was going to need was in fact the new heart that He had already given me, the new life that comes through being indwelt and filled with God's Holy Spirit.*
>
> *When I became a believer, the Bible says that I died to everything I once was, that I died to sin and embraced a new life characterized by holiness when the Holy Spirit came to live within me. So living out of a "whole heart" then is living with the realization that I stand in grace fully without condemnation (Romans 8:1) and have faith in the inner working of God*

to create in me who He has declared me to be (Philippians 2:13), and as I set my mind on this new reality (Colossians 3:1-4), I then begin to see changes manifest in me naturally as a part of my new nature. This new "heart" that now beats for God is not the result of my working hard to achieve it, but is the natural overflow of the relationship I have with God.

I paused to collect my thoughts.

It became clear to me tonight that, when God told me I would need my whole heart for what was coming, He was calling me to remember and embrace my true identity, to choose truth and live out of the reality of the new life I have in Christ. Jesus called it the "abundant life" in John 10:10. Paul called it "walking in the Spirit," where through intimacy with Christ you can experience the fruit of your relationship with God through such things as love, joy, peace, patience, kindness, etc. (Galatians 5:16-25). It's also a life where Jesus teaches me how to be his disciple—because like the early disciples, when I was born again, I wasn't born automatically knowing how to walk and live out this new heart of mine. So through the Holy Spirit as I walk intimately with God, Jesus teaches me how to hear His voice, and learn from Him as He teaches me more about Himself and who I am in Christ, as well as how to live and carry out his will. In short, he teaches me how to live out of my whole heart.

Until that first time I heard God speak, I

didn't really believe that God could or would speak directly to anyone today. I'd been raised and trained in a church setting that taught that such things do not exist in our day and time, that they were only for the first century. As a minister I had preached numerous sermons with that very conclusion. But after everything our family has been through over the last few months, how could I not believe? I'm learning that it's when I am seeking an intimate relationship with God and am sensitive to the ways He speaks to me, that I begin to discern the things He's trying to teach me and call me to do. Hearing God, I'm learning, is intimately tied to relationship.

Primarily God speaks to us through the Bible, as the plumb line of God's Truth. That's first and foremost. But the same Spirit who wrote the Bible is also living in us, and one of His primarily roles in our lives is to guide us into all truth (John 16:13). So not only does God guide us into all truth through the Bible, but He also guides us through prayer, the church, others, from discerning events that are happening around us, and from hearing Him directly, in our hearts, through a "still small voice," audibly, or through dreams and visions, etc.

As we walk with God daily, He uses such things (often a number of them to confirm a matter) to answer our prayers, give us wisdom and insight, help us discern and make decisions, and help us to live the life He has called us to live.

What I'm learning is that as a disciple I

need both wisdom and revelation, wisdom from God's word and revelation through the Spirit. I need wisdom to know God's concrete will on things, to see who God is and who I am in relationship with Him and Jesus. And I also need revelation—from the Spirit who is in me—to understand the truths of scripture, to reveal God's truth to my heart, to make it real for me as He empowers me to live the life spoken about in His Word, and to guide me as He walks with me through the daily activities, decisions, and difficulties of my day to day life.

I am also learning that, like with any relationship, good communication skills take time, especially as I am learning the heart of God. But as I learn to listen to Him and discern the things that He is saying to me, I can then better align my life to join Him in whatever it is He is doing around me, the things He is calling me to do.

So in short, "You are going to need your whole heart," I now know, was God's way of saying that I needed to walk intimately with Him as His disciple with my whole heart, to hear His voice, and live out the new life He's called me to live.

I paused again, and readied myself as I thought about the second part of the phrase.

"You are going to need your whole heart for what is coming." This is where God's revelation took me by surprise as I realized some things I had never really considered before.

Everything that I just described—all of it happens in the context of a war. We believers still live in a fallen world permeated with sin. We inhabit a place that is under the influence of an Enemy, the Devil who is dead set on keeping us from knowing the truth, about God, about ourselves, about our new heart, about the reality of the world we live in. Jesus reminds us that Satan's primary goal is to steal, kill, and destroy the abundant life that he came to give us (John 10:10).

When it comes to living our lives as believers, Satan wants us to believe that we ourselves are the best arbiters of our own destiny—that our willpower, our intellect, our perceptions, our ability to get through life is all we need. And of course the more he can get us to listen to him, the more we will fall into his traps and the more ineffective for God we then become.

I am coming to realize that, to walk with God as a disciple, I must listen for God's voice in the midst of spiritual warfare, in the middle of a great battle where I don't know, from day to day, what lies ahead—what pitfalls, landmines, right or wrong choices, twists and turns, or things that might cause me to stumble lie just outside the reach of my human wisdom.

God's desire is not for us to blindly stumble and fall into every temptation, every flaming arrow from the Enemy, and every bad judgment that sends us on a downward trajectory in life. Yes, we will have tests and trials, but that is not the same thing as temptation and attacks from the Enemy. The former God allows for our growth. The latter, the Enemy, desires for our destruction. God of course can and does make good a whole host of bad choices on our parts, but that doesn't mean that it's His desire for us to have to always experience them! His desire is that we walk closely to Him, hear His voice, follow His lead, and let Him lead us into abundant life.

On this note, Job 33:15-18 comes to mind: "In a dream, in a vision of the night, when deep sleep falls on people as they slumber in their beds, He may speak in their ears and terrify them with warnings, to turn them from wrongdoing and keep them from pride, to preserve them from the pit, their lives from perishing by the sword."

I'm convinced that all of this too, is to take place in the context of community. The abundant life is not to be lived alone. Yes there are times, like Jesus, when we are called to solitude, to go up to the mountain to be alone and pray. And these times are vitally important for us to be able to hear and discern God's voice for our lives. But you cannot hear God as fully and experience Him as you should until you hear Him and experience Him in the context of community. As people of faith have come around us from all kinds of different backgrounds and walks of life, we've been able to see firsthand how important it is for God's people to stand togeth-

> er. It is precisely because we live in a world at war that we need to band together and fight for each other's hearts, to help each other in the midst of trial or adversity, to share each other's strengths and help with each other's weaknesses, as we listen for God's voice for each other together.
>
> So living life with a whole heart for what's coming, I believe, is about getting out of the way and letting Christ lead me because only He knows what's coming down the road in my life. Only God is Sovereign. Only He knows which directions in life are best. It's about going wherever He wants me to go and avoiding everything He warns me to avoid. It's about looking for and expecting God's activity all around me and being sensitive to the fact that He is communicating with me all the time, in ways that I won't miss, if I know how to hear Him and if my heart is aligned to Him. "Man does not live on bread alone," Jesus said, "but on every word that comes from the mouth of God." (Matthew 4:4).

As I stopped typing, I felt exhausted. I couldn't believe that I'd written all that in just one sitting. I wanted to go back and process it all, but I was too tired. I leaned back in my chair and sat completely still, my eyes closed as I continued to listen.

"Tim, I knew beforehand that you and Tiffany were not in a place to hear My voice. And like I previously told you, though I would never have wanted Caleb to have been struck by that rock, I knew that he would. I knew that you would not hear My warnings, that you would be at the bottom of the falls at the wrong place at the wrong time, and that the Enemy would use the occasion to try to destroy your family. But I decided that I would not let Caleb's life be taken from him. I chose to let him live. And in the process there were many things I planned behind the scenes that you didn't know about. I had many lessons that I was and am still teaching to numerous people through the accident and through Caleb's life. And part of my lesson for you and Tiffany is that now, you know by experience what it means to walk with Me, to hear My voice, to receive My counsel and instruction and live by My Spirit. So just remember, you are going to need your whole heart for what is coming."

After my quiet time with God, I felt humbled. Very humbled. And somewhere in the midst of this encounter that I'd had with God, as I continued to feel God's love surround me, I suddenly felt a welcome sense of release from the guilt and pain that I had been feeling.

I felt forgiveness for myself.

CHAPTER TWENTY-SEVEN

"It Wasn't an Accident"

With Valentine's Day only a couple of days away, I thought back to why I had married my wife nearly ten years ago. Tiffany was a woman of faith. Early on, when I'd tended to live more pessimistically, Tiffany had an uncanny ability to see the good in everything. She always lifted my spirits. Although it was her emerald green eyes that first took my breath away, it had been her deep committed faith and Christian example that I continued to fall in love with more and more each passing day. This would be an excellent time, I thought, to renew our focus on each other.

Tiffany beat me to it. She arranged for Todd and Emily to stay with the kids and made a hotel reservation for that night. We'd sleep in late on Sunday morning, she said, returning home in time to attend the annual dinner banquet at the Piney Fire Department down in Spencer, Tennessee. Piney had been the first responders to Fall Creek Falls that October day and they had invited us to be their honored guests at this year's banquet. Tiffany and I had agreed, looking forward to another opportunity to connect and thank those who had helped us through the initial hours of that dreadful day.

We were a little nervous about leaving the boys, particularly Colby, in case he might be frightened that we were leaving him again. I took him aside and explained what we were doing and how it wasn't the same as when we'd gone to the hospital with Caleb.

"Caleb will be here with you," I said. "Mommy and Daddy are just going to stay in a hotel, like a date, so we can have some special time together. We're going to stay there tonight and then come back in the morning, and then we'll all go to the fire department dinner together."

Colby, contrary to our fears, wasn't the least bit concerned. Instead, he appeared thrilled at the chance to show off his Xbox skills to Todd and Emily.

The next day, we got the boys dressed and drove to Spencer, a little town situated about seven miles from Fall Creek Falls National Park. The Piney Fire Department and their families greeted us with open arms. We gave Tiwanna Bricker and Will Maxwell, who were the first to respond that day, huge hugs, thanking them for their roles in helping to save our son's life. The boys were ecstatic to be the center of attention as they were presented with Piney Fire Department Fireman badges, proclaiming them to be the department's first ever honorary firefighters.

"Hi Tim, I'm Ray Cutcher," a man said to me, holding out his hand. "I don't know if you remember me or not, but I'm a park ranger over at Fall Creek Falls. You and I spoke briefly that day. I just wanted to say how glad I am that your son is okay and getting better. I remember going home that night and telling my wife what had happened. We've kept up with Caleb's progress since then, and I just wanted to say we continue to think of you all and pray for Caleb." We shook hands. We chatted for a few moments and then Ray hesitated.

"Did you know we have the rock?"

I stood, eyes wide, as he continued.

"I knew the police would want to collect any evidence they could, so the next morning I hiked down to the bottom of the trail and retrieved it." He shook his head. "I gotta tell you, that was one heavy rock. It must've weighed at least thirty-five or forty pounds. It's in evidence right now."

"How do you know it was the right rock?"

"Uh, well, there was a lot of blood at the site, and there was blood and tissue on the rock so it was pretty easy to tell which rock it was."

I felt the blood drain from my face and for a moment I felt lightheaded.

"I hope I haven't upset you," he said, looking at me with concern. "Like I said, we're just so glad to see how well Caleb's doing. I probably wouldn't have told you about the rock except that he's doing so well. I just thought you might like to know."

"Can I ask how big was it?"

Ray held up his hands. "Oh, easily eighteen inches across and about eight to ten inches wide. Like I said, it easily weighed thirty or forty pounds. It was big. How he survived is truly a miracle." Ray's voice trailed off and we both glanced at Caleb, who was playing with Will's fire helmet. "So, do you know what really happened that day?" he asked.

I looked at him, confused.

"Well, the police said it might have been a natural rockfall or that someone at the top of the gorge either accidently or deliberately dislodged the rock, maybe teenagers. But they don't really know."

"Well, I can understand their caution, but we're pretty sure we know what happened. It wasn't an accident."

I stared at him.

"We had a witness who came forward the day after the accident," Ray explained. "I'd gone back to the park to find the rock and started asking around if anyone had seen anything, anyone acting strange or doing something they shouldn't. A man came forward to say he'd been walking down an adjacent trail when he'd overheard a couple of teenagers. They were being loud, making a lot of noise about something. That's when he heard it, the thud of the rock as it rolled down. He saw the panicked faces of the kids when the screams came from below. He said they asked if there were people down there and he replied, 'Of course there are.' When they heard that, they ran off."

"So they rolled the rock on purpose? Why would they do that?"

"My guess is it was a couple of kids who weren't really thinking and they thought it would be neat to try to roll a rock down into the water. They never stopped to think that there might be people down there."

I felt a surge of anger.

I thought of just how close I'd come to losing not just my son but my wife as well. And for what? Because of some irresponsible kids looking for a laugh?

I thought about the devastating consequences this had had, not just on Caleb, but on all of us. Caleb, for all his progress, still might never return to being the same little boy he'd been before the accident, and the extent of his difficulties were yet unknown. We had no idea what he would be like as he got older. I also thought of the nearly four hundred thousand dollars in expenses that were crushing us, and how the stress had taken a toll on us all.

When I later shared the story with Tiffany, she handled it in her typical optimistic fashion.

"Tim, let's focus on the good, and the blessings that we have. We still have Caleb. He's alive, and he's doing well. We have Colby and Connor, who are safe and happy, and we have each other. And we have God."

I looked at my wife. There was more forgiveness in her heart than I'd ever known in anyone. For me, letting go was harder. Much harder. That surge of anger I felt when Ray Cutcher told me it hadn't been an accident grew more and more intense. I discovered that somehow not knowing for sure what had happened, with the *possibility* it had been just a freak accident, had smoothed over my feelings of anger underneath. But now, knowing it had not been an accident, that it *could* have been prevented—I was beside myself. It was then I knew I had to unburden my heart of all the things I desperately wanted to say to those teenagers.

That night, after spending some quiet time alone with God, I sat down and wrote them a letter. I wrote and I wrote and I wrote. And as I wrote, I felt my anger begin to fade as God brought to my memory all the things that He had shown us. In the letter I poured out my anguish and how it had nearly consumed me these past few months. I wrote of how our lives had been forever changed and the struggles that not only we faced, but also that Caleb would conceivably face for the rest of his life. I wrote of how it affected not only Caleb and his mother and I, but his two brothers, both too young to understand the reasons why something this horrific could happen. That even I, as an adult, struggled to understand and accept it. I described what had happened when the rock struck Caleb, how his precious life's blood had poured out of him and drenched all of us, and how he almost didn't survive. How my wife almost didn't escape. I described how Caleb has had to learn to walk and talk and feed himself all over again and how tough it had been for him to do so, how hard he struggled every single day to do the kinds of things most of us take for granted. How the doctors had told us that, in the years to come, he might suffer learning, memory, and behavioral problems, that he might never be able to function normally in society. How his ability to relate to other people, including his family, had changed, possibly forever.

As I finished writing the letter, I explained that God had

released me from the anger that I had been feeling toward them, that He was beginning to heal my heart. "Because of what Jesus did for me on the cross," I wrote, "because he forgave me, I can forgive you." I wrote that most likely they had no idea what was going to happen that day, that they simply hadn't been thinking, and that, most likely, they were completely unaware of the consequences that would result from their actions, and how I could only imagine the pain and guilt they must feel. I encouraged them to turn to God for healing and forgiveness and come forward to take responsibility for their actions in order to forgive themselves and move forward.

I had no way of sending the letter, of course, unless they later chose to come forward. But I found myself hoping that, one day, should it be God's will, my letter would make it into the hands of those teenagers.

Perhaps, one day it will.

CHAPTER TWENTY-EIGHT

An Unexpected Surprise

Despite my fears about Caleb's future we continued to see encouraging signs of progress in our son. By the end of February, just six weeks before his third birthday, Caleb's physical and occupational therapy skills were evaluated. His results showed that he was now functioning developmentally at about the age of a twenty-four-month old. Tiffany and I were determined to be positive in light of the fact that, in just the last three months since we'd returned home, Caleb had regained roughly one year's development. When it came to visual motor skills, the kinds of activities that involve using the eyes to accomplish a task, Caleb was graded at twenty months, so his sight was still proving to be the real challenge to his development. When we did visual tracking exercises with him at home, he would still lose an object at about 40 degrees in his left field of vision, indicating the point at which he couldn't see very well. Overall his sight was better but he still needed a lot of work. His fine motor skills, on the other hand, his general dexterity, was ranked age appropriate, which gave us tremendous hope. Even so, we were unprepared for what would come next.

"I think we can cut Caleb's physical and occupational therapy sessions down from three per week to two," Kelley said. "Today was his best physical therapy session ever. He's walking now, and his balance is better. His movements are becoming much more fluid, and he's much more aware of his surroundings.

And his sight has improved. In fact, he's starting to rebel against the daily therapy routines, not terribly surprising considering his age. But the hard work is really paying off."

Caleb didn't waste any time demonstrating that he was improving. He had been getting increasingly more verbal, especially over the last couple of weeks. One night we'd been playing with one of his trains when it tipped over on its side. I almost fell over when he blurted, "Uh, oh. Oh, no, I got it!"

During a recent therapy session, Caleb blurted out, "Come on!" and grabbed the therapist's hand as Tiffany watched.

"Where are we going?" she said as she laughed.

"We go church!"

"Well, honey," I said, chuckling, when Tiffany told me the story, "we must be doing something right. He's already preaching and trying to lead others to Christ!"

∼

We started the month of March with Tiffany complaining of nausea. She spent several days in bed and I found myself being a single parent, juggling meals and diaper changes as well as Caleb's therapy homework. By Sunday, Tiffany had dragged herself out of bed to come with us to church. It was evident she wasn't feeling well and I'd begun to wonder if it might be a reaction to stress instead of an actual virus. She and I had both been through quite a bit over the last few months, and we'd both been emotional at times. But nothing could have prepared me for what I learned after church that day.

"I'm pregnant."

Four kids, I thought to myself. We'd originally hoped to stop at two. Connor had been a sweet surprise. And now, another one? How could we afford and provide for them, I wondered. Caleb still required a lot of attention. On any given day, taking care of Caleb was like taking care of two kids, so in many ways it was already like having four.

Over the next few days Tiffany and I both ran the gamut of emotions, from frustration and fear to uncertainty and anxiety. Eventually our fears began to subside as we opened up to each other.

"I was scared at first when I found out," Tiffany admitted. "I mean, how could we possibly manage to take care of Caleb along with Colby and Connor, and a newborn? But the more I think and pray about it, the more I realize how much of a blessing from God this baby is going to be." We'd given up on the idea of ever having a little girl. Maybe this would be our chance.

"You remember how hard it was the year before Caleb's accident when you didn't have a job and we didn't have any money?" Tiffany prodded. "That was the time when we felt closer to God than ever before, when He first spoke to you and started revealing all those things to us about faith. We were seeing Him do things all around us."

"And then I got scared," I said. "I ran out, grabbed the first job I could find, and got into another ministry, all out of fear."

"We were both afraid. Do you remember one of the big things that drove our fear?"

I nodded. I knew where Tiffany was going with this.

"You were pregnant with Connor then. And all I could say to God was, 'Thank you for all the amazing insights You've given us; thank you for showing us all these things about faith, but right now we're about to have a baby and I need an income!' Within two months I had a full-time job, a ministry, and a startup business I worked on at night while everyone slept. It consumed me."

Tiffany grimaced at the memory.

"And neither of us were listening to God much after that.

We grew apart, our marriage suffered, and then everything happened with Caleb." She clasped my hand. "Tim, let's not make that same mistake. Let's not let fear get in the way of the blessings God wants to give us." She gave me a shy smile. "I really feel like everything is coming full circle. It's like God is giving us another chance. Everything is just the same as it was. We've never felt closer to God but, at the same time, we're starting to feel the financial stress again, with all the medical bills. And now, here we are, expecting another baby."

She was right. Although the pressures and fears we'd experienced before felt the same as now, things were different. We were different.

"This time," I said, "I want to respond out of faith. I want to put God and family first. And I want to seek God's wisdom as to what our next steps should be."

I leaned my head back onto the couch.

"Last year I was leaning very heavily on my own understanding, of what I thought I needed to be doing with my life. I had good intentions, but I let fear take control. I put work and trying to provide for my family above my relationship with God and actually being a husband and a father. Now, after everything we've been through and all God has shown us, I am starting to learn how to just simply walk with Christ, to put Him first, to let Him do whatever He wants with me, to join Him in whatever it is He wants me to do, and to listen to Him, no matter how uncomfortable or how against common sense it may feel. I'm also learning that no matter what, even when times are hard financially, like they are now, spending time with you and our kids has to come before work. There has to be balance."

I paused for a moment.

"I am going to live out of a whole heart, for what's coming."

Tiffany nestled into my shoulder.

"I really feel like this baby is a whole new blessing in our lives. It's as if God is saying to us, 'Last year at this time you nearly lost Caleb, but this year, I am not only going to restore your son's life, but I am also going to bless your family with new life.'" She looked up at me. "A new life, Tim. In more ways than one, huh?"

"Yes. In more ways than one."

I thought about Caleb's third birthday coming up on the fourteenth of April. No doubt it was going to be a very special occasion since it was the birthday that, for weeks last year, we feared would never come. Tiffany and I had already decided to make it as an open invitation to anyone and everyone who wanted to come celebrate with us. We had scheduled the party for the last weekend in April and booked a picnic shelter at a park in Brentwood Tennessee, which would easily accommodate a large crowd. Channel 5 WTVF and Channel 4 WSMV had already made plans to be there and we'd invited all of the heroes who'd played a part in Caleb's rescue and recovery, hoping most would attend. It was going to be a very special birthday indeed.

CHAPTER TWENTY-NINE

Happy Birthday!

April had been another good month for achievements as Caleb continued his uphill battle for improvement. His physical therapist commented on how much better Caleb was walking, how much more stable he was on his feet, and how he was starting to show signs of wanting to run.

"I really think he'll get there soon," Kelley said. "I just know it. It won't be long before he's running up and down the halls."

Caleb's vision therapist had us practically dancing when he said that, since his previous evaluation, Caleb had experienced dramatic improvement.

"In my opinion, I see no reason why Caleb shouldn't regain most, if not all, his vision." All of this, he said, was due to the concentrated effort we continued to pour into Caleb's daily therapy at home. His other therapists concurred, saying he was consistently surpassing every goal they set for him, and that one big thing Caleb had going for him was that he loved learning. We just needed to keep up the effort, they said. That was just what we needed to hear. There were days it seemed that we ate, drank, slept, and planned therapy activities. Everything was a potential learning experience. How true for all of us, I thought.

Following Easter, we experienced some of the worst rainstorms we'd had all season. But thankfully, when the weekend of Caleb's birthday finally arrived, the weather cleared up dramatically. Saturday, April 30th, dawned clear, bright, sunny, and warm. The skies were a deep azure blue, with only a few wisps of clouds scattered about. The grass was beautiful, a lush green carpet beneath our feet. The trees were full of life, their vivid emerald branches swaying gently in the soft breeze.

"Tim, this is great!" Tiffany exclaimed. "We couldn't have asked for a better day."

We arrived at the park at nine-thirty that morning, the boys tumbling out of the van in excitement to greet the family members who'd come to help us set up. The boys gasped when they saw the huge playground. Colby raced toward it as Caleb and Connor did their best to catch up. As I watched Caleb play I couldn't help but notice how much he'd learned over the last few months. It was a testament to just how far Caleb had come, I thought, watching him as he navigated the various tubes, stairs, slides and uneven ground. But this wasn't therapy to Caleb. This was fun.

As the boys played under my watchful eye, a man, a woman, and two children I didn't recognize approached. The woman stuck out her hand.

"I'm Melissa Lyons. I was one of the nurses there that day at Fall Creek Falls."

"The pediatric trauma nurse from Vanderbilt?" I cried. "Oh my goodness, it's so good to finally meet you! I can't tell you how thankful we are for you and for all that you did for our son that day!" I shook her hand and asked, "Can I hug you?" We hugged and then Tiffany hugged her as I shook her husband's hand.

"Sir," I said to Bob, "Your wife is a hero. She has been in our thoughts ever since."

"I don't know if you remember or not," Melissa interjected, putting a hand on her husband's arm, "but Bob was there, too. He helped carry Colby back up the trail behind you."

I shook his hand again, even more vigorously.

"Thank you again, so much, for helping us and for helping Colby. I can't tell you how much that means to us." Melissa picked Caleb up, her eyes damp, and hugged him.

"You are doing so good, little man!" She looked at us. "I just can't believe it. I mean, the last thing I remember was seeing him lying there on the ground with his face so blue and lifeless, and now, well, to see him like this, it's nothing short of amazing."

More and more people arrived, filling the park. The news crews had set up and had begun filming. It was a good time to sing "Happy Birthday."

Everyone clustered beneath the canopied picnic area. Caleb sat in the center of a picnic table blanketed with a multicolored, star-studded tablecloth. To his right was an impressive mound of presents, which he was itching to start opening. In front of him was a brightly speckled chocolate birthday cake with three tall, yellow candles, flames flickering. As the sun flooded the covered shelter with warm, welcoming light, Caleb's eyes shone, sparkling bluer than ever before. His eyes were alive, a testament to the life we were celebrating.

"Okay, Caleb, let's blow out the candles." Caleb still didn't grasp how to blow out candles yet, but it didn't matter. As we stood on either side of him, Tiffany and I each held one of Caleb's hands, leaned in close and blew. Caleb's face lit up as everyone applauded.

After the cake, as the last news crew was readying to leave, we stepped aside for one final interview. The reporter positioned us in front of the camera.

"So, what do you think you've learned as a family?"

Tiffany and I looked at each other. For a moment we were at a complete loss for words. Where to begin? I smiled and nodded for Tiffany to answer first.

"The greatest lesson I've learned," she began, haltingly, "is that loving God and loving family is most important. It's the thread that's held us together. We knew those things before, of course, but now we know them so much more. We know them by experience."

"I agree," I added, when the reporter pointed his microphone at me. "The greatest lesson we've learned by far is the lesson of love, loving God and loving each other, and being there for each other."

"Open! Open!" Caleb yelled, as his brothers helped him open one present after another. Caleb couldn't wait to start playing with them.

"Hold on sweetie, let's open the rest of your presents first" Tiffany said.

"Open! Open!" he shouted.

After opening all the presents, and enjoying some playtime after our guests left, Tiffany and I grabbed a moment alone under a nearby tree. I slipped my arm around her waist.

"You know, I really meant what I said.

"What's that?"

"That it's all about love." Tiffany wrapped her arms around me.

"When I think about all we've been through together, and all the lessons we've learned—to me what it all boils down to is love. The greatest lesson we've learned is receiving God's love for us, and then loving Him with all our hearts. It's about loving each other, you and me, and loving our kids. And it's about loving others as God loves us. Love truly is not about what you receive, but what you give to others freely."

We looked over at Colby, Caleb, and Connor playing with their aunts, uncles, and grandparents. Tiffany leaned her head on my shoulder.

"I think that, for me, one thing God has made very clear is that we should never take life for granted. We should enjoy it at every moment, at every turn. We should never live in the hopes of tomorrow or in the memories of yesterday. We should only live in the joys of today." We watched the boys as they ran, laughed, and played together.

"It's so beautiful to see them playing like that, playing together," Tiffany said.

We talked for a time about how easy it was to fall into the trap of thinking that joy and happiness is a place, where if we worked hard enough, made enough money, and sacrificed enough time, then we would eventually get *there*, to that ever elusive place of happiness.

"Never again will we live like that," I promised. "God has shown us that the beauty of life is not arriving at a place where your circumstances fit your hopes or ideals. The beauty of life is being able to enjoy the most important things of life as you journey together, with Him." I gazed down at Tiffany.

"I love you, honey."

"I love you too," she whispered, as our lips met.

∽

Later that day, after we had put the boys down for their afternoon nap, we sat in our living room, surrounded by family and close friends. We had decided weeks earlier that there could be no better way to end such an incredible day of celebration than to worship God with our family and dearest friends. Todd, with his guitar in hand, sat next to his wife Emily on the living room floor and began to sing. Many of the songs were the same ones we'd sung back in the PICU at T.C. Thompson. There were also some new songs, including one Todd had written especially for Caleb, based on Psalm 91.

"This is what it's all about," Tiffany said, looking around at our guests. "Giving God glory for what he's done for Caleb and for our family."

"Amen!"

After everyone had said their goodbyes and gone, I glanced at the clock. There was still one very important guest who hadn't arrived yet, one for whom we'd set aside the rest of the afternoon.

There was a knock at the door.

"Tiffany, he's here. Do you want to get Caleb up from his nap?"

I opened the door to Michael Tagert and his family. We hugged. Michael hadn't been able to accept our invitation to come earlier as our honored guest at the party, but he'd gotten there as soon as he could. As it turned out, the quieter and more intimate meeting at home was better, giving us all a chance to spend time and talk with each other.

"Hey, little man!" Michael said as he picked up a still half-asleep Caleb. "Goodness, you've gotten heavier since the last time I saw you." Caleb grinned, all traces of tiredness disappearing. He sat contentedly, playing with Michael's goatee. "Wow, just look at you. You're doing so well!"

After Caleb opened Michael's gifts, we relaxed on the back deck of our home for several hours, recounting our shared experiences and catching up on all that had happened over the last few months. When the Tagerts eventually got up to leave, we walked them to the front lawn and snapped a few photos and said our goodbyes.

"Michael, I hope you know you're always welcome here in our home. Let's stay in touch."

"Thank you," Michael grinned, ruffling his hand through Caleb's hair. "I'm so glad to see Caleb doing as well as he is. He is one strong little guy, that's for sure." Michael knelt down and looked Caleb in the eye.

"And you, you keep doing what you're doing, little man. You're going to be just fine." Michael ruffled Caleb's hair again. Another exchange of hugs and they were on their way.

"What a perfect day," Tiffany sighed, Connor in her arms as we stood out on the lawn and watched the receding taillights.

Colby gave me a hopeful look.

"Hey Dada, wanna play with me?"

"You bet, buddy. Just give me and Caleb a couple of minutes and I'll be right in, okay?" Colby nodded. "Okay, Dada!"

Colby raced toward the front door. Tiffany leaned over and gave me a kiss. "I'm going to take Connor and go make dinner." See you in a minute."

After everyone went inside, I looked down at Caleb, and felt my chest swell with pride. I picked him up and gave him a kiss.

"Buddy, you are such an amazing little boy. You have taught Daddy and Mommy so much, you know that?" I pressed my lips against his ear. "You have taught so many people so many things. You are a miracle and I'm so proud that you're my son. I love you, little buddy." With a last kiss, I set Caleb down on the grass. With all the recent rains, the rows of bushes and trees behind us had grown enormously lush and green. I'd just mown the grass but it was sprouting again already. Caleb walked ahead of me, toward the shrubs, his right hand brushing against the soft leaves. I followed behind, admiring how well he was navigating the uneven ground.

The sun was starting to set. I could see the warm glow of light through the kitchen window. Caleb reached up and touched one of the leaves and smiled.

"All right, buddy, it's time to go in. Let's go back inside,"

I said and tickled him. Caleb gave me a mischievous look and started walking as fast as he could, his hands clasped together. I sprinted ahead so I was in front of him and began walking backwards, our eyes locked together. Then for the first time, instead of walking fast, Caleb began to run. In the waning daylight, his face was outlined, his chubby cheeks threatening to push his eyes closed as he giggled with delight. As we approached the front porch, I applauded at how well he was running. "Yay Caleb! Good job!" Caleb followed suit, clapping and cheering excitedly. As he slowed down, he again clasped his hands together briefly before letting go.

My breath caught in my throat and my heart began to pound. My knees felt weak.

"The fourth vision," I gasped. "I just saw the fourth vision!" I clapped my hand against my mouth. "Oh, thank you, God," I whispered as I wept, looking up at the sky, now dusted in beautiful shades of orange, warm red, and soft lilac. "Thank you, Father. I know now that everything is going to be okay. I know You are with us. Thank you!"

As I reached for the door handle, smiling from ear to ear, these words of Scripture fell to my lips as I whispered.

And now these three remain: faith, hope, and love, but the greatest of these is love.

EPILOGUE

You are going to need your whole heart for what is coming.

I had no idea what that had meant. And in these five years since the accident, I'm still learning. God has taught me so many valuable lessons over these last few years—about marriage, family, what it means to have a relationship with God, and how that relationship plays out in our day-to-day lives, living life for God's glory, no matter what the circumstances, through prayer, forgiveness, faith, miracles, discovering how God still works and speaks today, and, most important, His lessons on love.

God has frequently made His presence known in our lives, and His fingerprints have been hard to miss. There've been numerous encounters with Him over the years, some subtle and some not so subtle. Take, for example, our three boys' names. We had chosen our first three children's names simply because they appealed to us. But when Chloe came along, a year after Caleb's accident, we wanted one that held special meaning for us. "Chloe," as it turned out, was the perfect name as it means a green shoot, symbolizing a new beginning. Curious, I searched online, looking for Caleb's name. I knew it appeared in the Bible, but not much more.

"You are not going to believe this," I exclaimed. "Caleb," I read aloud to Tiffany, "as a boy's name, is of Hebrew origin. In the Bible, Caleb was a companion of Moses and Joshua, and was noted for his astute powers of observation and fearlessness in the face of overwhelming odds. The meaning of the name Caleb is 'Devotion, faithful…'" I looked up at Tiffany. "'Wholehearted.'" I put the book down, leaned back, and shook my head, marveling at this. "Tiffany we named our son 'wholehearted.' His name means to live out of a whole heart for God!" Her eyes sparkled as we exchanged delighted smiles.

God has continued to remind us daily that we are not alone, that He is present with us, and that He loves and cares for us, no matter what we go through in life, a lesson that was reiterated to us rather unexpectedly by none other than Caleb himself, when he was six years old. I was sitting on the kitchen floor, playing with two-year-old Chloe.

"Hey, Dad," Caleb blurted. "Remember when we went camping?"

We'd gone camping several times in the five years since the accident at Fall Creek Falls, so I didn't give his question much thought.

"Dad," he persisted. "Remember when we went camping? The rock hit me in the head, like this."

Caleb smacked his hand against his head. I stared at him. Neither Tiffany nor I had ever once spoken to Caleb about the accident. We didn't think he'd remembered it. Tiffany and I glanced at each other and then back at Caleb.

"We took a lot of pictures."

I did recall having taken a lot of pictures the first part of that day, all the way down to the base of the falls.

"Jesus was in the lightning and thunder. He took care of me." Caleb's expression was serious. I hung on every word. For the first time since the accident, Caleb was clearly recalling images, memories, and despite his brain injury, was trying to tell us what happened from his perspective.

"I fell in the water, but I came back up."

I was puzzled. He hadn't fallen into the water. What was he talking about? Caleb looked at me earnestly.

"But He took me to the top. He carried me."

He must be talking about Michael Tagert, I realized, the firefighter who'd carried him to the top. Perhaps the blood pouring out of his head and down his face after the impact made him think he'd been under water. But what did he mean by Jesus being there, in thunder and lightning? It had been a beautiful autumn day. Beautiful, that is, until that boulder came crashing down through the trees. Actually, it had thundered through the trees.

I thought about the many times since he'd been released and came home how frightened he would be by any sudden loud noise—the sound of a truck shaking a dumpster, fireworks exploding on the Fourth of July, or the crack of thunder. Every time he heard something loud, it would leave him in tears, screaming in terror. Sometimes it took hours to get him to calm down.

Jesus was in the lightning and thunder. And He took care of me.

I looked at my boy and nodded. Yes, I did remember. And, yes, Jesus had taken care of him. He had taken care of all of us. And now that Caleb was starting to remember some of the details of the accident, it was comforting knowing that Jesus was there, that Caleb knew God was with him, and that he wasn't alone.

Our family has gone through many changes in the last five years. Not only were we later blessed with a daughter, Chloe, but we are now expecting our fifth child, Camden, in February 2016.

Caleb is seven as I write this and attends second grade, in a special needs class. He continues to improve, though his progress has slowed since the days when he first returned from Scottish Rite. He continues to go to therapy and we work with him at home every evening. He's nearly mastered the alphabet and numbers, he can write his name, ride his bike, and talk your ear off. He still loves Thomas the Train, his favorite thing to do is to eat (I think we personally keep our local Chick-fil-A open for business), and he has a knack for music. Caleb's greatest interest though is his love for God and other people. He has the gentlest heart I know and can frequently be found singing Christians songs throughout the day.

Although Caleb cognitively lags behind his peers by a few years, you would never suspect he had suffered a brain injury just by looking at him. He rambunctiously laughs and plays right along with the rest of the kids.

The doctors and therapists remain optimistic about Caleb's future. He personally knows no limitations, tenaciously tackling any task, undaunted by challenges. He is not one to give up. And, despite the emotional, mental, and financial tolls we have experienced as a result of that fateful day, his tenacity inspires us.

Though life hasn't been easy these last five years, God's love and presence has remained with us, demonstrating that He is always near, always present in the midst of our trials. God continues to teach us and speak to us in numerous ways, reminding us that no matter where the journey takes us, if it is traveled with Him, it is a journey worth taking.

As we consider all we've learned as a family and all that still lies ahead, by God's grace we will continue to look to God and to Caleb's beautiful life-example and seek to live every day, wholehearted.

ACKNOWLEDGEMENTS

This book would not be in existence if it were not for the many people whom our family has come to affectionately call Caleb's Heroes. There were many of these heroes—too many to name—and each of them played a role in saving our son, helping him on his journey to recovery, and supporting us as a family. We cannot thank these people enough for their example of love, generosity, and support. When our family went through the darkest of valleys they were there to help us through. We will always remember them and cherish them in our heart.

At Fall Creek Falls

To Caleb's greatest hero, I want to thank Michael Tagert, the young firefighter who was there the moment Caleb was struck by the rock, and who ran with our son to the top of the trail. Because of his quick decisions our son is alive today.

I also want to thank the many others who were present that day and helped, people like Philip Martin who tried to help me carry Caleb at the bottom of the Falls, and Robert Potter, Michael's uncle, who aided Michael in carrying Caleb at one point near the top of the gorge. I also want to give thanks to Melissa Lyons, a Pediatric Trauma nurse, who helped Michael by continuing to check Caleb's vital signs as we waited for the ambulance to arrive. To Bob Lyons and Dallas Rice who helped carry our oldest son Colby and who helped me back to the top of the trail. To Summer Kelly who helped Tiffany up the trail and who stayed by her side and prayed with her as we waited for the ambulance to arrive. To Kevin and Paige Thompson, who was there at the bottom of the trail when the rock fell, and who also helped us up the trail and stayed by Tiffany and prayed with her. Thank you for being there for us and for all the times you visited us at T.C. Thompson.

I also want to thank the many people who were there with us at the top of the trail who prayed and tried to help us as best as they could, as well as the many doctors and nurses who happened to be hiking the trail that day. I want to thank Ray Cutcher, the park ranger at Fall Creek Falls National Park, and others like Ron Parres and Wendy Krause, as well as Philip and Dawn Martin, who worked to keep the trail open and the path cleared as Michael ran to the top of the trail. I want to thank Stephanie Rainey and Beth Duryea for stepping forward and laying hands on Caleb and praying for him, and then driving us to the LifeForce helicopter landing area in the park.

I want to thank the first responders, Tiwanna Bricker and Will Maxwell from the Piney Fire Department, as well as Nick Abraham, Brian Campbell, Joey Grisson and Preston Denney from the Van Buren County EMS, who prepped Caleb for his LifeForce flight to T.C. Thompson. I also want to thank Robert Berger, Adam Jones, and Ron Bethleff, and all those with LifeForce who cared for our son during his flight to T.C. Thompson. And finally I would like to thank Officer Jamie Walling who not only personally drove us all the way to Chattanooga, but who stayed with us in the hospital for a time and continued to check on Caleb throughout his entire journey to recovery.

At T.C. Thompson

For our time at T.C. Thompson I want to thank all the doctors and nurses who saved our son's life and who carefully nursed him back to health to get him ready for rehab. I want to thank Dr. Marvin Hall, Dr. Mark Rowin, Dr. Gregory Talbott and Dr. Patrick Keegan, as well as Dr. Erin Reade and Dr. Jennifer Hamm. I also want to thank nurses, Josh Black, Kristy Johnson, Devin Gobble, Kami Litchfield, Kimberly Smith,

ACKNOWLEDGEMENTS

Coleen Martin, Audret Whiting, and Rhesa Rodriguez, Nicole Bridges, Kysha Friedrich, Suzanne Miller, Jessica Fosbinder, Barb Rhyne, and Susan Mitchell. I especially want to thank Pat Pearson and Lori Atchley, who went out of their way not only to care for our son, but to care for Tiffany and I as well.

There were many others who came alongside to help us during our time while we were at T.C. Thompson. I want to thank Jason Mckay and Brian Smith who led the charge in spreading the news about prayer, both over social media and through traditional media. Jason also helped us numerous times with communicating to the public, the media, and helping us with whatever needs we had. I also want to thank Assistant Chief Mike Williams of the Chattanooga Police Department and Darvin Oakes, owner of Sunrise Christian Campground, where we had camped, for also taking a lead in spreading the news about Caleb and asking for prayer. I want to thank Scott Arnold, reporter from WTVF Channel 5 in Nashville and John Madewell, reporter from WTVC Channel 9 in Chattanooga, and those from the many other news outlets in and around the Nashville and Chattanooga communities. Thank you for helping us and taking a personal interest in our son.

We also want to thank all the people who came to visit us, who stopped by to pray, encourage, and share their own stories to give us strength and hope. Among these we will never forget is Camille Ward whose bright smile and personal story about her own family's struggle and victory over TBI gave us hope right when we needed it most. Also Mike and Jodi Cook who's story about their son also greatly encouraged us.

We want to thank the numerous churches and people who came to pray and support us, too many to count. Among some of these were the White's Creek Church of Christ, as well as Chris Barnett, Minister from East Brainerd Church of Christ, and John and Rea Douglas from the Middle Valley Church of Christ. Also Michael and Ruth Ann Johnson, from Ridgedale Baptist Church. Also Steve Lusk and Jason Brazier, Minister and Youth Minister from the Red Bank Church of Christ. Also Tim Frizzell, my longtime mentor and friend, as well as the leadership from the Crieve Hall Church of Christ. Also Jeff and Bobbie Ford, and everyone at Alexandria Church of Christ for organizing Caleb's Run and making it such a success. Also all those from the James Avenue Church of Christ. I also want to thank Simplex Healthcare and my previous co-workers, for also being an integral part of helping with Caleb's Run, as well as helping our family when I could no longer return to my job. We also want to thank Chuck Payne and all those with him who helped organize a fundraising effort to give us a car when we were about to go to Atlanta for rehab and didn't have transportation. We also want to thank Dewayne and Regina Cordell, for organizing the Southern Gospel Singing Fundraiser for our family, along with the artists who performed and all who came out to support our family.

We also want to thank Michele Carter and everyone at the Chattanooga Ronald McDonald House, for feeding us and giving us a place to call home while we were away from our home.

At Scottish Rite

For our time at Scottish Rite, at Children's Healthcare of Atlanta, I want to thank Dr. Maurice Sholas, and all the other doctors and staff who cared for Caleb, as well as nurses Amy Tarnosk, Tina Crivellone, and Scott Legnon.

I also want to thank all the many therapists who painstakingly worked to help our son relearn how to eat, walk, play and be a kid again: John Tilley, Kristen Lidstone Howell, Cori Snyder, Beth Collier, Cindy Lou Manning, Theresa Stewart, Erin McFarling, Karen Keegan, and Julie Hagar.

I also want to thank the many people who visited and encouraged us during our time at Scottish Rite, and those that helped us, like Jane Waits who opened up her home to us so we could have a place to stay (away from the hospital) for when our kids would come to visit. We also want to thank Charles and April Tinch, and their son Isaac Tinch, as well as Costello Reese and his son Pinky Reese, whose own stories encouraged us as we walked the journey of rehab together with our children.

At Vanderbilt

I also want to thank all the doctors, therapists and staff at Vanderbilt Pediatric Rehabilitation who have continued to help Caleb excel in all of his various therapies: Kelley Siegert, Donna Trotter, Ellen Hobbs, Gladys Harms, Renee Ingle, Dr. Richard D. Durocher, Kate Nelson, Dr. Alan Fry, and everyone else since who has played a role in helping Caleb recover.

At School

I also want to thank all the therapists, teachers, and staff over the last few years who've played such a pivotal role in helping Caleb in school, who've worked with us and with the therapists at Vanderbilt to give Caleb the very best care possible. I also want to thank Amy Biggs, our representative from The Arc of Davidson County, who has been such an amazing advocate and help for us as Caleb has begun his journey in Elementary school.

At Home

When it comes to our close friends and family, to those who gave so much to help us, not only after Caleb's accident, but even still to this day, we don't have the words to thank you enough. To Ken and Carol Raetz and for all the volunteers who helped to renovate our home and get it ready for Caleb's return from rehab in Atlanta. Thank you for all your love and support. To Steve Austin, Allen Morrell, Ryan Kennedy, their wives, and all the staff at 180 Degrees Ministries, for all the wisdom, love, and encouragement, and for helping raise money to support our family. Had it not been for 180 Degrees Ministries we would have never known what it meant to see God's activity in our lives, recognize His fingerprints, and live life abundant and free. You guys are "smackin' daddy awesome."

We want to thank James and Tammy Rabun and their family, for the encouragement and sacrifices they made for us, often giving up their weekends to be with us and help us with our children. For Donna Wood, June Price, and all the ladies from Tiffany's Wednesday evening Bible class, who were a rock and support for Tiffany. We also want to thank my best friend Todd Jacobs and his wife Emily, who were there with us every step of the way, whom God used to strengthen and support our marriage, as well as to help us on the weekends with our children then and later when we returned home to Nashville. They are a great help to us even today, still strengthening our marriage and still encouraging us to look to God for everything we need.

We want to thank Tiffany's sisters, Chassi Hall and her husband Josh, and also Misty King and her husband Ryan, for watching and caring for Colby and Connor during the two months we were away from home, as well as for attending to our needs while at the hospital and helping us as we transitioned back home. Their love and sacrifice were great and we can never thank them enough for caring for our two other precious boys while we were away.

Finally, we want to thank our entire family and all of our friends who helped us during this journey, and who continue to help us today. I want to thank my parents Tim Sr. and Trina Brown, my brothers Todd, Travis, and Thomas, and sister Tiffany Brown. I want to thank my grandmother Audrey Denham, and Aunt Lynn Jones as well as her husband Tim. My cousins Tammy Thatcher and her husband Aaron, Christie Gilliam and her husband Tim, and Amy Briggs and her husband Chris. I want to thank Tiffany's parents, Terry and Sherron Trimble, as well as her uncle John Trimble. We could not have made it without you. We will never forget those long nights together in the PICU waiting room, crying, laughing, talking, praying and worshipping together. In times of testing like we experienced, you learn the value of family and close friends, and I can truly say that we value and love each and every single one of you. Thank you.

Caleb's Prayer Warriors

I can't thank enough the people who have prayed for Caleb and who continue to pray for him to this day, to the now nearly 10,000 people who follow Caleb's story on Facebook, to the hundreds of churches and to the countless thousands of people across the world. Thank you.

For Those Who Helped With the Book

I also want to thank the many people who lent a hand to help me write this book. To the many friends and family who helped me recall all the events as they happened, to the many people from Caleb's Facebook page who volunteered to read the numerous revisions of the manuscript and to offer their critiques and input to help me get it to the form it is in now. I want to especially thank Siobhan Gallagher who was the editor of this book and who worked with me from the beginning. Your professionalism, attention to detail, as well as personal desire to tell Caleb's story made the editing process fun, educational, and very rewarding. I also want to especially thank Ann Williams and Audrey Denham (my grandmother), as well as the many others who helped financially support the publishing of this book through our Kickstarter campaign. Lastly, I'd like to thank Emem Habuti for the cover design and Sarah Thomsen for the internal layout design of this book. Thank you.

To My Wife and Children

I also want to thank my amazing wife and children who have loved and supported me these last five years as I've labored to write, revise, edit, and re-write this book. I would not have been able to finish this book had it not been for the collaboration and hard work of my wife, Tiffany, as she helped me to remember and write down everything that our family experienced and learned. You prayed for me and believed in me every step of the way. You will never know how much you mean to me. I love you with all of my heart.

To God

And finally I want to thank my God and Father, who is truly the Author of this story and book, and to Jesus His Son, and to the Spirit who has been present with us since the beginning. To God be all the glory. Amen.

ABOUT THE BROWNS

Timothy M. Brown, Jr is an author, blogger, speaker, minister and entrepreneur. After a life-transforming personal encounter with God in early 2009, and nearly losing one of their five children from a rock fall at Fall Creek Falls in late 2010, God led Tim's family on a journey of discovering Him in real, personal, tangible ways – ways they never thought possible. In the years following their son's accident as Caleb has continued to heal and overcome the impossible, God has taught the Brown family many valuable life lessons and shown them that miracles do indeed still happen. God Still Speaks: The Miracle at Fall Creek Falls is Tim's record of their family's journey and the lessons they've learned along the way.

Tim writes regularly on his personal blog which is followed by thousands, and is the launching pad for Wholehearted Ministries, a teaching ministry devoted to helping people learn how to live out of a whole heart for God. As a result of the life-transformation that happened both during and after their son's accident, Tim's passion is to write on topics such as: how to grow in one's relationship with God, how to hear God's voice and walk with Him, how God still works today, how we can live the abundant life in Him, as well as finding God in the midst of trials and suffering. Tim also writes on other themes such as faith, prayer, forgiveness, issues related to marriage and family and men's leadership. You can visit Tim's blog by going to: www.timothybrownjr.com

Tim and his wife Tiffany live in Gallatin, TN with their five children: Colby, Caleb, Connor, Chloe and Camden who is due to be born in early 2016. Over the last fourteen years Tim has served in ministry and is currently the full time minister for a congregation in Gallatin, TN. Tim has also worked and preached in 4 African countries: Ivory Coast, Guinea, Tanzania, and Nigeria. Tim graduated Lipscomb University in 2001 where he received his B.A. in Biblical Languages and Preaching, and then again in 2003 where he received an M.A. in Biblical Studies. Tim has written over 1,000 sermons, bible class curricula, scholarly papers, articles and blog posts and is an experienced public speaker, routinely speaking to groups large and small since 2001.

Tim speaks regularly about his family's story and about the things they have learned in the last five years since their son's accident and subsequent recovery. Tim is currently writing his second book, A Faith That Moves Mountains: What Happens When Faith Finds the Miraculous, a follow up to the book God Still Speaks: The Miracle at Fall Creek Falls.

Tiffany, also an entrepreneur, works from home and runs their family's home business. Tiffany's favorite work however is being a full time mom and is passionate about being involved in her children's education and spiritual growth. She has a gift for children's ministry and serves as a bible class teacher and member of the Education Team at her church. Tiffany also uses her unique experience and background to counsel women and teens. Tiffany loves to read and one of her favorite hobbies is photography as she loves to take lots of pictures of her kids.

Tim's greatest passion is his family where, when he is not speaking or writing, he can be found playing with Thomas the Train toys on the floor with Caleb, dolls with his daughter Chloe, or playing video games or engaging in Nerf wars around the house with Colby and Connor. And when he can find a babysitter willing to watch his four rambunctious children, Tim loves to go on dates and romance his wife of fourteen years, Tiffany (who is glowingly pregnant with their fifth child, a boy, Camden).

More information at
www.godstillspeaksbook.com
www.timothybrownjr.com
and www.helpcaleb.com

A POEM FOR CALEB BROWN

by Siobhan Hickerson
Given to us while we were at T.C. Thompson, two weeks after Caleb's accident.

God we cannot always understand
Why things happen the way they do
Sometimes the only comfort we have
Is knowing we serve a God like You

You will always take every single thing
And somehow figure out how
To use everything for our own good
Even if we can't see it right now

Doctors are doing all that they can
But we are trusting in Your healing grace
Because no one can do what You do
No doctor can take Your place

Be with and heal this sweet little boy
With whom we have all fallen in love
Because he is a precious child of Yours
An incredible gift from above

Give his parents all that they need
To get through each and every day
Keep their faith and hearts strong
Be a blessing to them in every way

Because none of us could imagine
The burden they have, the pain they see
Yet they continue to remain faithful
What an example they have come to be

An example to every person
Who has heard their story
An example of trusting, faithfully
That all will be used for Your glory

And this beautiful, innocent child
Fighting a hard fight, though so small
He is following his mommy and daddy
In being an example for us all

Bless this family beyond compare
Whatever they do, wherever they go
Because they are changing lives
Of people they don't even know

People are praying for sweet Caleb
People who have never prayed before
Because He is helping people realize
That there has to be something more

Doctors don't always have the answers
And humans can't always understand
But there is more, we are learning
A heavenly, helping hand

No one will ever be able to count
The number of lives he has rearranged
Just by his story and his fight
Which gives us a reason to be changed

Because no matter what else happens
Through all the pain in this life
We serve a God who is faithful
And will see us through every strife

PHOTOS

Early Photos of Caleb

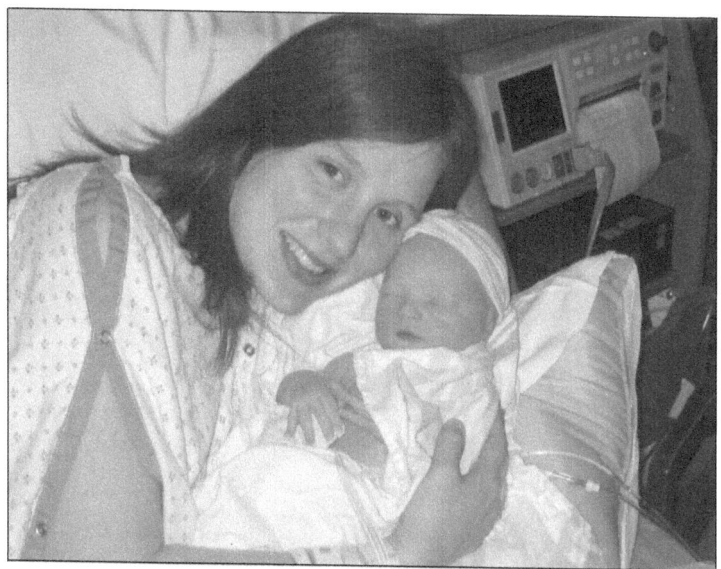

Caleb Timothy Brown, born April 14th, 2008

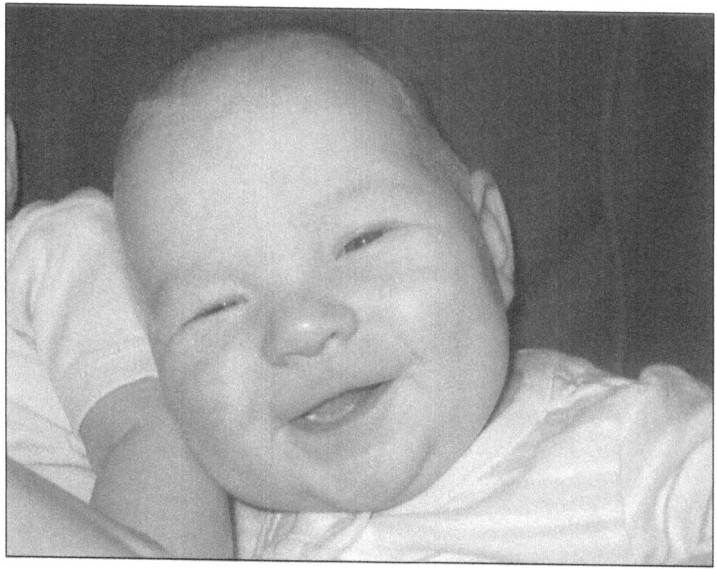

Three-month-old Caleb, July 2008

Caleb having fun swinging at the park, March 2010

Caleb's second birthday, April 2010

Photos Taken the Day of the Accident at Fall Creek Falls

Cleaning up after breakfast, October 16th, 2010

Teaching Colby and Caleb how to play baseball for the first time, October 16th, 2010

Caleb excited to see the falls, October 16th, 2010

One of the last pictures before the accident, October 16th, 2010

Photos Taken at T.C. Thompson Children's Hospital

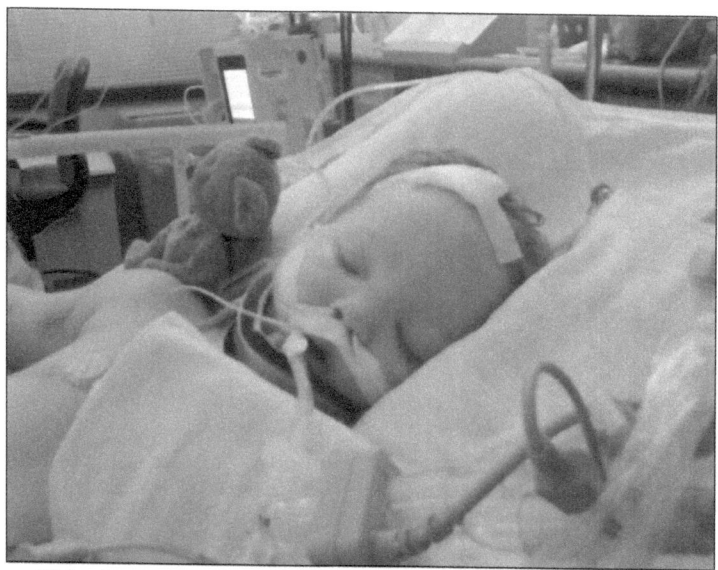

This photo was taken after we learned the news that Caleb was going to live, October 2010

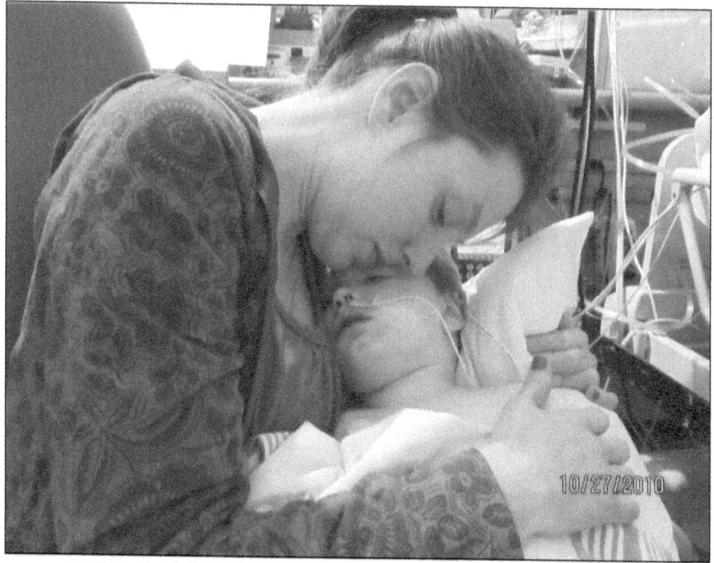

Tiffany holding Caleb for the first time after the accident, October 27th, 2010

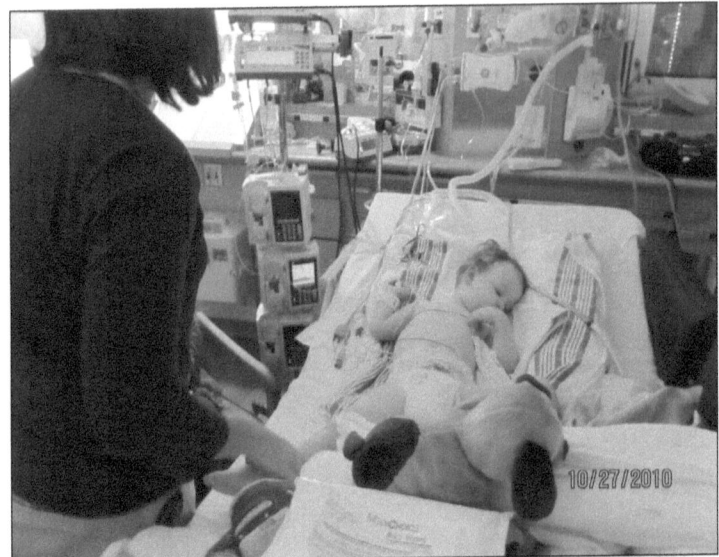

Caleb's first day of therapy, October 27th, 2010

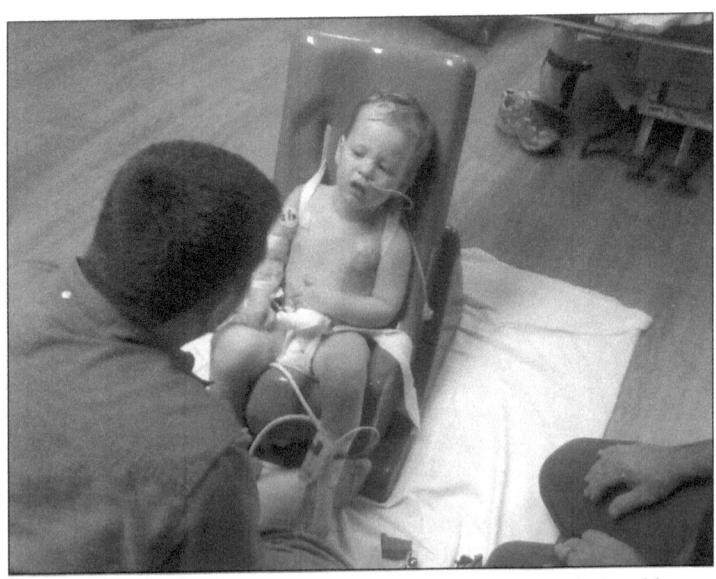

Tim helping Caleb learn how to sit up and hold up his head by himself, November 4th, 2010

Tim helping Caleb learn how to walk again, November 2010

Tiffany enjoying some time outside with Caleb, November 2010

Our nightly therapy time in our room, November 2010

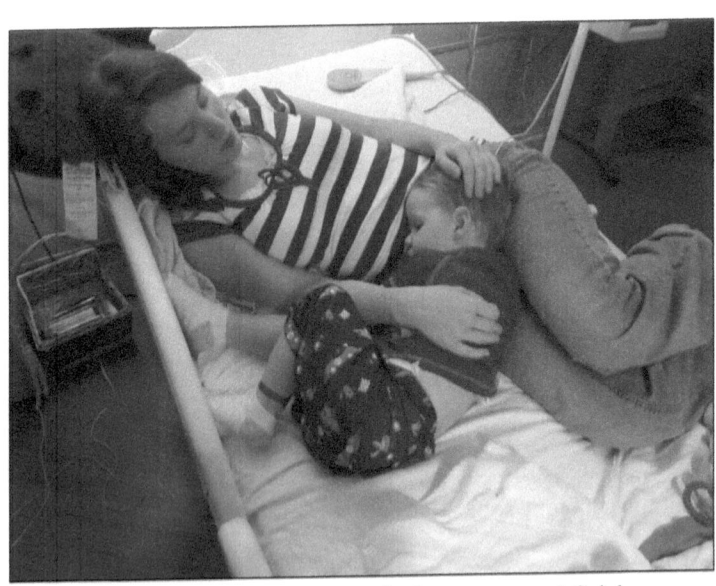
The day's therapy wears out both mommy and Caleb,
November 2010

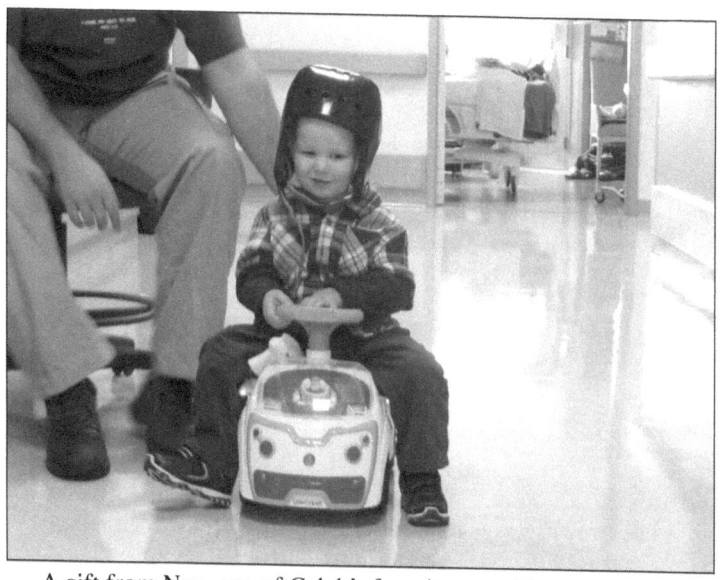

A gift from Nan, one of Caleb's favorite toys, November 2010

Photos Taken on the Way Home to Nashville & Caleb's 3rd Birthday

Caleb waves good-bye at our press conference on the way home to Nashville, December 8th, 2010

The Browns arrive home after being away for two months,
December 8th, 2010

Caleb is being interviewed by WTVF,
Channel 5 News Nashville, December 8th, 2010

Caleb eating birthday cake at his third birthday party celebration, April 2011

Caleb sliding down a slide on his third birthday, at the park, April 2011

Michael Tagert, the firefighter who saved Caleb's life, holds him on his 3rd birthday, April 2011

Photos Taken Since Caleb's Accident

Caleb having fun outside, February 2011

Caleb holding his baby sister, Chloe, when she was born, November 2011

Caleb hugging one of his favorite therapists, Kristen, at the Scottish Rite Rehab Reunion, August 2011

Caleb's Kindergarten class picture, Fall 2012

Caleb opening presents at his four-year-old birthday party, April 2012

Tim, Tiffany, Colby, Caleb, Connor, and Chloe Easter family picture, April 2013

The kids enjoying some ice cream outside, June 2013

Caleb's first grade class picture, September 2014

Family picture at Gallatin Church of Christ, February 2015

Family vacation at Legoland Florida, July 2015

www.ingramcontent.com/pod-product-compliance
Lightning Source LLC
Chambersburg PA
CBHW022227010526
44113CB00033B/550